The Search for Peace

THE WORLD STUDIES SERIES

VOLUMES PUBLISHED

Malaysia and its Neighbours, J. M. Gullick.

The European Common Market and Community, Uwe Kitzinger, Fellow of Nuffield College, Oxford.

The Politics of John F. Kennedy, Edmund Ions, Department of History, Columbia University, New York.

Apartheid: A Documentary Study of Modern South Africa, Edgar H. Brookes.

Israel and the Arab World, C. H. Dodd, Department of Government, University of Manchester, and M. E. Sales, Centre for Middle Eastern and Islamic Studies, University of Durham.

The Theory and Practice of Neutrality in the Twentieth Century, Roderick Ogley, Department of International Relations, University of Sussex.

Soviet Foreign Policy since the Death of Stalin, H. Hanak, School of Slavonic and East European Studies, University of London.

The Search for Peace

D. W. Bowett
The President, Queens' College, Cambridge

LONDON AND BOSTON
ROUTLEDGE & KEGAN PAUL

First published 1972
by Routledge & Kegan Paul Limited
Broadway House, 68–74 Carter Lane
London EC4V 5EL and

9 Park Street
Boston, Mass. 02108, U.S.A.

Printed in Great Britain
by C. Tinling & Co. Ltd
London and Prescot

ISBN – 0 7100 7216 3

Contents

CONTENTS

CONTENTS

viii

General Editor's Preface

The World Studies Series is designed to make a new and important contribution to the study of modern history. Each volume in the Series will provide students in sixth forms, Colleges of Education and Universities with a range of contemporary material drawn from many sources, not only from official and semi-official records, but also from contemporary historical writing from reliable journals. The material is selected and introduced by a scholar who establishes the context of his subject and suggests possible lines of discussion and inquiry that can accompany a study of the documents.

Through these volumes the student can learn how to read and assess historical documents. He will see how the contemporary historian works and how historical judgments are formed. He will learn to discriminate among a number of sources and to weigh evidence. He is confronted with recent instances of what Professor Butterfield has called 'the human predicament' revealed by history; evidence concerning the national, racial and ideological factors which at present hinder or advance man's progress towards some form of world society.

The quiet realism with which Dr Bowett makes these documents speak to the condition of modern man is admirable. The vigour and archaism of the sovereign state, the need for peaceful settlement of international disputes, the peace-keeping role of the United Nations Organization—aid to developing countries and disarmament—all these elements in the search for peace are convincingly demonstrated by means of quotation from appropriate sources. In the author's introduction to Part VII the basic question raised by this volume is stated: 'Must we assume that centralization of authority stops at the nation state? Why not centralize still further in a world community?'

JAMES HENDERSON

Volume Editor's Preface

This volume attempts a quite impossible task. It simply is not possible to convey any real understanding of the problem of maintaining world peace in so slender a volume. What may be possible, however, is to give an inkling of what is involved, to spark an interest in the minds of the young people who, it is hoped, will read this book and, above all, to convince them that the problem is soluble.

Of course the prospect for peace is faint; of course the historical evidence suggests that mankind will again be bundled into wholesale war, whether by accident or design; and, of course, we must face the likelihood that such a war will be fought with nuclear weapons. But there can be no possible justification for any counsel of despair. There is no inevitability about war, and the problem of maintaining peace—at least in the sense of avoiding global war—is soluble like any other problem. It will take time and great ingenuity and, probably, a large amount of pure faith to arrive at the solution. It is for this reason that this little book is designed for, and addressed to, young people. The solution is likely to be in their hands, simply because it will be achieved, if at all, in the longer term rather than the shorter term. To achieve it they will need a great deal of understanding, far more than this book can give; all this can do is to stimulate their awareness of the problem and the need for understanding and effort to arrive at its solution. Perhaps the greatest enemies of peace are apathy and despair.

Acknowledgments

The author and publishers wish to thank the following for kind permission to print in this volume extracts from the works cited:

Foreign Affairs for 'On Peaceful Co-existence' by Nikita S. Khrushchev, 1959. Copyright by the Council on Foreign Relations, Inc., New York

The Macmillan Company and Weidenfeld (Publishers) Ltd for *Venceremos: The Speeches and Writings of Che Guevara* ed. by John Gerassi. Copyright John Gerassi, 1968

The University of Chicago Press for *A Study of War* by Quincy Wright

The Hague Academy of International Law for 'General Course of International Law' by R. Y. Jennings, from *Recueil des Cours*, II, 1967

The David Davies Memorial Institute of International Studies for *Report of a Study Group on the Peaceful Settlement of International Disputes*, 1966, and for *United Nations Forces* by D. W. Bowett, Stevens & Sons, 1964

The Journal of Conflict Resolution for 'The Peaceful Limitation of Disputes: Police Powers and System Problems' by Walter Goldstein, 1962

The American Society of International Law for 'The Role of the United Nations in Civil Wars' by Louis B. Sohn, from *The Proceedings of the Annual Meeting of the Society*, 1963

Praeger Publishers, Inc. for *In Pursuit of World Order* by Richard N. Gardner

Harvard University Press for *World Peace through World Law* by Grenville Clark and Louis B. Sohn

The Center for the Study of Democratic Institutions for *Constitution for the World* by Elisabeth Mann Borgese

Introduction

All forms of human society contain conflicts of interest. This book is concerned with those conflicts of interest which, if not contained and regulated, are likely to lead to violence between States. To illustrate the problems involved in restraining international violence, documents, quotations and extracts from many and varied sources are used in this book. The reader will find writings by Nikita Khrushchev, Mao Tse-tung, Che Guevara, Ho Chi-minh, Dag Hammarskjöld and U Thant; extracts from treaties, declarations of State policy, UN documents; and academic contributions from distinguished authors.

The 'search for peace', by which we mean the task of devising the techniques of restraint, is many-faceted and law plays a part in this task. But law cannot, of itself, resolve these conflicts. Within a State whole areas of conflicts—over race relations, industrial disputes, religious issues—may only marginally be subject to legal regulation, and it is to education, science, sociology, ethics and economics that society must turn to find the answer to its problems. International society is not much different. Conflicts between States are not resolved simply by legal rules, for these conflicts have causes and it is only by the elimination of these causes that the conflicts can ultimately be resolved.

However, all societies face the need to impose limits on the *methods* which parties may use to promote their interests which are at variance with the interests of others. In other words, whilst society may accept the existence of a conflict of interests and may realize that the resolution of the conflict calls for long-term measures of education and economic readjustment, society may equally take the view that pending a true resolution of the conflicts of interests certain *methods* of promoting their own interests shall not be available to the parties. Resort to

I

force is a method commonly outlawed in most civilized societies and outlawry of force within a modern State presupposes two things: first, the availability of legal remedies before properly constituted courts and, second, the existence of an effective law-enforcing machinery—the police—capable of enforcing compliance with the law. It cannot be said that the modern State society necessarily assumes that, having provided both these things, the conflict will be resolved. The legal remedies may be quite 'unjust' in the view of one party, so that his ultimate aim becomes a change in the law. This aim he may pursue through political action, pressure-groups (trade unions, professional associations, etc.), information media (books, TV, newspapers), but *not* through resort to force. Ultimately, if sufficient people share his view of the inequity of the present law, there is a Parliament with power to change the law. Of course, even within State societies, the techniques of peaceful change occasionally fail to afford an adequate substitute for violence: groups of people, frustrated in their search for peaceful change, are then prone to take to the streets. The contemporary wave of civil unrest, illustrated by civil-rights demonstrations, student riots and the like, which has swept the globe, is one illustration: the extreme illustration is civil war. It is for this reason that, without adequate techniques for peaceful change, the adoption by international society of the characteristic features of the State society—law, courts, enforcement agencies, legislatures, etc.—cannot of itself be expected to prevent international war, any more than these features within the State prevent civil war.

Within international society this degree of sophistication in the rules and techniques for avoiding violence is currently lacking. The members of this society are 'sovereign' States, relatively large and powerful units as compared with the members of the State society and whilst, as we shall see, legal rules prohibiting recourse to force have evolved, there is neither a system for the compulsory settlement of disputes nor an effective, centralized law-enforcing machinery. International society bears the hallmarks of any relatively primitive, decentralized society—akin to England under the feudal barons. Moreover, in so far as the present state of international law may not afford 'just' remedies to a State whose interests are prejudiced, there is no international legislature capable of changing the law with binding effect on all the members of the international community.

Given these defects in international society, it is not surprising that, prior to the present century, international law conceded to the sovereign State the right to wage war. True, scholars and writers like Aquinas, Grotius, Gentili and Vattel had attempted on the basis of notions of natural law to limit this right to 'just' wars, when a State had a 'just' cause. But by the nineteenth and early twentieth centuries such theories found little reflection in State practice. Indeed, war was seen as an instrument for defending a State's rights, perfectly legitimate in the absence of procedures for compulsory settlement of disputes through international courts and of an international police force capable of protecting those rights. In addition, war was seen as having the somewhat incompatible function of changing the law—or legal rights—where the State regarded the prevailing position as 'unjust' or 'unfair'. Thus, an inequitable distribution of territory or economic wealth might be challenged by resort to war, having as its aim the acquisition of more territory or a fairer share of economic resources. And, indeed, given the absence of an international legislature, the need for some instrument of change could scarcely be denied.

However, the situation in international society was basically anarchical. Since each State remained judge of its own cause, it became impossible to limit resort to war to the defence of legal rights or, alternatively, to challenges to existing rights which were 'just'. International society lacked the courts and the legislature which, in municipal society, serve to give objective judgments on such issues. And, therefore, in an era of virtually unfettered subjectivism—fettered only rarely by public opinion—the State waged war with impunity in the knowledge that military victory would be decisive of all the issues: 'might' became 'right'.

Abhorrence and revolt against such a system was in early times based largely upon conscience: hence the attempts of the theologians and scholastics to invoke the restrictions of divine or natural law. The First World War of 1914–18 added new dimensions to the abhorrence of the system. The technological advances of armaments' production had created weapons with unprecedented power to inflict death and destruction: *that* war caused forty million casualties.[1] Even apart from the frightful slaughter of human beings, the lives of millions of ordinary people became involved in the struggle. War had ceased to be the affair of princes and their private, mercenary armies. Military conscription, conscription of civilian labour for war production, rationing, the vulnerability of the civilian population to air attack or starvation from blockade: all these combined to produce an era of 'total' war in which the classical distinction between combatants and non-combatants became almost meaningless. And techniques of modern propaganda served to inculcate the hatred of the enemy as a nation which was necessary to inspire a population to continue so deadly a struggle.

The Second World War of 1939–45 demonstrated that the new pattern was no freak but rather the form which any major conflict would be likely to assume: total casualties have been estimated at sixty million.[2] Moreover, with the advent of the atomic weapon, mankind was forced to contemplate the destruction of human life on a scale never before imagined. Today, one Polaris-equipped submarine is capable of delivering missiles with a destructive power twice the total bomb-loads delivered by all the air-forces employed in the Second World War; and the long-lasting effects of nuclear radiation are capable of injuring generations yet unborn. The ultimate irony lay in the realization that in modern war there are no 'victors': the human and material cost to victor and vanquished alike is on so large a scale that the idea of the 'fruits of Victory' becomes meaningless.

Given this appalling situation, it behoves intelligent people to ask themselves certain basic questions about international society, and, since these questions can be perfectly well comprehended by the young (and since they have a vested interest —their own survival—in seeing that society finds the right answers) it is the purpose of this book to pose certain of these

[1] Quincy Wright, *A Study of War*, University of Chicago Press, London, 1965, p. 1543, suggests that only one-quarter of these were the direct result of military action.

[2] Quincy Wright, *ibid.*, suggests that, of these sixty million, seventeen million were military, thirty-four million were civilian casualties resulting directly from the war and the remainder were civilian casualties from war-borne epidemics.

questions in a way which will assist in understanding and discussing them.

These questions are the following. Can rules be formulated which will limit the State's right to resort to war or other forms of coercion as a method of pursuing its policies? Can substitute procedures for the peaceful settlement of disputes or techniques for the avoidance of conflicts be provided? Can some form of international police force or 'peace-keeping' machinery be instituted? Can measures be taken which will eliminate the causes of these conflicts? Can international society develop a degree of centralization akin to that which prevails within a State so as to control individual member States? Can the destructive power of individual States be limited or controlled by arms control or disarmament? Can mankind devise a better structure for international society than the present conglomeration of sovereign States, loosely linked by co-operation through international organizations?

The discerning student will discover within this book a vast oversimplification of some of these questions and the problems involved within them. The desire to rely on 'source material' and sheer limitations of space in part account for this. However, it is hoped that such a student will be encouraged to delve further, beyond this book, into the many ramifications of these questions. And yet, it would be a pity if, in exploring these ramifications, the student were to become obsessed by the complications and the technicalities. None of them is insuperable, certainly to a species capable of placing a man on the moon. What is needed is a clear faith in man's ability to solve the technical problems and in man's intelligence and will to survive, overcoming the dangers of a system with in-built potential for mass suicide; and a belief that, in the final analysis, the questions are basic and comprehensible and need not be clouded over by technicalities and difficulties. In short, what mankind lacks is not the capacity to solve these problems, but merely the will.

PART I

The Sovereign State and Resort to War

(a) THE ATTEMPTS TO OUTLAW WAR AND FORCE BY FORMAL PROHIBITION

The 1914–18 World War shattered any illusion that the precepts of natural law or the dictates of conscience or even the 'balance of power' sufficed to prevent States from using war as a means of pursuing their self-interest. The remedy was therefore seen in the Covenant of the League of Nations as one of 'collective security': a system which would both prohibit war and organize the international community to deal collectively with the aggressor. The terms in which the prohibition of war was framed indicate clearly that States were to be offered peaceful techniques of settlement of their disputes as alternatives to war. Thus, reference of any dispute was to be made *either* to arbitration or judicial settlement (treating the dispute as a 'legal' dispute) *or* to the League Council (treating the dispute as a 'political' dispute). It was essentially the refusal to accept these alternatives which constituted the breach of the Covenant and therefore made a State's resort to war illegal: the Covenant did not attempt to characterize a war as illegal by reference to its aims or purposes.

DOCUMENT I. EXTRACT FROM THE COVENANT OF THE LEAGUE OF NATIONS, 1919

Article 10. The Members of the League undertake to respect and preserve as against external aggression the territorial integrity and existing political independence of all Members of the League. In case of any such aggression or in case of any threat or danger of such aggression the Council shall

6

advise upon the means by which this obligation shall be fulfilled.

Article 11. 1. Any war, or threat of war, whether immediately affecting any of the Members of the League or not, is hereby declared a matter of concern to the whole League, and the League shall take any action that may be deemed wise and effectual to safeguard the peace of nations.

In case any such emergency should arise the Secretary-General shall on the request of any Member of the League forthwith summon a meeting of the Council.

2. It is also declared to be the friendly right of each Member of the League to bring to the attention of the Assembly or of the Council any circumstance whatever affecting international relations which threatens to disturb international peace or the good understanding between nations upon which peace depends.

Article 12. 1. The Members of the League agree that, if there should arise between them any dispute likely to lead to a rupture, they will submit the matter either to arbitration *or judicial settlement* or to inquiry by the Council, and they agree in no case to resort to war until three months after the award by the arbitrators *or the judicial decision*, or the report by the Council.

2. In any case under this Article the award of the arbitrators *or the judicial decision* shall be made within a reasonable time, and the report of the Council shall be made within six months after the submission of the dispute.

Article 13. 1. The Members of the League agree that, whenever any dispute shall arise between them which they recognize to be suitable for submission to arbitration *or judicial settlement*, and which cannot be satisfactorily settled by diplomacy, they will submit the whole subject-matter to arbitration *or judicial settlement*.

2. Disputes as to the interpretation of a treaty, as to any question of international law, as to the existence of any fact which, if established, would constitute a breach of any international obligation, or as to the extent and nature of the reparation to be made for any such breach, are declared to be among those which are generally suitable for submission to arbitration *or judicial settlement*.

3. *For the consideration of any such dispute, the court to which the case is referred shall be the Permanent Court of International Justice,*

established in accordance with Article 14, or any tribunal agreed on by the parties to the dispute or stipulated in any convention existing between them.

4. The Members of the League agree that they will carry out in full good faith any award *or decision* that may be rendered, and that they will not resort to war against a Member of the League which complies therewith. In the event of any failure to carry out such an award *or decision*, the Council shall propose what steps should be taken to give effect thereto.

Article 14. The Council shall formulate and submit to the Members of the League for adoption plans for the establishment of a Permanent Court of International Justice. The Court shall be competent to hear and determine any dispute of an international character which the parties thereto submit to it. The Court may also give an advisory opinion upon any dispute or question referred to it by the Council or by the Assembly.

Article 15. 1. If there should arise between Members of the League any dispute likely to lead to a rupture, which is not submitted to arbitration *or judicial settlement* in accordance with Article 13, the Members of the League agree that they will submit the matter to the Council.

Any party to the dispute may effect such submission by giving notice of the existence of the dispute to the Secretary-General, who will make all the necessary arrangements for a full investigation and consideration thereof.

2. For this purpose the parties to the dispute will communicate to the Secretary-General, as promptly as possible, statements of their case with all the relevant facts and papers, and the Council may forthwith direct the publication thereof.

3. The Council shall endeavour to effect a settlement of the dispute, and, if such efforts are successful, a statement shall be made public giving such facts and explanations regarding the dispute and the terms of settlement thereof as the Council may deem appropriate.

4. If the dispute is not thus settled, the Council either unanimously or by a majority vote shall make and publish a report containing a statement of the facts of the dispute and the recommendations which are deemed just and proper in regard thereto.

5. Any member of the League represented on the Council

may make public a statement of the facts of the dispute and of its conclusions regarding the same.

6. If a report by the Council is unanimously agreed to by the Members thereof other than the Representatives of one or more of the parties to the dispute, the Members of the League agree that they will not go to war with any party to the dispute which complies with the recommendations of the report.

7. If the Council fails to reach a report which is unanimously agreed to by the members thereof, other than the Representatives of one or more of the parties to the dispute, the Members of the League reserve to themselves the right to take such action as they shall consider necessary for the maintenance of right and justice.

8. If a dispute between the parties is claimed by one of them, and is found by the Council, to arise out of a matter which by international law is solely within the domestic jurisdiction of that party, the Council shall so report, and shall make no recommendation as to its settlement.

9. The Council may in any case under this Article refer the dispute to the Assembly. The dispute shall be so referred at the request of either party to the dispute, provided that such request be made within 14 days after the submission of the dispute to the Council.

10. In any case referred to the Assembly, all the provisions of this Article and of Article 12 relating to the action and powers of the Council shall apply to the action and powers of the Assembly, provided that a report made by the Assembly, if concurred in by the Representatives of those Members of the League represented on the Council and of the majority of the other Members of the League, exclusive in each case of the Representatives of the parties to the dispute, shall have the same force as a report by the Council concurred in by all the members thereof other than the Representatives of one or more of the parties to the dispute.

Article 16. 1. Should any Member of the League resort to war in disregard of its covenants under Articles 12, 13 or 15, it shall *ipso facto* be deemed to have committed an act of war against all other Members of the League, which hereby undertake immediately to subject it to the severance of all trade or financial relations, the prohibition of all intercourse between their nationals and the nationals of the covenant-breaking State, and the prevention of all financial, commercial or personal intercourse between the nationals of the covenant-breaking State and the nationals of any other State, whether a Member of the League or not.

2. It shall be the duty of the Council in such case to recommend to the several Governments concerned what effective military, naval or air force the Members of the League shall severally contribute to the armed forces to be used to protect the covenants of the League.

3. The Members of the League agree, further, that they will mutually support one another in the financial and economic measures which are taken under this Article, in order to minimize the loss and inconvenience resulting from the above measures. and that they will mutually support one another in resisting any special measures aimed at one of their number by the covenant-breaking State, and that they will take the necessary steps to afford passage through their territory to the forces of any Members of the League which are co-operating to protect the covenants of the League.

4. Any Member of the League which has violated any covenant of the League may be declared to be no longer a Member of the League by a vote of the Council concurred in by the Representatives of all the other Members of the League represented thereon.

*

A marked shift of emphasis came with the Kellogg-Briand Pact of 1928 (the Paris Pact) which, in two brief articles, confirmed the obligation to settle disputes or conflicts by pacific means but condemned war 'as an instrument of national policy', thus introducing a substantive rather than a procedural criterion for determining its illegality.

DOCUMENT 2. THE KELLOGG-BRIAND PACT OF 1928 (GENERAL TREATY FOR THE RENUNCIATION OF WAR AS AN INSTRUMENT OF NATIONAL POLICY)[1]

[1] This pact came about as the result of the initiative of France and the United States. The latter was *not* a party to the League Covenant but desired to be associated with some general treaty prohibiting aggressive war. It was signed by fifteen Governments and, over the years, more than sixty States adhered to it.

Article 1. The High Contracting Parties solemnly declare in the names of their respective peoples that they condemn recourse to war for the solution of international controversies, and renounce it as an instrument of national policy in their relations with one another.

Article 2. The High Contracting Parties agree that the settlement or solution of all disputes or conflicts of whatever nature or of whatever origin they may be, which may arise among them, shall never be sought except by pacific means.

*

Whatever hopes for peace were created by these two documents were soon destroyed. The Japanese invasion of Manchuria in 1931, the Italian invasion of Abyssinia in 1935, the German invasions of Austria in 1937 and Czechoslovakia in 1938, the Japanese attack on China in 1937 and the Soviet Union's attack on Finland in 1939 demonstrated a total disregard for any such prohibition of war. True, Japan, Germany and Italy withdrew from the League so as to disembarrass themselves of the obligations of membership (though they remained bound by the Paris Pact). However, the most disheartening feature of the entire inter-war period was the apathy of the League membership. The great concept of 'collective security' degenerated into pathetic gestures of condemnation: Japan, Italy and Russia were all condemned for breach of the Covenant by the Council of the League, and half-hearted sanctions of an economic character were initiated against Italy. A policy of appeasement towards Hitler, coupled with the 'neutralism' of the USA (which had never joined the League), made it appear that there was no collective will to resist aggression. Thus Germany felt confident in her pursuit of aggressive aims and only with the invasion of Poland in 1939 did France and Britain finally decide to make a stand, a stand in which, after the Japanese attack on Pearl Harbour in 1941, they were joined by the USA. Hitler's attack on the Soviet Union in 1941 (which had acted as joint invader of Poland in 1939) brought into alliance Great Britain, the USA, the Soviet Union, China and France (fighting through the Free French forces under de Gaulle after France's capitulation in 1940). This wartime alliance defeated the Axis Powers (Germany, Italy and Japan) and in the celebrated Nuremberg Trials a tribunal established by the Soviet Union, Britain and the USA vindicated the Paris Pact of 1928. The major German war leaders were indicted for 'crimes against the peace', very largely on the basis that the Paris Pact had not only made war illegal but also a criminal act for which the leaders of a State responsible for its planning and execution were individually responsible. The concept of individual, criminal responsibility aroused great controversy because of its novelty. However, in principle it was clearly right to establish the principle that 'crimes against international law are committed by men, not by abstract entities, and only by punishing individuals who commit such crimes can the provisions of international law be enforced'.

DOCUMENT 3. EXTRACTS FROM THE CHARTER AND JUDGMENT OF THE INTERNATIONAL MILITARY TRIBUNAL AT NUREMBERG, 1946

Charter of the IMT at Nuremberg

Jurisdiction and General Principles

Article 6. The Tribunal established by the Agreement referred to in Article 1 hereof for the trial and punishment of the major war criminals of the European Axis countries shall have the power to try and punish persons who, acting in the interests of the European Axis countries, whether as individuals or as members of organisations, committed any of the following crimes.

The following acts, or any of them, are crimes coming within the jurisdiction of the Tribunal for which there shall be individual responsibility:

(a) Crimes against peace: namely, planning, preparation, initiation or waging of a war of aggression, or a war in violation of international treaties, agreements or assurances, or participation in a common plan or conspiracy for the accomplishment of any of the foregoing.

(b) War crimes: namely, violations of the laws or customs of war. Such violations shall include, but not be limited to, murder, ill-treatment or deportation to slave labour or for any other purpose of civilian population of or in occupied territory, murder or ill-treatment of prisoners of war or persons on the seas, killing of hostages, plunder of public property, wanton destruction of cities, towns or villages, or devastation not justified by military necessity.

(c) Crimes against humanity: namely, murder, extermination, enslavement, deportation, and other inhumane acts committed against any civilian population, before or during the war, or persecutions on political, racial or religious grounds in execution of or in connection with any crime within the jurisdiction of the Tribunal, whether or not in violation of the domestic law of the country where perpetrated.

Leaders, organisers, instigators, and accomplices participating in the formulation or execution of a common plan or conspiracy to commit any of the foregoing crimes are responsible for all acts performed by any persons in execution of such plan.

Article 7. The official position of Defendants, whether as Heads of State or responsible officials in Government Departments, shall not be considered as freeing them from responsibility or mitigating punishment.

Article 8. The fact that the Defendant acted pursuant to order of his Government or of a superior shall not free him from responsibility, but may be considered in mitigation of punishment if the Tribunal determines that justice so requires.

The Nuremberg Judgment

Kellogg-Briand Pact

The Pact of Paris was signed on the 27th August 1928, by Germany, the United States, Belgium, France, Great Britain, Italy, Japan, Poland and other countries; and subsequently by other powers. The Tribunal has made full reference to the nature of this Pact and its legal effect in another part of this judgment. It is therefore not necessary to discuss the matter further here, save to state that in the opinion of the Tribunal this Pact was violated by Germany in all the cases of aggressive war charged in the Indictment. It is to be noted that on the 26th January 1930, Germany signed a Declaration for the Maintenance of Permanent Peace with Poland, which was explicitly based on the Pact of Paris, and in which the use of force was outlawed for a period of ten years. . . .

The Law of the Charter

The jurisdiction of the Tribunal is defined in the Agreement and Charter, and the crimes coming within the jurisdiction of the Tribunal, for which there shall be individual responsibility, are set out in Article 6. The law of the Charter is decisive, and binding upon the Tribunal. . . .

The Charter makes the planning or waging of a war of aggression or a war in violation of international treaties a crime; and it is therefore not strictly necessary to consider whether and to what extent aggressive war was a crime before the execution of the London Agreement. But in view of the great importance of the questions of law involved, the Tribunal has heard full argument from the Prosecution and the Defence, and will express its view on the matter.

It was urged on behalf of the defendants that a fundamental principle of all law—international and domestic—is that there can be no punishment of crime without a pre-existing law. 'Nullum crimen sine lege, nulla poena sine lege.' It was submitted that ex post facto punishment is abhorrent to the law of all civilised nations, that no sovereign power had made aggressive war a crime at the time the alleged criminal acts were committed, that no statute had defined aggressive war, that no penalty had been fixed for its commission, and no court had been created to try and punish offenders.

In the first place, it is to be observed that the maxim nullum crimen sine lege is not a limitation of sovereignty, but is in general a principle of justice. To assert that it is unjust to punish those who in defiance of treaties and assurances have attacked neighbouring states without warning is obviously untrue, for in such circumstances the attacker must know that he is doing wrong, and so far from it being unjust to punish him, it would be unjust if his wrong were allowed to go unpunished. Occupying the positions they did in the government of Germany, the defendants, or at least some of them must have known of the treaties signed by Germany, outlawing recourse to war for the settlement of international disputes; they must have known that they were acting in defiance of all international law when in complete deliberation they carried out their designs of invasion and aggression. On this view of the case alone, it would appear that the maxim has no application to the present facts.

This view is strongly reinforced by a consideration of the state of international law in 1939, so far as aggressive war is concerned. The General Treaty for the Renunciation of War of 27th August 1928, more generally known as the Pact of Paris or the Kellogg-Briand Pact, was binding on sixty-three nations, including Germany, Italy and Japan at the outbreak of war in 1939. . . .

The question is, what was the legal effect of this Pact? The nations who signed the Pact or adhered to it unconditionally condemned recourse to war for the future as an instrument of policy, and expressly renounced it. After the signing of the Pact, any nation resorting to war as an instrument of national policy breaks the Pact. In the opinion of the Tribunal, the solemn renunciation of war as an instrument of national policy necessarily involves the proposition that such a war is illegal in international law; and that those who plan and wage such a war, with its inevitable and terrible consequences, are committing a crime in so doing. War for the solution of international controversies undertaken as an instrument of national policy certainly includes a war of aggression, and such a war is therefore outlawed by the Pact. . . .

But it is argued that the Pact does not expressly enact that such wars are crimes, or set up courts to try those who make such wars. To that extent the same is true with regard to the laws of war contained in the Hague Convention. The Hague Convention of 1907 prohibited resort to certain methods of waging war. These included the inhumane treatment of prisoners, the employment of poisoned weapons, the improper use of flags of truce, and similar matters. Many of these prohibitions had been enforced long before the date of the Convention; but since 1907 they have certainly been crimes, punishable as offences against the laws of war; yet the Hague Convention nowhere designates such practices as criminal, nor is any sentence prescribed, nor any mention made of a court to try and punish offenders. For many years past, however, military tribunals have tried and punished individuals guilty of violating the rules of land warfare laid down by this Convention. In the opinion of the Tribunal, those who wage aggressive war are doing that which is equally illegal, and of much greater moment than a breach of one of the rules of the Hague Convention. In interpreting the words of the Pact, it must be remembered that international law is not the product of an international legislature, and that such international agreements as the Pact of Paris have to deal with general principles of law, and not with administrative matters of procedure. The law of war is to be found not only in treaties, but in the customs and practices of states which gradually obtained universal recognition, and from the general principles of justice applied by jurists and practised by military courts. This law is not static, but by continual adaptation follows the needs of a changing world. Indeed, in many cases treaties do no more than express and define for more accurate reference the principles of law already existing.

The view which the Tribunal takes of the true interpretation of the Pact is supported by the international history which preceded it. . . . Crimes against international law are committed by men, not by abstract entities, and only by punishing individuals who commit such crimes can the provisions of international law be enforced. . . .

The principle of international law, which under certain circumstances, protects the representatives of a state, cannot be applied to acts which are condemned as criminal by international law. The authors of these acts cannot shelter themselves behind their official position in order to be freed from punishment in appropriate proceedings. Article 7 of the Charter expressly declares:

> The official position of defendants, whether as Heads of State or responsible officials in government departments, shall not be considered as freeing them from responsibility, or mitigating punishment.

On the other hand the very essence of the Charter is that individuals have international duties which transcend the national obligations of obedience imposed by the individual State. He who violates the laws of war cannot obtain immunity while acting in pursuance of the authority of the State if the State in authorising action moves outside its competence under international law.

It was also submitted on behalf of most of these defendants that in doing what they did they were acting under the orders of Hitler, and therefore cannot be held responsible for the acts committed by them in carrying out these orders. The Charter specifically provides in Article 8:

> The fact that the defendant acted pursuant to order of his Government or of a superior shall not free him from responsibility, but may be considered in mitigation of punishment.

The provisions of this Article are in conformity with the law of all nations. That a soldier was ordered to kill or torture in violation of the international law of war has never been recognised as a defence to such acts of brutality, though, as the Charter here provides, the order may be urged in mitigation of the punishment. The true test, which is found in varying degrees in the criminal law of most nations, is not the existence of the order, but whether moral choice was in fact possible.

*

The victorious alliance had, as early as 1941, begun calling themselves 'the United Nations' and they pledged themselves to create a new collective security organization after the war. At the San Francisco Conference in 1945 this new organization, the United Nations Organization (UNO), was established. This provided a far greater degree of centralization than did the League in that, instead of leaving it to individual member States to decide upon what sanctions they would take against an aggressor, the new Security Council was to be endowed with 'primary responsibility' for the maintenance of international peace and the decisions of the Council were to be binding on all members. The Security Council was to fulfil this responsibility *either* by recommending procedures or terms for the settlement of disputes (Chapter VI of the Charter) *or* by deciding upon preventive or enforcement action (Chapter VII of the Charter). However, there was one fundamental requirement for all important (or, more accurately, 'non-procedural') decisions and that was that the Big Five—the permanent members, Britain, France, China, USSR, USA—should concur: each has a power of veto. The assumption made in 1945 that the war-time alliance would maintain its basic agreement on all vital matters affecting world peace has, of course, proved quite false: far from continuing in alliance the split between East and West—the 'Cold War'—became the most marked feature of the post 1945 era. Thus, the Security Council has never worked as intended. As one consequence of this breakdown of political unity, the Security Council has never been able to agree upon the kind of agreements which were to be made under Article 43 of the Charter so as to commit member States to providing the armed forces with which the Council could then combat aggression. To date, no State is legally obliged to provide armed forces and, indeed, armed enforcement action has never been taken against any State under Article 42. Economic sanctions were ordered against Rhodesia in 1966 and, as we shall see in Part III, the Security Council has also developed a notion of 'peace-keeping operations' involving the use of military forces voluntarily contributed by members, although not to be used as a fighting force against any State. However, this falls very far short of the scheme originally envisaged in Chapter VII of the UN Charter.

DOCUMENT 4. EXTRACTS FROM THE UNITED NATIONS CHARTER, 1945

Article 1. The purposes of the United Nations are:

1. To maintain international peace and security, and to that end: to take effective collective measures for the prevention and removal of threats to the peace, and for the suppression of acts of aggression or other breaches of the peace, and to bring about by peaceful means, and in conformity with the principles of justice and international law, adjustment or settlement of international disputes or situations which might lead to a breach of the peace;

2. To develop friendly relations among nations based on respect for the principle of equal rights and self-determination of peoples, and to take other appropriate measures to strengthen universal peace;

3. To achieve international co-operation in solving international problems of an economic, social, cultural, or humanitarian character, and in promoting and encouraging respect for human rights and for fundamental freedoms for all without distinction as to race, sex, language or religion; and

4. To be a centre for harmonizing the actions of nations in the attainment of these common ends.

Article 2. The Organization and its Members, in pursuit of the Purposes stated in Article 1, shall act in accordance with the following Principles.

1. The Organization is based on the principle of the sovereign equality of all its Members.

2. All Members, in order to ensure to all of them the rights and benefits resulting from membership, shall fulfil in good faith the obligations assumed by them in accordance with the present Charter.

3. All Members shall settle their international disputes by peaceful means in such a manner that international peace and security, and justice, are not endangered.

4. All Members shall refrain in their international relations from the threat or use of force against the territorial integrity or political independence of any state, or in any other manner inconsistent with the Purposes of the United Nations.

5. All Members shall give the United Nations every assistance in any action it takes in accordance with the present Charter, and shall refrain from giving assistance to any state against which the United Nations is taking preventive or enforcement action.

6. The Organization shall ensure that states which are not Members of the United Nations act in accordance with these Principles so far as may be necessary for the maintenance of international peace and security.

7. Nothing contained in the present Charter shall authorize the United Nations to intervene in matters which are essentially within the domestic jurisdiction of any state or shall require the Members to submit such matters to settlement under the present Charter; but this principle shall not prejudice the application of enforcement measures under Chapter VII.

The Security Council

Composition

Article 23. 1. The Security Council shall consist of fifteen Members of the United Nations. The Republic of China, France, the Union of Soviet Socialist Republics, the United Kingdom of Great Britain and Northern Ireland, and the United States of America shall be permanent members of the Security Council. The General Assembly shall elect ten other Members of the United Nations to be non-permanent members of the Security Council, due regard being specially paid, in the first instance to the contribution of Members of the United Nations to the maintenance of international peace and security and to the other purposes of the Organization, and also to equitable geographical distribution.

2. The non-permanent members of the Security Council shall be elected for a term of two years. In the first election of the non-permanent members after the increase of the membership of the Security Council from eleven to fifteen, two of the four additional members shall be chosen for a term of one year. A retiring member shall not be eligible for immediate re-election.

3. Each member of the Security Council shall have one representative.

Functions and Powers

Article 24. 1. In order to ensure prompt and effective action by the United Nations, its Members confer on the Security Council primary responsibility for the maintenance of international peace and security, and agree that in carrying out its duties under this responsibility the Security Council acts on their behalf. . . .

Article 25. The Members of the United Nations agree to accept and carry out the decisions of the Security Council in accordance with the present Charter.

Voting

Article 27. 1. Each member of the Security Council shall have one vote.

2. Decisions of the Security Council on procedural matters shall be made by an affirmative vote of nine members.

3. Decisions of the Security Council on all other matters shall be made by an affirmative vote of nine members including the concurring votes of the permanent members; provided that, in decisions under Chapter VI, and under paragraph 3 of Article 52, a party to a dispute shall abstain from voting. . . .

Chapter VI
Pacific Settlement of Disputes

Article 33. 1. The parties to any dispute, the continuance of which is likely to endanger the maintenance of international peace and security, shall, first of all, seek a solution by negotiation, enquiry, mediation, conciliation, arbitration, judicial settlement, resort to regional agencies or arrangements, or other peaceful means of their own choice.

2. The Security Council shall, when it deems necessary, call upon the parties to settle their dispute by such means.

Article 34. The Security Council may investigate any dispute, or any situation which might lead to international friction or give rise to a dispute, in order to determine whether the continuance of the dispute or situation is likely to endanger the maintenance of international peace and security.

Article 35. 1. Any Member of the United Nations may bring any dispute, or any situation of the nature referred to in Article 34, to the attention of the Security Council or of the General Assembly.

2. A state which is not a Member of the United Nations may bring to the attention of the Security Council or of the General Assembly any dispute to which it is a party if it accepts in advance, for the purposes of the dispute, the obligations of pacific settlement provided in the present Charter.

3. The proceedings of the General Assembly in respect of matters brought to its attention under this Article will be subject to the provisions of Articles 11 and 12.

Article 36. 1. The Security Council may, at any stage of a dispute of the nature referred to in Article 33 or of a situation of like nature, recommend appropriate procedures or methods of adjustment.

2. The Security Council should take into consideration any procedures for the settlement of the dispute which have already been adopted by the parties.

3. In making recommendations under this Article the Security Council should also take into consideration that legal disputes should as a general rule be referred by the parties to the International Court of Justice in accordance with the provisions of the Statute of the Court.

Article 37. 1. Should the parties to a dispute of the nature referred to in Article 33 fail to settle it by the means indicated in that Article, they shall refer it to the Security Council.

2. If the Security Council deems that the continuance of the dispute is in fact likely to endanger the maintenance of international peace and security it shall decide whether to take action under Article 36 or to recommend such terms of settlement as it may consider appropriate.

Article 38. Without prejudice to the provisions of Articles 33 to 37, the Security Council may, if all the parties to any dispute so request, make recommendations to the parties with a view to a pacific settlement of the dispute.

Chapter VII
Action with Respect to Threats to the Peace, Breaches of the Peace, and Acts of Aggression

Article 39. The Security Council shall determine the existence of any threat to the peace, breach of the peace, or act of aggression and shall make recommendations, or decide what measures shall be taken in accordance with Articles 41 and 42, to maintain or restore international peace and security.

Article 40. In order to prevent an aggravation of the situation, the Security Council may, before making the recommendations or deciding upon the measures provided for in Article 39, call upon the parties concerned to comply with such provisional measures as it deems necessary or desirable. Such provisional measures shall be without prejudice to the rights, claims, or position of the parties concerned. The Security Council shall duly take account of failure to comply with such provisional measures.

Article 41. The Security Council may decide what measures not involving the use of armed force are to be employed to give effect to its decisions, and it may call upon the Members of the United Nations to apply such measures. These may include complete or partial interruption of economic relations and of rail, sea, air, postal, telegraphic, radio, and other means of communication, and the severance of diplomatic relations.

Article 42. Should the Security Council consider that measures provided for in Article 41 would be inadequate or have proved to be inadequate, it may take such action by air, sea, or land forces as may be necessary to maintain or restore international peace and security. Such action may include demonstrations, blockade, and other operations by air, sea, or land forces of Members of the United Nations.

Article 43. 1. All Members of the United Nations, in order to contribute to the maintenance of international peace and security, undertake to make available to the Security Council, on its call and in accordance with a special agreement or agreements, armed forces, assistance, and facilities, including rights of passage, necessary for the purpose of maintaining international peace and security.

2. Such agreement or agreements shall govern the numbers and types of forces, their degree of readiness and general location, and the nature of the facilities and assistance to be provided.

3. The agreement or agreements shall be negotiated as soon as possible on the initiative of the Security Council. They shall be concluded between the Security Council and Members or between the Security Council and groups of Members and shall be subject to ratification by the signatory states in accordance with their respective constitutional processes. . . .

Article 47. 1. There shall be established a Military Staff Committee to advise and assist the Security Council on all questions relating to the Security Council's military requirements for the maintenance of international peace and security, the employment and command of forces placed at its disposal, the regulation of armaments, and possible disarmament.

2. The Military Staff Committee shall consist of the Chiefs

of Staff of the permanent members of the Security Council or their representatives. . . .

Article 51. Nothing in the present Charter shall impair the inherent right of individual or collective self-defence if an armed attack occurs against a Member of the United Nations, until the Security Council has taken measures necessary to maintain international peace and security. Measures taken by Members in the exercise of this right of self-defence shall be immediately reported to the Security Council and shall not in any way affect the authority and responsibility of the Security Council under the present Charter to take at any time such action as it deems necessary in order to maintain or restore international peace and security.

*

Although Article 39 of the UN Charter refers to 'threats to the peace, breach of the peace or act of aggression' by way of defining the circumstances in which it would be permissible to use the Council's powers under Chapter VII, it will be noted that what is actually prohibited for States under Article 2(4) is the 'threat or use of force'. To date, the UN has failed to achieve any accepted definition either of the concept of 'aggression' or of the 'threat or use of force'. This failure reflects one of the most difficult contemporary problems of regulating violence in international society.

The traditional method of attacking a State lay in the use of military force: there was an overt act of invasion or bombardment. True, there remained the difficult task of deciding which of the two or more combatant States was the aggressor and which the victim acting in self-defence—a right expressly preserved for all member States under Article 51 of the Charter. But, assuming a State's plea of self-defence could not be justified, there was little difficulty in characterizing the open use of military force as 'aggression'.

(b) THE CONTEMPORARY PROBLEM OF SUBVERSION AND INTERVENTION

Today, though acts of overt military aggression continue, we face the problem of the infinitely varied, subtler techniques of 'subversion' by which one State may destroy the independence of another. These range from hostile propaganda to espionage, sabotage, providing training, financial and material support for armed bands operating either from the territory of the 'aggressor' or within the territory of the 'victim' (or both) and the use of political or even economic pressure. These insidious forms of coercion are in fact ideally suited to a situation, such as now exists in the world, in which great powers strive for political control over areas occupied by weaker powers. The western powers and the communist powers demonstrate an obvious reluctance to extend their areas of influence by military conquest: to do so would involve condemnation by the world at large and possibly a risk of open conflict with each other. Hence these other forms of pressure become preferable either as a means of persuading a Government to accept alliance or of overthrowing a Government which opposes alliance. It is in this context of a struggle for influence that the question arises whether methods of coercion or pressure are to be outlawed. Clearly, the blandishments of promises of economic or military aid are generally regarded as permissible, but the doubts over other forms of coercion are amply revealed in the following extract from the report of a UN Special Committee which failed to reach complete agreement on the scope of the prohibition of Article 2(4).

DOCUMENT 5. EXTRACTS FROM THE REPORT OF THE UN SPECIAL COMMITTEE ON PRINCIPLES OF INTERNATIONAL LAW CONCERNING FRIENDLY RELATIONS AND CO-OPERATION AMONG STATES, 1967 (UN DOC. A/6799)[1]

1. *General prohibition of force*

There was agreement on the following statement:

(i) Every State has the duty to refrain in its international relations from the threat or use of force against the territorial integrity or political independence of any State, or in any other manner inconsistent with the purposes of the United Nations.

It was also agreed that:

[1]See now the Declaration adopted by the General Assembly in Resol. 2625 (1970).

Consequently, such a threat or use of force shall never be used as a means of settling international issues.

2. *Consequences and corollaries of the prohibition of the threat or use of force*

(i) There was agreement in principle that a war of aggression constitutes a crime against the peace.

(ii) There was also agreement in principle on the inclusion of the concept of responsibility for wars of aggression.

(iii) There was no agreement whether a statement on war propaganda should be included.

3. *Use of force in territorial disputes and boundary problems*

There was agreement in principle that every State has the duty to refrain from the threat or use of force to violate the existing boundaries of another State or as a means of solving international disputes, including territorial disputes and problems concerning frontiers between States. There was no agreement whether there should be a reference to international lines of demarcation in this connection.

4. *Acts of reprisal*

There was agreement that every State has the duty to refrain from acts of armed reprisal, but agreement was not reached on whether a statement to this effect should refer as well to acts of this nature not involving the use of armed force.

5. *Organization of armed bands*

There was agreement in principle that every State has the duty to refrain from organizing or encouraging the organization of irregular or volunteer forces for incursion into the territory of another State.

No agreement was reached whether a statement to this effect should be included under the principle concerning the threat or use of force, or under the principle of non-intervention.

Nor was agreement reached on the application of this rule to situations where force is used to deprive peoples of dependent territories of the right to self-determination.

6. *Instigation of civil strife and terrorist acts*

There was agreement in principle that every State has the duty to refrain from involvement in civil strife and terrorist acts in another State. However, agreement was not reached as to whether a statement to this effect should be included under the principle concerning the threat or use of force or under the principle of non-intervention. Nor was agreement reached with regard to its application to situations where force is used to deprive peoples of dependent territories of the right to self-determination.

7. *Military occupation and non-recognition of situations brought about by the illegal threat or use of force*

There was no agreement on the inclusion of a statement to the effect that the territory of a State may never be the object of military occupation or other measures of force on any grounds whatsoever.

Nor was there agreement whether a statement should be included requiring that situations brought about by an illegal threat or use of force would not be recognized.

8. *Armed forces or repressive measures against colonial peoples, the position of territories under colonial rule, and the Charter obligations with respect to dependent territories*

There was no agreement on the inclusion of a statement on a duty of States to refrain from the use of force against peoples of dependent territories.

9. *Economic, political and other forms of pressure*

There was no agreement whether the duty to refrain from the threat or use of 'force' included a duty to refrain from economic, political or any other form of pressure against the political independence or territorial integrity of a State. Nor was agreement reached on the inclusion of a definition of the term 'force' in a statement of this principle.

*

The problem of 'subversion' is germane not only to the prohibition of force under Article 2(4) but also to the duty of non-intervention, a duty not specifically mentioned in the Charter. Many States have in fact preferred to see Article 2(4) confined to traditional, military force and to deal with these other forms of impermissible interference or coercion under this other concept of non-intervention. It is, moreover, this concept which is particularly relevant to situations of civil strife in which outside powers may seek to intervene in order to ensure the triumph of that faction which is friendly towards their own policies. The intervention thus aims at ensuring the victory of a future ally or, at the least, of ensuring that a potentially antagonistic Government does not succeed to power.

A particularly sensitive problem has been that of the 'colonialist' régime faced with a 'liberation movement' backed by outside powers. The Soviet bloc and most of the Afro-Asian powers have taken the view that a struggle for liberation, in the exercise of the right of self-determination, is not only in itself lawful, but that any outside power may legitimately assist such a liberation movement. This view is opposed not only by States like South Africa, Portugal and Great Britain but by many others who sympathize with the aim of terminating colonialism but are opposed to outside intervention as a means, and this largely because of the threat to world peace created by such intervention. The other ground for opposition is that, for the Soviet bloc, a 'colonialist' régime can only exist in the overseas territories of the western powers: the Soviet bloc denies that 'colonialism' or the right of self-determination, or the right of intervention, can exist in relation to the territories of eastern Europe under Soviet control.

The UN Special Committee has, not surprisingly, so far failed to secure general agreement on the scope of the principle of non-intervention. The General Assembly has, however, formulated its own views in a resolution of 1965: this is not an agreed statement of law, binding on States, but it is indicative of the general desire to prohibit these techniques of interference.

The problem is obviously crucial to world peace: it is simply not enough to outlaw the use of conventional force International society must achieve a set of 'ground-rules' which will safeguard the independence of States from these other forms of coercion and maintain a state of 'peaceful coexistence' between the rival power blocs.

DOCUMENT 6. DECLARATION ON THE INADMISSIBILITY OF INTER-
VENTION IN THE INTERNAL AFFAIRS OF STATES AND THE PROTEC-
TION OF THEIR INDEPENDENCE AND SOVEREIGNTY: RESOLUTION
2131 (XX) OF THE GENERAL ASSEMBLY OF THE UNITED NATIONS,
21 DECEMBER 1965

1. No State has the right to intervene, directly or indirectly,
for any reason whatever, in the internal or external affairs of
any other State. Consequently, armed intervention and all
other forms of interference or attempted threats against the
personality of the State or against its political, economic and
cultural elements, are condemned.

2. No State may use or encourage the use of economic,
political or any other type of measures to coerce another State
in order to obtain from it the subordination of the exercise of
its sovereign rights or to secure from it advantages of any kind.
Also, no State shall organize, assist, foment, finance, incite or
tolerate subversive, terrorist, or armed activities directed
towards the violent overthrow of the régime of another State,
or interfere in civil strife in another State.

3. The use of force to deprive peoples of their national
identity constitutes a violation of their inalienable rights and
of the principle of non-intervention.

4. The strict observance of these obligations is an essential
condition to ensure that nations live together in peace with one
another, since the practice of any form of intervention not only
violates the spirit and letter of the Charter of the United Nations
but also leads to the creation of situations which threaten
international peace and security.

5. Every State has an inalienable right to choose its political,
economic, social and cultural systems, without interference in
any form by another State.

6. All States shall respect the right of self-determination and
independence of peoples and nations, to be freely exercised
without any foreign pressure, and with absolute respect to
human rights and fundamental freedoms. Consequently, all
States shall contribute to the complete elimination of racial
discrimination and colonialism in all its forms and mani-
festations.

7. For the purpose of the present Declaration, the term

'State' covers both individual States and groups of States.

8. Nothing in this Declaration shall be construed as affecting in any manner the relevant provisions of the Charter of the United Nations relating to the maintenance of international peace and security, in particular those contained in Chapters VI, VII and VIII.

*

This Declaration was passed overwhelmingly by the General Assembly, by 109 votes to nil, with one abstention (UK). The question is, do States really intend to abide by any set of 'ground-rules' which the principle of non-intervention involves? Many people would regard the policies of the United States in Vietnam, in Latin America (the Bay of Pigs invasion of Cuba in 1961, the landing of marines in the Dominican Republic in 1965, etc.), and even in the Middle East as 'interventionist'. Equally in question is the Soviet Union's record in Hungary in 1956, or in Czechoslovakia in 1968; or the Anglo-French invasion of Suez in 1956; or the Chinese invasion of Tibet in 1959—all these incidents cause the smaller powers to question the intentions of the great powers. Of course, in most cases a great power seeks to justify its actions as 'counter-intervention', i.e. that it was forced to intervene in order to protect the independence of a State threatened by the prior intervention of the other side. At this point, clearly, the problem is not only one of defining what we mean by prohibited intervention but also of ascertaining the facts: essentially, the question is 'Who started intervening?'

The core of the problem lies in the fact that neither East nor West really believes the other is prepared to abandon intervention as a means of extending, or perpetuating, its influence in foreign countries. And, given the records of both sides, this is not surprising.

From the western point of view there remains the basic question of whether communism is committed to a policy of destruction of the capitalist systems of the West by means of war, subversion or intervention. Soviet interpretation of Marxism has changed since the days of Trotsky and, currently, the Soviet Union renounces force as an instrument for the destruction of capitalism: the present emphasis is on 'peaceful coexistence' between East and West and a rejection of the inevitability of conflict. It is, however, unclear how far China subscribes to this view. Moreover, there remain many advocates of the communist cause who are convinced that revolution and subversion are legitimate and necessary means of overthrowing capitalism abroad. Indeed, many in the West would regard the Soviet Union's rejection of these techniques as false and insincere since, whilst the Soviet Union might itself refrain from war or active, open intervention within the western world, it remains prepared to encourage, finance and abet it when carried out by others.

From the communist point of view, western capitalism retains a continuing domination of many parts of the world, denying to the peoples of those countries the right of self-determination and the right to elect for socialism (communism) in place of the present, oppressive, capitalist régimes. This therefore represents, from that point of view, a continuing intervention which must be eliminated: the only real question, as indicated above, is as to the means legitimate for this purpose. The next three documents, all extracts from communist writers, show how widely divergent are their views on this issue, and how differently they construe 'peaceful co-existence'.

DOCUMENT 7. EXTRACTS FROM AN ARTICLE ON 'PEACEFUL CO-EXISTENCE' BY NIKITA S. KHRUSHCHEV IN *Foreign Affairs* (SEPT. 1959)

I have been told that the question of peaceful coexistence of states with different social systems is uppermost today in the minds of many Americans—and not only Americans. The question of coexistence, particularly in our day, interests literally every man and woman. We all know well that tremendous changes have taken place in the world.

Gone, indeed, are the days when it took weeks to cross the ocean from one continent to the other or when a trip from Europe to America, or from Asia to Africa, was an extremely complicated undertaking. By the scale of modern technology our planet is not very big; in this sense, it has even become somewhat congested. And if in our daily life it is a matter of considerable importance to establish normal relations with our neighbours in a densely inhabited settlement, this is so much the more necessary in the relations between states, especially states belonging to different social systems.

You may like your neighbour or dislike him. You are not obliged to be friends with him or visit him. But you live side by side, and what can you do if neither you nor he has any desire to quit the old home and move to another town? All the more so in relations between states. It would be unreasonable to assume that you can make it so hot for your undesirable neighbour that he will decide to move to Mars or Venus. And vice versa, of course.

What else can be done? There may be two ways out: either war—and war in the age of rockets and H-bombs is fraught with the most dire consequences for all nations—or peaceful coexistence. Whether you like your neighbour or not, nothing can be done about it, you have to find some way of getting on with him, for we live on one planet.

But the very concept of peaceful coexistence, it is said, frightens certain people who have lost the habit of trusting their neighbours and who see a double bottom in every suitcase, by its alleged complexity. On hearing the word 'coexistence', people of this kind begin to juggle about with it one way and another, sizing it up and applying various yardsticks to it— could it be a fraud? or a trap? Does existence, perhaps, signify a division of the world into areas separated by high fences, which do not communicate with each other at all? And what is going to happen behind those fences?

The more such questions are piled up artificially by the 'cold war' warriors, the more difficult it is for the ordinary man to make head or tail of them. It would therefore be timely to divest the essence of this question of all superfluous elements and to attempt to look soberly at the most pressing problem of our day—the problem of peaceful coexistence. . . .

What is the policy of peaceful coexistence?

In its simplest expression it signifies the repudiation of war as a means of solving controversial issues. However, this does not by any means exhaust the concept of peaceful coexistence. Apart from commitment to non-aggression, it also presupposes an obligation on the part of all states to desist from violating each other's territorial integrity and sovereignty in any form and under any pretext whatsoever. The principle of peaceful coexistence signifies a renunciation of interference in the internal affairs of other countries with the object of altering their political system or mode of life, or for any other motives. The doctrine of peaceful coexistence also presupposes that political and economic relations between countries are to be based upon complete equality of the parties concerned, and upon mutual benefit.

It is quite often said in the West that peaceful coexistence is nothing but a tactical move of the socialist states. There is not a grain of truth in such allegations.

Our desire for peace and peaceful coexistence is not prompted by any time-serving or tactical considerations. It springs from the very nature of socialist society in which there are no classes or social groups interested in profiting by means of war or by seizing and enslaving foreign territories. The Soviet Union and other socialist countries, thanks to their socialist system, have an unlimited home market and, for this reason, they have no need to pursue an expansionist policy of conquest and subordination of other countries to their influence.

It is the people who determine the destiny of the socialist countries. The socialist countries are ruled by the working people themselves—the workers and the peasants, the people who themselves create all the material and spiritual values of society. And working people cannot want war. For to them war spells grief and tears, death, devastation and misery. Ordinary people have no need for war.

Contrary to what certain propagandists hostile to us say, the coexistence of states with different social systems does not mean that they will only fence themselves off from one another by a high wall and undertake the mutual obligation not to throw stones over the wall and not to pour dirt upon each other. No, peaceful coexistence does not merely mean cohabiting side by side in the absence of war but with the constantly remaining threat of its breaking out in the future. *Peaceful coexistence can and should develop into peaceful competition in the best possible satisfaction of all man's needs.*

We say to the leaders of the capitalist states: Let us try out in practice whose system is better, let us compete without war. That is much better than competing in who produces more arms and who smashes whom. We stand, and always will stand, for such competition as will help to raise the well-being of the peoples to a higher level.

The principle of peaceful competition does not at all demand that a country abandon its accepted system and ideology. It goes without saying that the acceptance of this principle cannot lead to the immediate end of disputes and contradictions, which are inevitable between countries adhering to different social systems. But the main thing is ensured: the states which have decided to take the path of peaceful coexistence repudiate the use of force in any form and agree on the peaceful adjustment of possible disputes and conflicts with due regard for the mutual interests of the parties concerned. And in our age of H-bomb and atomic techniques this is the main thing of interest to every man. . . .

The Communist Party of the Soviet Union at its Twentieth Congress has made it perfectly clear and obvious that the allegations that the Soviet Union intends to overthrow capitalism in other countries by 'exporting' revolution are absolutely groundless. I cannot refrain from reminding you of my words at the Twentieth Congress. They ran as follows: 'It goes without saying that among us Communists there are no adherents of capitalism. But this does not mean at all that we have interfered or plan to interfere in the internal affairs of those countries where capitalism exists. Romain Rolland was right when he said that 'freedom is not brought in from abroad in baggage trains like the Bourbons'. It is ridiculous to think that revolutions are made to order.

We Communists believe that the idea of communism will ultimately triumph throughout the world, just as it has triumphed in our country, in China, and in many other states. Many readers of *Foreign Affairs* will probably disagree with us. Perhaps they think that it is the idea of capitalism that will ultimately triumph. It is their right to think so. We may argue, we may disagree with one another. *The main thing is to keep to the sphere of ideological struggle, without resorting to arms in order to prove that one is right.* The point is that with military techniques what they are today, there are now no spots in the world that are out of reach. Should a world war break out, no country will be able to shut itself off in any way from a crushing blow.

We believe that ultimately that system will be victorious on the globe which will offer the nations greater opportunities for improving their material and spiritual life. It is socialism that creates unprecedentedly great prospects for the inexhaustible creative enthusiasm of the masses, for a genuine flourishing of science and culture, for the realisation of man's longing for a happy life, a life without destitute and unemployed people, for happy childhood and tranquil old age, for the realisation of the most audacious and ambitious human projects, for man's right to create in a truly free manner in the interests of the people.

But when we say that in the competition between the two systems, the capitalist and the socialist, our system will win, this does not signify by any means, of course, that we shall achieve victory by interfering in the internal affairs of the capitalist countries. . . .

We believe that in the long run all the peoples will embark on the path of struggle for the building of socialist society.

You disagree with us? Prove in practice that your system is superior and more efficacious, that it is capable of ensuring a higher degree of prosperity for the people than the socialist system, that under capitalism man can be happier than under socialism. It is impossible to prove this. I have no other explanation for the fact that talk of violently 'rolling back' communism never ceases in the West. Not long ago the U.S. Senate and House of Representatives saw fit to pass a resolution calling for the 'liberation' of the socialist countries allegedly enslaved by communism and, moreover, of a number of Union Republics constituting part of the Soviet Union. The authors of the resolution call for the 'liberation' of the Ukraine, Byelorussia, Lithuania, Latvia, Estonia, Armenia, Azerbaijan, Georgia, Kazakhstan, Turkmenistan and even the 'Ural Area'.

I would not be telling the full truth if I did not say that the adoption of this ill-starred resolution was regarded by the Soviet people as an act of provocation. Personally, I agree with this appraisal. . . .

So we come back to what we started with. In our day there are only two ways—peaceful coexistence or the most destructive war in history. There is no third way.

The problem of peaceful coexistence between states with

different social systems has become particularly pressing in view of the fact that after the Second World War the development of relations between states has entered a new phase. Now we have approached a period in the life of mankind when there is a real chance of excluding war once and for all from the life of society.

How can this be done?

The new alignment of international forces which has developed since the Second World War offers ground for the assertion that a new world war is no longer fatally inevitable, that it can be averted.

First, today not only all the socialist states, but many countries in Asia and Africa which have embarked upon the road of independent national statehood, and many other states outside the aggressive military groupings, are actively fighting for peace.

Secondly, the peace policy enjoys the powerful support of the broad masses of people all over the world.

Thirdly, the peaceful socialist states are in possession of very potent material means, which cannot but have a deterring effect upon the aggressors.

Prior to the Second World War, the U.S.S.R. was the only socialist country, with only about 17 per cent of the area, about 9 per cent of the population, and about 10 per cent of the output of the world. At present, the socialist countries cover about one-fourth of the area of the globe inhabited by one-third of the world population, and their industrial output accounts for about one-third of the world output.

This is precisely the explanation of the indisputable fact that throughout the recent years, seats of war arising now in one and now in another part of the globe—in the Middle East and in Europe, in the Far East and in South-East Asia—were nipped in the bud.

And what lies ahead?

As a result of the fulfilment and overfulfilment of the Seven-Year Plan of Economic Development of the U.S.S.R., and of the plans of the other socialist countries of Europe and Asia, the countries of the socialist system will account for somewhat more than half of the world output. Their economic power will grow immeasurably, and this will serve to an even greater extent to consolidate world peace: the material might and moral influence of the peace-loving states will be so great that any bellicose militarist will have to think ten times before risking war. It is the good fortune of mankind that there has emerged a community of socialist states which are not interested in new wars, because to build socialism and communism the socialist countries need peace. Today the community of socialist countries which has sprung up on the basis of complete equality holds such a position in the development of all branches of economy, science and culture as to be able to exert an influence towards preventing the outbreak of new world wars.

Hence, we are already in a practical sense near to that stage in the life of humanity when nothing will prevent people from devoting themselves wholly to peaceful labour, when war will be wholly excluded from the life of society.

But if we say that there is no fatal inevitability of war at present, this by no means signifies that we can rest on our laurels, fold our arms and bask in the sun in the hope that an end has been put to wars once and for all. Those in the West who believe that war is to their benefit have not yet abandoned their schemes. They control considerable material forces, military and political levers, and there is no guarantee that some tragic day they will not attempt to set them in motion. All the more necessary is it to continue an active struggle in order that the policy of peaceful coexistence may triumph throughout the world not in words but in deeds.

Of much importance, of course, is the fact that this policy has in our day won not only the widest moral approval but also international legal recognition. The countries of the socialist camp in their relations with the capitalist states are guided precisely by this policy. The principles of peaceful coexistence are reflected in the decisions of the Bandung Conference of Asian and African countries. Furthermore, many countries of Europe, Asia and Africa have solemnly proclaimed this principle as the basis of their foreign policy. Lastly, the idea of peaceful coexistence was unanimously supported in the decisions of the twelfth and thirteenth sessions of the United Nations General Assembly. . . .

What is still needed to make the principles of peaceful coexistence an unshakeable international standard and daily practice in the relations between the West and East?

Of course, different answers may be given to this question. But to be quite frank, the following still has to be said: *Everybody should understand the irrevocable fact that the historic process is irreversible.* It is impossible to bring back yesterday. It is time to understand that the world of the twentieth century is not the world of the nineteenth century, that two diametrically opposite social and economic systems exist side by side in the world today, and that the socialist system, in spite of all the attacks upon it, has grown so strong, has developed into such a force, as to make any return to the past impossible.

Real facts of life in the last ten years have shown convincingly that the policy of 'rolling back' communism can do no more than poison the international atmosphere, heighten the tension between states and work in favour of the 'cold war'. Neither its inspirers nor those who conduct it can turn back the course of history and restore capitalism in the socialist countries. . . .

One cannot help seeing that the policy of peaceful coexistence acquires a firm foundation only in the event of extensive and absolutely unrestricted international trade. It may be said without exaggeration that there is no good basis for improving relations between our countries other than the development of international trade. . . .

No ideological differences have prevented, for instance, a considerable extention of trade relations between the Soviet Union and Britain and other Western states in recent years.

We make no secret of our desire to establish normal commercial and business contacts without any restrictions, without any discriminations, with the United States as well. . . .

Peaceful coexistence is the only way which is in keeping with the interests of all nations. To reject it would under existing conditions mean to doom the whole world to a terrible and destructive war, whereas it is quite possible to avoid it. . . .

Precisely because we want to rid mankind of war, do we urge the Western Powers to peaceful and noble competition. We say to all: Let us prove to each other the advantages of one's own system not with fists, not by war, but by peaceful economic competition in conditions of peaceful coexistence.

As for the social system in a country, that is the domestic affair of its people. We have always stood, and stand today, for non-interference in the internal affairs of other countries.[1] We have always abided, and shall abide, by this standpoint. The question, for example, of what system shall exist in the United States or in other capitalist countries cannot be decided by other peoples or states. This question can and will be decided only by the American people themselves, only by the people of each country.

The existence of the Soviet Union and of the other socialist countries is a real fact. It is also a real fact that the United States of America and other capitalist countries live in different social conditions, in the conditions of capitalism. Then let us recognise this real situation and proceed from it in order not to go against reality, against life itself. Let us not try to change this situation by interference from without, by means of war on the part of some states against other states.

I repeat, there is only one road to peace, one way out of the existing tension—peaceful coexistence.

DOCUMENT 8. QUOTATIONS FROM CHAIRMAN MAO TSE-TUNG, 1937–57, IN *The Little Red Book* (FOREIGN LANGUAGES PRESS, PEKING, 2ND ED., 1967)

War is the highest form of struggle for resolving contradictions, when they have developed to a certain stage, between classes, nations, states, or political groups, and it has existed ever since the emergence of private property and of classes ('Problems of Strategy in China's Revolutionary War' (December 1936), *Selected Works*, Vol. I, p. 180).

'War is the continuation of politics.' In this sense war is politics and war itself is a political action; since ancient times there has never been a war that did not have a political character. . . .

But war has its own particular characteristics and in this

[1] See below, Part IV for the Documents on the Soviet intervention in Czechoslovakia in 1968. Has Soviet policy changed or was this statement insincere even when Khrushchev wrote it? It must be remembered that the Soviets intervened by force in Hungary only three years before this article was written.

sense it cannot be equated with politics in general. 'War is the continuation of politics by other . . . means.' When politics develops to a certain stage beyond which it cannot proceed by the usual means, war breaks out to sweep the obstacles from the way. . . . When the obstacle is removed and our political aim attained, the war will stop. But if the obstacle is not completely swept away, the war will have to continue till the aim is fully accomplished. . . . It can therefore be said that politics is war without bloodshed while war is politics with bloodshed ('On Protracted War' (May 1938), *Selected Works*, Vol. II, pp. 152–3).

History shows that wars are divided into two kinds, just and unjust. All wars that are progressive are just, and all wars that impede progress are unjust. We Communists oppose all unjust wars that impede progress, but we do not oppose progressive, just wars. Not only do we Communists not oppose just wars, we actively participate in them. As for unjust wars, World War I is an instance in which both sides fought for imperialist interests; therefore the Communists of the whole world firmly opposed that war. The way to oppose a war of this kind is to do everything possible to prevent it before it breaks out and, once it breaks out, to oppose war with war, to oppose unjust war with just war, whenever possible (*ibid.*, p. 150).

Revolutions and revolutionary wars are inevitable in class society, and without them it is impossible to accomplish any leap in social development and to overthrow the reactionary ruling classes and therefore impossible for the people to win political power ('On Contradiction' (August 1937), *Selected Works*, Vol. I, p. 344).

Every Communist must grasp the truth, 'Political power grows out of the barrel of a gun' ('Problems of War and Strategy' (6 November 1938), *Selected Works*, Vol. II, p. 224).

The seizure of power by armed force, the settlement of the issue by war, is the central task and the highest form of revolution. This Marxist-Leninist principle of revolution holds good universally, for China and for all other countries (*ibid.*, p. 219).

We are advocates of the abolition of war, we do not want war; but war can only be abolished through war, and in order to get rid of the gun it is necessary to take up the gun (*ibid.*, p. 225).

Over a long period we have developed this concept for the struggle against the enemy: strategically we should despise all our enemies, but tactically we should take them all seriously. This also means that we must despise the enemy with respect to the whole, but that we must take him seriously with respect to each and every concrete question. If we do not despise the enemy with respect to the whole, we shall be committing the error of opportunism. Marx and Engels were only two individuals, and yet in those early days they already declared that capitalism would be overthrown throughout the world. But in dealing with concrete problems and particular enemies we shall be committing the error of adventurism unless we take them seriously. In war, battles can only be fought one by one and the enemy forces can only be destroyed one by one. Factories can only be built one by one. The peasants can only plough the land plot by plot. The same is even true of eating a meal. Strategically, we take the eating of a meal lightly—we know we can finish it. But actually we eat it mouthful by mouthful. It is impossible to swallow an entire banquet in one gulp. This is known as a piecemeal solution. In military parlance, it is called wiping out the enemy forces one by one (Speech at the Moscow Meeting of Communist and Workers' Parties (18 November 1957)).

It is my opinion that the international situation has now reached a new turning point. There are two winds in the world today, the East Wind and the West Wind. There is a Chinese saying, 'Either the East Wind prevails over the West Wind or the West Wind prevails over the East Wind.' I believe it is characteristic of the situation today that the East Wind is prevailing over the West Wind. That is to say, the forces of socialism have become overwhelmingly superior to the forces of imperialism (*ibid.*).

DOCUMENT 9. EXTRACTS FROM THE WRITINGS OF CHE GUEVARA[1]
FROM *Venceremos: the Speeches and Writings of Che Guevara*, ED.
JOHN GERASSI (WEIDENFELD & NICOLSON, LONDON, 1968)

What is to be done? We reply: Violence is not the exclusive preserve of the exploiters; the exploited can use it, and what is more, should use it at the proper time. Martí said: 'He who furthers an avoidable war in a country, and he who fails to further an unavoidable one, is a criminal.'

Lenin, on the other hand, stated:

Social democracy has never approached war from a sentimental point of view, nor does it now. It absolutely condemns war as a violent means of settling differences among men, but it knows that wars are inevitable as long as society is divided into classes, as long as man exploits man. And in order to end this exploitation we shall be unable to avoid war, which, whenever and wherever it occurs, is started by the dominant oppressive exploiters themselves.

He said this in 1905.

Later, in *The Military Program of the Proletarian Revolution*, where he profoundly analyzed the nature of the class struggle, he asserted:

He who accepts the class struggle cannot help accepting civil wars, which in every class society represent the continuation, development, and recrudescence—natural and under certain circumstances inevitable—of the class struggle. All the great revolutions confirm this. To reject civil wars or to forget them would be to lapse into extreme opportunism and to deny the socialist revolution.

That is to say, we must not fear violence, the midwife of new societies. But that violence must break out at the precise moment when the leaders of the people have found circumstances favorable.

What will these conditions be? They depend, where subjective elements are concerned, on two factors which com-

---

[1] Che Guevara, a revolutionary guerrilla fighter, became a cult figure for the youthful Left: an Argentinian, he fought with Castro in Cuba and was shot on 8 October 1967 whilst leading a peasant revolution in Bolivia, apparently betrayed by a woman.

42

plement each other, and which in turn deepen in the course of the struggle: the awareness of the need for change and the certainty of the possibility of this revolutionary change. These, combined with the objective conditions—extremely favorable in almost all of Latin America for the development of the struggle—and with the firm will to achieve it, along with the new correlations of forces in the world, create the time for action.

However distant the socialist countries may be, their beneficent influence on the struggling peoples will always be felt, and their instructive example will give the latter greater strength. Fidel Castro said last July 26:

> And the duty of the revolutionaries, above all at this moment, is to know how to be perceptive, to know how to grasp the changes which have occurred in the world in the correlation of forces, and to understand that this change facilitates the struggle of the different peoples. The duty of revolutionaries [of Latin American revolutionaries] does not consist in waiting for the change in the correlation of forces in order to perform the miracle of social revolutions in Latin America, but in taking full advantage of all the ways in which that change in the correlation of forces favors the revolutionary movement. Above all it consists in creating the revolutions!

There are those who say: 'Let us grant that revolutionary war is the proper means, in certain specific instances, of succeeding in seizing power. Where will we get the great leaders, the Fidel Castros, who will lead us to triumph?' Fidel Castro, like every human being, is a product of history. The military and political heads who lead insurrectionary struggles in Latin America, if they can possibly be united in one single person, will learn the art of war by the waging of war itself. There is no trade or profession that can be learned only from textbooks. Struggle, in this case, is the great teacher. . . . ('Guerrilla Warfare: A method').

America, a forgotten continent in the last liberation struggles, is now beginning to make itself heard through the Tricontinental and, in the voice of the vanguard of its peoples, the Cuban Revolution, will today have a task of much greater relevance:

creating a Second or a Third Vietnam, or the Second *and* Third Vietnam of the world.

We must bear in mind that imperialism is a world system, the last stage of capitalism—and it must be defeated in a world confrontation. The strategic end of this struggle should be the destruction of imperialism. Our share, the responsibility of the exploited and underdeveloped of the world is to eliminate the foundations of imperialism: our oppressed nations, from where they extract capitals, raw materials, technicians and cheap labor, and to which they export new capitals—instruments of domination—arms and all kinds of articles; thus submerging us in an absolute dependance [*sic*].

The fundamental element of this strategic end shall be the real liberation that will be brought about through armed struggle in most cases and which shall be, in Our America, almost indefectibly, a Socialist Revolution.

While envisaging the destruction of imperialism, it is necessary to identify its head, which is no other than the United States of America.

We must carry out a general task with the tactical purpose of getting the enemy out of·its natural environment, forcing him to fight in regions where his own life and habits will clash with the existing reality. We must not underrate our adversary; the U.S. soldier has technical capacity and is backed by weapons and resources of such magnitude that render him frightful. He lacks the essential ideologic motivation which his bitterest enemies of today—the Vietnamese soldiers—have in the highest degree. We will only be able to overcome that army by undermining their morale—and this is accomplished by defeating it and causing it repeated sufferings.

But this brief outline of victories carries within itself the immense sacrifice of the people, sacrifices that should be demanded beginning today, in plain daylight, and which perhaps may be less painful than those we would have to endure if we constantly avoided battle in an attempt to have others pull our chestnuts out of the fire.

It is probable, of course, that the last liberated country shall accomplish this without an armed struggle and the sufferings of a long and cruel war against the imperialists—this they might avoid. But perhaps it will be impossible to avoid this struggle or its effects in a global conflagration; the suffering would be the same, or perhaps even greater. We cannot foresee the future, but we should never give in to the defeatist temptation of being the vanguard of a nation which yearns for freedom, but abhors the struggle it entails and awaits its freedom as a crumb of victory.

It is absolutely just to avoid all useless sacrifices. Therefore, it is so important to clear up the real possibilities that dependent America may have of liberating itself through pacific means. For us, the solution to this question is quite clear: the present moment may or may not be the proper one for starting the struggle, but we cannot harbor any illusions, and we have no right to do so, that freedom can be obtained without fighting. And these battles shall not be mere street fights with stones against tear-gas bombs, or of pacific general strikes; neither shall it be the battle of a furious people destroying in two or three days the repressive scaffolds of the ruling oligarchies; the struggle shall be long, harsh, and its front shall be in the guerrilla's refuge, in the cities, in the homes of the fighters— where the repressive forces shall go seeking easy victims among their families—in the massacred rural population, in the villages or cities destroyed by the bombardments of the enemy.

They are pushing us into this struggle; there is no alternative: we must prepare it and we must decide to undertake it.

The beginnings will not be easy; they shall be extremely difficult. All the oligarchies' powers of repression, all their capacity for brutality and demagoguery will be placed at the service of their cause. Our mission, in the first hour, shall be to survive; later, we shall follow the perennial example of the guerrilla, carrying out armed propaganda (in the Vietnamese sense, that is, the bullets of propaganda, of the battles won or lost—but fought—against the enemy). The great lesson of the invincibility of the guerrillas taking root in the dispossessed masses. The galvanizing of the national spirit, the preparation for harder tasks, for resisting even more violent repressions. Hatred as an element of the struggle; a relentless hatred of the enemy, impelling us over and beyond the natural limitations that man is heir to and transforming him into an effective, violent, selective and cold killing machine. Our soldiers must

45

be thus; a people without hatred cannot vanquish a brutal enemy.

We must carry the war into every corner the enemy happens to carry it: to his home, to his centers of entertainment; a total war. It is necessary to prevent him from having a moment of peace, a quiet moment outside his barracks or even inside; we must attack him wherever he may be; make him feel like a cornered beast wherever he may move. Then his moral fiber shall begin to decline. He will even become more beastly, but we shall notice how the signs of decadence begin to appear.

And let us develop a true proletarian internationalism; with international proletarian armies; the flag under which we fight would be the sacred cause of redeeming humanity. To die under the flag of Vietnam, of Venezuela, of Guatemala, of Laos, of Guinea, of Colombia, of Bolivia, of Brazil—to name only a few scenes of today's armed struggle—would be equally glorious and desirable for an American, an Asian, an African, even a European.

Each spilt drop of blood, in any country under whose flag one has not been born, is an experience passed on to those who survive, to be added later to the liberation struggle of his own country. And each nation liberated is a phase won in the battle for the liberation of one's own country.

The time has come to settle our discrepancies and place everything at the service of our struggle.

We all know great controversies rend the world now fighting for freedom; no one can hide it. We also know that they have reached such intensity and such bitterness that the possibility of dialogue and reconciliation seems extremely difficult, if not impossible. It is a useless task to search for means and ways to propitiate a dialogue which the hostile parties avoid. However, the enemy is there; it strikes every day, and threatens us with new blows and these blows will unite us, today, tomorrow, or the day after. Whoever understands this first, and prepares for this necessary union, shall have the people's gratitude.

Owing to the virulence and the intransigence with which each cause is defended, we, the dispossessed, cannot take sides for one form or the other of these discrepancies, even though sometimes we coincide with the contentions of one party or the other, or in a greater measure with those of one part more than

46

with those of the other. In time of war, the expression of current differences constitutes a weakness; but at this stage it is an illusion to attempt to settle them by means of words. History shall erode them or shall give them their true meaning.

In our struggling world every discrepancy regarding tactics, the methods of action for the attainment of limited objectives should be analyzed with due respect to another man's opinions. Regarding our great strategic objective, the total destruction of imperialism by armed struggle, we should be uncompromising.

Let us sum up our hopes for victory: total destruction of imperialism by eliminating its firmest bulwark: the oppression exercized by the United States of America. To carry out, as a tactical method, the people's gradual liberation, one by one or in groups: driving the enemy into a difficult fight away from its own territory; dismantling all its sustenance bases, that is, its dependent territories.

This means a long war. And, once more we repeat it, a cruel war. Let no one fool himself at the outstart and let no one hesitate to start out for fear of the consequences it may bring to his people. It is almost our sole hope for victory. We cannot elude the call of this hour. Vietnam is pointing it out with its endless lesson of heroism, its tragic and everyday lesson of struggle and death for the attainment of final victory ('Message to the Tricontinental').

*

One relatively new development is worth attention, and this is the desire of mainly small States to avoid involvement in the struggle for power between communism and the West. This desire has been made manifest in their adherence to the political doctrine of 'non-alignment' and, in their common solidarity to maintain this posture against encroachment and involvement from either side, it may well be that the non-aligned powers are making a very substantial contribution to world peace. True, the non-aligned powers have castigated 'colonialism' and supported 'peaceful coexistence' in such terms as to give the impression that their policies coincide with those of the Soviet Union: but this may be quite misleading as to their eventual role. It is perfectly conceivable that in the future, and on major issues like peace-keeping, disarmament or economic aid, they will diverge fundamentally from the Soviet Union.

(c) THE ELIMINATION OF THE CAUSES OF WAR

Obviously, for society to content itself with formal prohibitions of war, force or intervention without tackling the more fundamental problem of the *causes* of conflict would be demonstrably foolish. Why do States fight? This simple question has no simple answer. For the communist the answer is certainly simple: war is a consequence of the capitalist system and therefore, once this is eliminated and a classless society emerges throughout the world, war will cease. The Soviet Union's own relations with Hungary, Czechoslovakia and China—all members of the socialist world—have not given any real assurance that the answer is as simple as that. For a sociologist and international lawyer like the American writer, Quincy Wright, the problem is certainly more complex. He does not resolve the problem, but he certainly clarifies it—albeit by demonstrating its complexity. His acceptance of the economic motivations for some wars is important, for this is a theme to which we must return in Part V when we shall consider the 'North-South rift', the gap between the rich and poor nations as a threat to peace. Again, it becomes clear that war can result from conflicts of ideology: indeed, the 'religious' wars of the past may not be dissimilar in cause from the conflicts between communists and capitalists of today. The ideology may change but they indicate the same order of intolerance in which men strive to ensure the dominance of their beliefs over those of other men by force rather than by example and argument.

Of particular interest, in his later appendix on 'The causes of war in the atomic age', is his conclusion that, even accepting the deterrent effect of nuclear weapons, the balance of power between the USSR and the USA (bipolarized world) affords no guarantee of peace—and a 'multipolar' balance even less so. Thus, to him, the primary problem remains one of 'organizing peace', in particular through disarmament and the strengthening of international law and organization, though he remains uncertain about whether this will be achieved by gradual transition or by sudden transformation of international relations following a new world war. That good sense may need to be proved to mankind by a nuclear war is a saddening, appalling, but necessary thought!

DOCUMENT 10. EXTRACTS FROM AN ARTICLE ON 'PROBLEMS OF WAR AND PEACE IN OUR AGE' BY N. PROKOPYEV IN *International Affairs* (MOSCOW), DECEMBER 1967.

Marxism-Leninism on the Sources and Essence of Wars

The history of class society abounds in wars which have taken an immeasurable toll of lives, caused senseless destruction, calamities and suffering. But the ideologists of the exploiting classes, doing the bidding of their masters, have tried to conceal from the people, the essence and real causes of wars, to justify them in one way or another. To these ends, various pseudo-scientific theories have been devised which seek the causes of wars in man's biological features, in mistakes and delusions of statesmen, and so on.

The servitors of the bourgeoisie assert that wars are an inevitable and eternal phenomenon, that mankind could not develop without them, that there will always be wars as long as human society exists. Stewart Alsop, a well-known American journalist, for example, claims that 'there will never be a time when poverty and war and the attendant miseries of both are wholly banished from the earth'.

Different variants of technocratic theories of war and armed violence in general are now in vogue in the West. These theories are used to prove that war is rooted in contemporary science and technology, not in private property or the imperialist system. In the opinion of Q. Wright, a U.S. sociologist, wars have always accompanied improvements in technology, and since technological progress will never end, war can never be abolished.

The ideologists of anti-Communism also have in their arsenal the extremely dangerous concept of the 'balance of terror', which justifies the arms race. Proponents of this idea seek to prove that thermonuclear weapons as such have become a prime factor in ensuring peace and preventing war.

The ideological armoury of imperialist expansion has other, no less reactionary theories to justify war. Irrespective of their initial premises, form of presentation and degree of frankness, they all aim at preventing the people from realising that imperialism is the sole source of war.

For the first time in the history of social thought, Marxism-Leninism elaborated a dialectical materialist doctrine of war and peace; harmonious, integrated and scientific, this theory reveals all aspects of the essence of war and its causes.

Unlike the unscientific fabrications of bourgeois ideologists, Marxism-Leninism proves that war is a socio-historic development connected with definite transient stages of human society. Wars appeared with the transition of mankind from the primitive communal system of slavery, with the appearance of private property, the division of society into classes and the formation of the state with its 'special bodies of armed men' which developed into a powerful machine of armed coercion.

The possibility of wars stems from the desire of the propertied classes to enrich themselves not only by intensifying the exploitation of the working people in their own country, but also by robbing other countries and peoples. Private ownership of the means of production gives rise to the economic and political inequality of people, to the system of class and national oppression and social and national antagonisms. War is the product and expression of these antagonisms. 'War does not contradict the fundamentals of private property,' Lenin wrote, 'on the contrary, it is a direct and inevitable outcome of those fundamentals.' The sources of war are rooted in the very core of exploiting society, whose ruling classes have always been the organisers and instigators of predatory wars.

Marxism-Leninism, revealing the sources of war, at the same time disclosed the social, class nature and essence of war. It is a many-sided phenomenon, but its main characteristic is its political content. That is why an analysis of the connection between war and politics is the key element for the scientific understanding of war's essence. German military theoretician Karl von Clausewitz coined the formula in his book *Vom Kriege*, that war is a continuation of politics by forcible means. But Clausewitz regarded politics as representing all interests of society as a whole. He deprived war of its class nature and drew the wrong conclusion that every war expressed the interests of all classes.

Lenin analysed Clausewitz's views, disclosing his bourgeois, idealistic approach to politics. He revealed the class content of politics and thereby placed the connection between war and politics on a scientific basis.

'All wars,' Lenin pointed out, 'are inseparable from the political systems that engender them.' But war is not only a continuation of politics, at the same time, as Lenin stressed, it is a sum total of politics, it is 'politics through and through'. War is not merely a continuation of politics, it is also a means of achieving definite political ends, it is an instrument of politics.

Politics gives rise to war, constitutes its class content and determines its essence. War is politics pursued with the help of a state's armed forces. 'With reference to wars,' Lenin wrote, 'the main thesis of dialectics . . . is that *"war is simply the continuation of politics by other* [i.e., violent] *means"*. . . . And it was always the standpoint of Marx and Engels, who regarded *any* war as the *continuation* of the politics of the powers concerned— and the *various classes* within those countries—in a definite period.'

Two organically interconnected sides—the socio-political and the military-technical—are given in dialectical unity in Lenin's definition of the essence of war. Hence it would be a gross error to identify war with armed struggle, to reduce the diverse phenomena of war to the mere military operations of the armies and navies of the belligerents. At the same time, the Marxist-Leninist understanding of the essence of war does not allow its reduction solely to politics. Politics, as a particular sphere of human relations and activity, is displayed not only by various actions of armed struggle, but also by different non-military forms of economic, diplomatic and ideological struggle.

An analysis of war's essence necessarily brings out the importance of properly understanding the relationship between politics and war in the age of nuclear-missile weapons. Bourgeois ideologists allege that nuclear-missile war has ceased to be a means of politics and that therefore the proposition that 'war is a continuation of politics by other means' has become obsolete.

Trying to implant a cult of nuclear war, the ideologists of contemporary imperialism vainly wish to prove that such a war is a struggle for the physical survival of nations and states. Thus U.S. Senator Fulbright states that 'there is no longer any validity in the Clausewitz doctrine of war as "a carrying out of policy with other means".'

It is easy to see that all these arguments show a far from scientific understanding of the relationship between politics and war. Nuclear-missile weapons have transformed not the essence of war, but the nature of the armed struggle. Therefore there are no grounds whatsoever for considering that war is no longer a continuation and instrument of politics.

The new element in the relationship between war and politics is that the imperialist aggressors no longer stand to gain politically or economically through a world nuclear war. Such a war can only spell the inevitable end of the reckless policy of those who would plunge mankind into a devastating conflict.

Lenin's definition of the essence of war as a continuation of politics by means of armed force stresses the specific nature of war as a phenomenon. This is important because of the assertions that war is first of all an 'economic phenomenon' and only then a political one. But that view is wrong, because war is not an economic phenomenon. It has an economic basis and economic causes, but its essence has always been politics pursued by means of armed force. Guided by only one criterion, the nature of political aims, Lenin established the division of wars into just and unjust. The international Communist movement and the working class absolutely support just wars of liberation.

Unjust wars express and continue the policies of the imperialist bourgeoisie. These include: forcible suppression of the revolutionary movements of the proletariat; aggression of imperialist states against Socialist countries; wars of imperialists for the expansion, preservation or restoration of the colonial system; predatory wars of imperialists for the redivision of colonies and for world domination. Communists have always opposed unjust, aggressive wars provoked by the imperialists.

Disclosing the political essence of war, Lenin always insisted on discrimination between the types of war characteristic of a definite epoch. He held that 'it is theoretically wrong and practically harmful *not* to differentiate the types of war'.

In the present epoch, the most typical wars are those of imperialist powers against peoples and countries fighting for their social and national liberation or defending the freedom and independence they have won, their right to build a new society. In our days, civil wars are possible and highly probable in capitalist countries. At the same time, the aggressiveness of imperialism and the anti-Communist trend of its war preparations predetermine the possibility of war being imposed on Socialism whose aim would be to defend the Socialist homeland and the whole Socialist community.

DOCUMENT II. EXTRACTS ON 'CAUSES OF WAR IN THE ATOMIC AGE' FROM *A Study of War* BY QUINCY WRIGHT (FIRST WRITTEN IN 1942 BUT WITH APPENDICES (OF WHICH THE FOLLOWING IS ONE) ADDED IN 1964) (UNIVERSITY OF CHICAGO PRESS, 1965)

Causes of War in the Atomic Age

The problem of war has become more acute since this book was written. Quantitative changes have been of such magnitude that the relations of nations have become qualitatively different. A new world has emerged. Nevertheless, my conclusions in regard to the causes of war still seem valid.

Among the specific causes of war frequently noted by historians, I referred (*a*) to reaction to perceived threats; (*b*) to enthusiasm for ideals; (*c*) to frustration over unsatisfactory conditions attributed to a foreign scapegoat; (*d*) to belief in the utility of threats of war or war itself as an instrument of independence, policy, prestige, or power; and (*e*) to conviction that military self-help is necessary to vindicate justice, law, and rights if peaceful negotiation proves ineffective.

(*a*) *Reaction to perceived threats* The urge to preserve the self and the territory, the group, the means of livelihood, and the way of life with which the self is identified threatened war after World War II, as it always had among animals, primitive peoples, and historic civilizations. Many people on both sides of the iron curtain were obsessed by the fear that the government on the other side was determined to attack or subvert them and that war might be necessary to assure their survival. Many Americans and Europeans perceived a threat from the superior land army of the Soviet bloc backed by the formidable missiles with nuclear warheads, and many Soviet citizens perceived a threat from the superior nuclear missiles controlled by the United States on submarines and land bases surrounding Soviet territory. Although the American government said these weapons were only for defense in a counterforce strategy, the Soviet Union interpreted this policy as designed to destroy Soviet retaliatory capability by a first strike after all launching sites had been pin-pointed by espionage from the air or outer space. The arms race resulting from these perceived threats tended to augment fear on each side and the demand for a position of strength, for superior power, or for dominance.

(b) *Enthusiasm for ideals* To some people, obsessed by ideological convictions, which have often been emphatic in proportion as the revolution that gave political support to their ideology was recent, war seemed laudable to contain or to eliminate a society, whether communist or capitalist, which they considered wicked or to convert the world to values which they considered good for everyone.

(c) *Frustration over unsatisfactory conditions* Frustrated by continued disorder and poverty after independence (Indonesia) or by the failure of economic planning inspired by revolution (China), some governments developed aggressive policies against their neighbors, their ideological opponents, or those 'imperialist' states generally considered responsible for their difficulties.

(d) *Belief in the utility of threats of war* To people demanding self-determination, such as the Vietnamese, Algerians, and Angolans, war seemed necessary if the demand was resisted, and to some mature states war or threats of war seemed useful for promoting the policy of the government, whether that of the Soviet Union in Korea or Hungary or that of the United States in Vietnam or Cuba.

(e) *Belief in the necessity of military self-help* Some governments thought military resistance or attack reasonable or necessary to maintain justice or a right, such as that claimed by France in

54

Indochina and Algeria, by the United States and the Soviet Union in Berlin, by Israel and the Arab states in Palestine, and by Britain and France in Suez.

It is still true that no single cause of war can be identified. Recent hostilities, although attributable primarily to specific causes, have arisen because of the changing relation of numerous factors—psychological, economic, ideological, social, political, and legal. It is still true that peace results from an equilibrium among many forces. Among these forces, appreciation of the cost of nuclear war and the intervention of international organizations assumed great importance after World War II.

Apart from specific causes of war, certain general conditions have made for war. Among these have been the lag of procedures for peaceful adjustment behind technological and ideological change. Such a lag was especially notable after World War II because of the extraordinary rapidity of such change. Neither diplomacy nor the United Nations was wholly adequate to deal with the problems posed by atomic energy and guided missiles, ideological differences, the break-up of empires, and territorial disputes. Military self-help at Suez in 1956 was said to be justifiable, in spite of the UN Charter prohibitions against the use or threat of force in international relations, because neither diplomacy nor the United Nations had been able to protect Israel against fedayeen raids or to settle the Suez dispute to the satisfaction of the British and French. In justification of the Cuban quarantine in 1962, some jurists suggested, in spite of the Charter limitation of the right of defense to armed attack, that modern military technology justified anticipatory defensive action.

Another general condition inducing war has been the inherent aggressiveness of particular rulers or states, like Hitler and Nazi Germany, and the attribution of such aggressiveness by their opponents to the communist and imperialist states during the 'cold war'.

A traditional feud between two states has frequently induced war in the past. Such a feud developed between Russia and the West at the time of the Soviet Revolution and was augmented by mutual provocations in spite of their alliance during World War II. Feuds have also developed between Israel and the

Arab states, between Greece and Turkey, and between India and Pakistan.

Another general condition unfavorable to peace has been the bipolarization of power through rival alliances. Bipolarization has in the past made the power situation extremely unstable because each side believes eventual war is inevitable and calculates the influence of time on its relative power position. The side that becomes convinced that time is against it is likely to initiate a preventive war. The conviction of each side in the 'cold war' that time is favoring it together with the extreme risks of nuclear war has made deliberate initiation of preventive war improbable in the nuclear age. But bipolarization has created great concern with relative power positions, has made each side unwilling to make the concessions necessary to settle disputes for fear they may compromise that position, and has developed a disposition in times of crises, as in Berlin and Vietnam, to retaliate, countering threats with threats and intervention with counterintervention. Furthermore bipolarization developed the concept of security through mutual deterrence by nuclear threats. But as counter-force strategy develops with the increased destructive power of weapons and the greater speed in delivering them, a premium is placed on the first strike which may destroy the enemy's retaliatory capacity; and pre-emptive war (i.e., preventive war, when it is believed the enemy is about to strike) becomes a real danger. Some hope to counter it by protective secondstrike capability of both sides in hardened bases or submarines so that devastating retaliation against a first strike is certain.

The most persistent condition of war, however, has been the inherent difficulty, which I have emphasized in this book, or organizing peace. In spite of earnest efforts, this difficulty has not been overcome in the postwar period. Peace has not been made the most important symbol or goal in the policy of governments and the opinions of peoples. Particular symbols, such as justice and self-determination, and particular drives, such as security and power, continue to urge action which produces hostilities. It is still impossible for all persons or groups to satisfy, and difficult for them to sublimate, the human urge to dominate over others, particularly the urge of great powers to dominate over small neighbors. Sovereign states are still reluctant to recognize that objective justice implies submission to impartial third-party adjudication.

It has proved no less difficult in recent years than in the past to maintain either a stable equilibrium of power or a system of collective security among the rapidly changing political and military forces within the state system. Each great power confronted by a rival deemed it necessary to increase its power in order to survive. Each could not negotiate from a position of superior strength, but each tried to do so, with the result of an arms race in which each became less secure. Power must balance power in a stable system but the balance must be complicated, utilizing elements other than military and centres of power other than states.

Today, as in the past, states, especially new states, have found it difficult to organize political authority sufficient to maintain internal order unless they are in hostile relations to outside states. War or fear of war has often been used to integrate states. On occasion, multinational states, like the Soviet Union, India, Pakistan, Israel, and Indonesia, have sought to maintain their solidarity by convincing all their people of the need for united defense from external enemies, actual or created. Regional organizations—NATO, the Warsaw Pact, and the Arab League—have manifested internal solidarity only when all members feared attack from outside. The world-society has no external enemy, so the United Nations, like the League of Nations, has found it difficult to maintain order and stability within that society. The advantages of co-operation must play a larger role than fear of aggression if states and international organizations are to enjoy both stability within and peace without.

It has always been difficult to develop the sources and sanctions of international law so as to keep that law an effective analysis of the changing interests of states, of the changing conceptions of justice, and of the changing values of humanity. This difficulty has continued in spite of the efforts of the International Court of Justice, the International Law Commission, and the United Nations. Each sovereign state still claims to be the legislator, judge, and executor of its own rights. If it acknowledges the existence of international law, it reserves the right to interpret it in its own interest, as did Britain in the Suez crisis of 1956, the United States in the Cuban crisis of 1962, and the Soviet Union in the Hungarian crisis of 1956, or to decide what matters are within its domestic jurisdiction, as did the United States Senate by the Connally amendment to its acceptance of the optional clause of the World Court Statute. There has been progress both in developing international law and international adjudication, but the balance of law and politics is still overweighted on the side of the latter.

These difficulties in the realms of psychology and opinion, of politics and power, of government and authority, and of law and sovereignty have in the past frustrated efforts to create conditions of secure peace. Until they are surmounted, states may continue, however irrationally in the atomic age, to regard war or threats of war as instruments of policy and necessary supports to diplomacy and justice. They may deem war necessary when political obstruction will not yield to persuasion or threats. These difficulties will never be wholly surmounted. Conditions of peace can never be taken for granted. They will have to be continually reconstructed and maintained by human efforts. Peace is artificial: war is natural.

Conditions of peace had not been established by 1964. In the score of years since World War II, hostilities were no less frequent than in the score of years between the two world wars. Nor were they less bloody, if one considers the protracted hostilities in Vietnam, Algeria, and Korea, the civil hostilities in China, Colombia, and the Congo, and the communal hostilities on the separation of India and Pakistan and the division of Palestine. . . .

Technological Change and War

The new technology has had a major influence on war, but that influence has been less on the conduct of war than on its utility. The wars since World War II have been fought not with nuclear but with conventional weapons. The recent literature has dealt less with the art of war than with the solution of conflict, the management of power, and the deterrence of war. In spite of the effort to develop new weapons, students have perceived the problem of war as basically psychological.

Modern weaponry has made war too dangerous for nuclear

powers to use as an instrument of policy. There appears to be no effective defense against missile or satellite-borne nuclear weapons; and none is likely to be invented, as stated by President John F. Kennedy in June, 1963. One megaton hydrogen-bomb explosion can destroy a city with blast, fire, and fall-out, and a score of them can destroy most countries. Although threats to use such weapons in first strike may support diplomatic demands, and threats to use them in second strike may deter a first strike, it is gradually dawning on statesmen that a threat must be credible to be effective and that if it is effective for deterrence it cannot also be effective as an instrument of policy. It cannot be both credible and incredible at the same time. The danger is not that a nuclear power will deliberately resort to major war as an instrument of policy, defense, or vindication but that a rival may fear it will do so. . . .

Writers have, in the past, often assumed that new weapons had made war obsolete. Artillery, smokeless powder, the machine gun, and poison gas have each, when first used, impressed some with this view. But defenses against each of these weapons have eventually been devised—fortifications, trenches, gas masks—and as a result, invention has tended in the long run to benefit the defensive more than the offensive.

The consequence of superiority of the defensive in war has been a stalemated peace or a stalemated war. Small states have been able to defend and to emancipate themselves against the distant power of empire. The number of independent states has increased as it did in the long period of invulnerable castles in the Middle Ages. When, however, total war occurred between states equipped with the most advanced weaponry, it tended, even when there were initial victories of one side because of surprise or superior strategy, to become a war of mutual attrition in which the side with the most available economic resources, morale, and reputation built up its forces, converted neutrals into allies, and eventually triumphed. The Crusades and the Hundred Years' War of the Middle Ages, the Napoleonic Wars, the American Civil War, and World Wars I and II were of this type. The side best prepared when the war began lost the war.

The consequence of offensive superiority over a considerable period of time, on the other hand, has been the tendency of states to expand in size and of the number of states in the system to decrease. Alexander and Caesar built great empires through the tactical superiority of the phalanx and the legion, and the European states built great empires through the use of gun powder against small states and overseas peoples not so equipped. The number of states decreased from the fifteenth to the twentieth centuries.

It has been remarkable that in the last twenty years, in spite of the tremendous offensive power of weapons, empires have broken up and the number of states has greatly increased. How can this be explained? It is because missiles, satellites, and nuclear weapons have introduced a new order of magnitude in the destructiveness and offensive capability of weapons. Instead of benefiting empire-builders, as have newly invented offensive weapons in the past, the most recent inventions appear to have made war useless as an instrument of either policy or defense for either empire-builders or empire-maintainers. Since peace based on a balance of terror appears to be inherently unstable, the new weapons may portend either destruction of civilization or a supersession of the simple military balance of power by an international law, resting on a complex equilibrium of power regulated by international organizations. . . .

The following questions left unanswered in the book deserve detailed consideration: (*a*) Has war lost its effectiveness as an instrument of national policy? (*b*) Has war lost its effectiveness as an instrument of defense? (*c*) Has the balance-of-power system lost its effectiveness as a means to maintain stability? (*d*) Can transition from a world order of power politics to one of international law and organization be made suddenly or only gradually?

(*a*) *War as an instrument of policy in the atomic age* The utility of war and threats of war as instruments of policy has varied in history according to the character of military technology, the character of the international system, the particular policy involved, and the power position of the group utilizing this instrument. When military technology has favored the offensive and has not been excessively destructive; when the international system has been a loosely organized balance of military power providing no forum in which economic, legal, or moral arguments might prevail against an opponent with a superior power position; and when policies have generally aimed at territorial adjustments, nationalistic integration, imperial expansion, increase of power, or other tangible interests with little attention to human welfare or world stability, war has been a useful instrument of policy for states in relation to those of inferior power. These conditions have often existed in modern civilization, and threats of war, implicit or explicit, have been the accepted backing of diplomatic demands especially by the 'great powers'. Diplomacy has usually been attempted first, but has often been followed by threats and by military expeditions, reprisals, blockades, or wars. When great powers or lesser powers of equal magnitude have fought each other, both might lose in a war of attrition, but one might win by superior tactics or strategy without excessive cost. . . .

Revolutionary changes in these conditions have occurred in the twentieth century, most dramatically since World War II, but they were perceived after World War I. Modern military technology, although it favors the offensive, is so devastatingly destructive that, if used between states each of which utilizes this technology, war is likely to prove suicidal. War might still be a useful instrument if fought only with conventional weapons, and threat of nuclear war might be effective if directed only against a non-nuclear power, but the international system makes it doubtful whether these limiting conditions can be maintained in a given situation. Conventional wars may escalate if both sides have nuclear weapons and may encourage intervention by nuclear powers even if one or both sides lack such weapons. In a world in which all states are vulnerable and interdependent, there is danger that small wars will become total. . . .

The use of nuclear weapons against a nuclear power, as an instrument of policy rather than of defense, would hardly be reasonable except as a first strike against the enemy's nuclear installations, with the hope of destroying his retaliatory capability and thus achieving relative immunity from his second strike and compelling his surrender. But with the relative invulnerability of hardened missile bases and submarine-borne missiles, such immunity seems unlikely. The United States and Russia have both declared that they will not use nuclear weapons to initiate hostilities. The Soviet Union has urged agreement never to use these weapons except in a second strike after a nuclear attack, but the United States seems to have adopted the policy of using at least tactical nuclear weapons with relatively slight fall-out against enemy conventional forces when hostilities actually exist. This policy has been criticized on the ground that it would be impossible to distinguish tactical from strategic nuclear weapons and that, consequently, the use of nuclear weapons in hostilities should be eliminated even though this ban might make war with conventional weapons a more useful instrument of policy. As long as countries have stocks of nuclear weapons and means of deploying them, conventional war may escalate. Disarmament, first in nuclear weapons and their means of delivery and eventually in conventional arms, along with the diminution in tensions which is a necessary condition of such disarmament, seems the only way to eliminate the danger of nuclear war. In the long run such agreement and the subsequent decline in the use or threat of war as an instrument seems probable.

(b) *War and defense in the atomic age*   The role of war as an instrument of defense has also varied in history according to the character of military technology, the character of the international system, the nature of the thing defended, and the relative power position of the defender and the aggressor. When military technology gave an advantage to the defense; when there were a number of great powers all tending to pursue balance-of-power policies, the great defending the weak against the aggressor; when territory was the major interest to be defended; and when no state was so powerful that it could defeat not only its victim but all other states which, under the balance-of-power systems, might come to the victim's rescue, war could often be useful for defense. In fact, this was so generally assumed that military defense against attack was considered a necessity, justifiable in international law, as indeed it is under Article 51 of the United Nations Charter.

The value of military force for defense, however, has greatly declined in the atomic age. . . .

It is now clear that there is no direct defense against missile-borne nuclear weapons. In total war with such weapons the offensive has an overwhelming advantage. The armed forces, economy, and population of every state are wholly vulnerable to such an attack. Total destruction of the nuclear forces of an enemy on the ground in a massive first strike or deterrence of nuclear attack by threats of retaliation appears to be the only military defense.

Military writers have sought to develop a system of arms control assuring mutual deterrence. Each side is to be equipped with invulnerable second-strike capability so that none will risk the initiation of nuclear war. The success of the system depends, however, upon the credibility of the second strike, a psychological problem. It is conceivable that a first strike against enemy bases, which would greatly reduce the enemy's second-strike capabilities, followed by a threat to destroy his cities if he retaliates, would induce him to surrender. A government might not sacrifice a large proportion of its population to prove that its threat of retaliation was credible. If it were certain that deterrence would always succeed, nuclear war would not occur, and nuclear threat would have proved useless as an instrument of policy but perfect as an instrument of defense against nuclear attack.

Such success, however, might make utilization of conventional arms in some situations an effective instrument of policy. Over large areas, the land forces, supported by the air and naval forces of one state, may have an offensive superiority, as demonstrated by Hitler in the early stages of World War II. Such a superiority by Russia and China, if nuclear weapons were eliminated, was feared by their neighbors in 1963. A threat of massive nuclear retaliation against a border attack with conventional arms, as made by Secretary of State John Foster Dulles in connection with the Indo-Chinese hostilities of 1954, is not likely to be credible if the attacker or its ally has nuclear arms, and so will not deter. Consequently, systems of graduated deterrence, providing for conventional defense forces in vulnerable areas and perhaps for tactical nuclear weapons if necessary, have been proposed. But if the enemy also has tactical nuclear weapons, such a war is almost certain to escalate into suicidal nuclear war if each side or its allies have nuclear weapons and perceive no substitute for victory. The half-dozen states which have remained divided for a decade or more since World War II demonstrate, however, that conventional defensive weapons on both sides of a frontier may maintain a cease-fire. But such a cease-fire line is likely to be unsatisfactory to both sides and so may constitute a continuing threat that hostilities will be renewed. . . .

(c) *War and the balance of power in the atomic age* The factors which have tended to deteriorate the stability of balances of power in the past led me to conclude in 1942 that 'it seems doubtful whether stability can be restored on the basis of a military balance of power'.

Since World War II it has become even more clear that the balance-of-power system cannot function effectively for either defense or deterrence when power is bipolarized. If power is equally divided, overwhelming power obviously cannot be mobilized to defend the victim of attack. From this point of view it would seem that a disintegration of the great alliances and the development of third, fourth, or fifth forces in China, western Europe, and the Commonwealth equal to those of the Soviet Union and the United States would increase the stability of the balance of power. But this consideration must be weighted against the danger of a diffusion of nuclear capabilities increasing the probabilities of accidental, pre-emptive, catalytic, or irresponsible war. Furthermore, as pointed out before, nuclear threats are inherently incredible if directed against a nuclear power or its ally and of dubious utility as instruments either of policy or of defense. Only if the possibility of nuclear war were eliminated might a multipolar balance of power function. . . .

(d) *War and international organization in the atomic age* For those who believe that a balance of military power cannot be stable under modern conditions, the rational solution of the problem of war lies in an effective international law of peaceful co-existence and an effective international organization to maintain the law and to provide for both collective security and for human progress.

But the problem remains: How can this transition be made? Must it be sudden or may it be gradual? . . .

It is still difficult to say whether the transition from a world of power politics and war to a world of law and peace can be effected by sudden or by gradual action, but with the increasing destructiveness of nuclear war and the impracticability of transition by sudden action without war, the weight of the argument is for gradualness. . . .

World government, in the narrower sense, comparing it with international organization and assuming that it implies a centralization of military force and a direct control of the individual in many matters, seems beyond the possibilities of the present international situation.

SUGGESTED STUDY QUESTIONS

1. Do you regard the prohibition of war by treaty as an effective means of preventing war?
2. What are the arguments for and against imposing on *individuals* a criminal responsibility for the planning or initiation of an aggressive war?
3. What are the contemporary circumstances which now lead to a preoccupation with the problem of 'intervention' rather than 'war'?
4. Explain what is meant by 'peaceful coexistence'. Is this concept one which is likely to contribute towards the maintenance of peace?
5. What evidence is there that if capitalism disappears war will disappear?

FURTHER READING

ARON, RAYMOND, *On War*, London: Secker & Warburg, 1958.
BOULDING, K., *Conflict and Defence*, New York: Harper Bros, 1962.
FALK, R. and MENDLOVITZ, S., *The Strategy of World Order*, Vol. I, 'Toward a Theory of War Prevention', New York: The World Law Fund, 1966.
FRANKE, W., *China and the West*, Oxford: Blackwell, 1967.
GRIFFITH, W. E., *Communism in Europe*, Oxford: Pergamon Press, 1967.
KENNAN, G. F., *On Dealing with the Communist World*, New York: Council on Foreign Relations, 1963.
LIPPMAN, WALTER, *The Communist World and Ours*, Boston: Little, Brown and Co., 1959.
SLESSOR, SIR JOHN, *What Price Coexistence?*, New York: Praeger, 1961.
STRACHEY, JOHN, *On the Prevention of War*, New York: St Martins, 1963.

PART II

The Peaceful Settlement of Disputes

We tend to think it axiomatic that the prohibition of self-help in any society must be accompanied by a system for the compulsory adjudication of disputes by courts. Thus, it is possible to outlaw forceful self-help in municipal law precisely because the citizen has available to him all the apparatus of the courts and their enforcement procedures: justice is available to him via the orderly, institutionalized procedures of the law.

In international society the prohibition of force has not been accompanied by a system of compulsory settlement of disputes. The International Court of Justice, sitting at The Hague as the principal judicial organ of the United Nations, cannot compel a State to appear before it and no State is bound to submit its disputes to that court: jurisdiction is always based upon the consent of both parties, whether expressed at the time the suit is filed or in advance (with reference to specified categories of cases) via what is called the 'Optional Clause'. Indeed, the ICJ deals with relatively few cases and none of them are of a kind which, if they were not so settled, would really endanger international peace.

Of course, States also have a choice of going to arbitration, equally based upon the consent of both parties and, as Professor Jennings points out in his lecture quoted below, there are many different kinds of tribunals, claims commissions and courts for dealing with particular categories of inter-State disputes.

However, as Professor Jennings warns, it is wrong to assume that all conflicts of interests between States can be classified as 'disputes' and regarded as suitable for judicial adjudication. In practice, those which are likely to lead to war can rarely be so classified. For example, although the Middle East situation or Vietnam contain quite a number of highly controversial legal

66

issues, no one would seriously suggest that the whole problem could be resolved by referring it to the International Court. Obviously, if a settlement is to be reached it will be by political negotiation and decision.

This is not to deny the utility of settling what are clearly legal controversies by means of international courts or tribunals, or to excuse the refusal of States to do so. The extracts from the David Davies Study show some of the factors which militate against a State's willingness to accept impartial, judicial settlement. But, in the final analysis, all discussion of courts and legal disputes is really rather marginal in the area of vital problems, which may pose a threat to world peace, which are now our concern.

Is international society then really so different from municipal society? Or is the 'axiom' with which we began this section equally untrue of municipal society? In a way it is, because within a State the really big issues which determine the whole structure of that society, and which could, if not resolved, destroy it, are also rarely appropriate for judicial decision. The major issues—claims for autonomy or secession from part of a State's territory, religious or political unrest, demands for nationalization of sectors of industry—tend to be resolved by political discussion and decision, either inside Parliament or outside, and *not* by judicial decisions. Thus, on reflection, the contrast between international and municipal societies may not be as great as is commonly supposed.

If this is so, then the real 'gaps' in international society in this area of the settlement of disputes lie in the absence of bodies capable of undertaking the task of political discussion and decision, and not in the lack of courts with compulsory jurisdiction.

However, in fact, there are no such 'gaps'. Not only do States have at their disposal the Security Council and General Assembly—which the extracts from the David Davies Study show to have a wide competence in disputes likely to endanger international peace—but, in addition, many States are parties to regional organizations like NATO, the Organization of American States, the Arab League, which also exercise power of conciliation in regional disputes. The real difference lies not so much in that international society lacks the political machinery for settlement but more in that this machinery is frequently incapable of taking effective *decisions* or that it is simply not used at all.

We have seen that, in the Security Council, whilst Chapter VI of the Charter provides a variety of techniques of settlement, the powers of the Council are restricted to making *recommendations* to the parties: the Council could only achieve a decision-making role indirectly by proceeding to use its powers of enforcement under Chapter VII. In any event, all Security Council action, either under Chapter VI or Chapter VII, is subject to a veto by any of the five Permanent Members.

Professor Goldstein gets to the heart of the problem when he demonstrates how, in practice, all the major 'disputes' which threaten world peace tend to involve the Cold War. Mostly in the present bipolarized world, either the USA or the USSR will tend to ensure that such disputes do not get before the UN or, if they do, that no effective decisions are taken. Indeed, his list of 'imperative needs', though it does mention the need to strengthen the ICJ, is concerned far more with issues of partial disarmament and the provision of ground rules to eliminate intervention, surprise attack and so forth.

The primary problem may therefore be to persuade the great powers that issues affecting world peace are not their peculiar prerogative and that there does exist a safeguard for peace in debating these issues before the organs of the world community—like the Security Council and General Assembly —and accepting the collective judgment of member States on the proper course to pursue.

DOCUMENT 12. EXTRACT FROM 'GENERAL COURSE OF INTERNATIONAL LAW' BY PROFESSOR R. Y. JENNINGS IN *Recueil des Cours* OF THE HAGUE ACADEMY, VOL. II, 1967, PP. 584–90

The problem is not one of drafting legal precepts controlling the use of force but one of devising international institutions through which the use of force in international relationships can be legally ordered and controlled on an international instead of a sovereignty basis. The problem therefore is not to bring about the abolition of force but to bring about the institutionalisation of the use or threat of force. And this in turn involves not only the harnessing of force to procedures for international order—such as has indeed in a modest way been partly achieved, by the organization of United Nations Forces, for example—but also, and perhaps more importantly, the devising of procedures for bringing about on an internationally ordered basis some of the changes that war and force have in the past been used to bring about.

It has long been realized that peace cannot be maintained by forbidding the use of force, whilst at the same time providing little or no means for peaceful change. But it is no less true that it is no use forbidding a State to resort to self-help against a law-breaker whilst failing to provide a compulsory means for testing the legalities of the situation. It is the weak who need to be compelled to go into court as well as the strong. At the same time it is important not to slip into the fallacy of supposing that all that is needed in the way of procedures for pacifist settlement is machinery for dealing with the kind of dispute that yields an 'issue' of the kind that can be argued before a court of law. To take a ready example: a principal problem at the present day is that of disarmament; but to this question an adversary procedure for the determination according to law of particular issues is almost totally irrelevant. Of course the categories of disputes, situations and problems often overlap, and a major problem of an essentially political kind may contain within itself important justiciable issues, and the determination of those issues by appropriate legal procedures may contribute importantly to the solution of the whole problem. Nevertheless it is important to keep always in mind the distinction between questions that call for adjudication and questions that call for political negotiation and decision; and to remember that advance in the compulsory adjudication of disputes in the narrow sense is only likely to be achieved if it moves parallel with the development of adequate procedures for the taking of these major political decisions.

It may be useful to carry this question a little further, looking first very briefly at the kind of dispute procedure that lawyers usually have in mind; and then at the question of establishing institutions for the taking of political decisions; and it will be convenient to refer to this difference—a difference but not a true dichotomy—in terms of traditional terminology which broadly distinguishes, rightly, and still highly relevantly, between legal and political disputes. The important truth behind this difference has tended to be obscured by the more lawyer-like but in many ways unfortunate alternative terminology which purports to distinguish justiciable and non-justiciable disputes: a terminology which immediately introduces a fallacy, because there is an important sense in which all disputes are justiciable.

The Obligation to Settle Disputes

Article 2 of the United Nations Charter, before it goes on to the legal regulation of the use of force or threat of force, provides first, in Section 3, that:

3. All Members shall settle their international disputes by peaceful means in such a manner that international peace and security, and justice, are not endangered.

By this provision, the obligation of members to settle their disputes is linked not only to the maintenance of peace and security but also to the doing of justice . . . the introduction of the notion of justice into Section 3 shows that the obligation contained in Section 3 is independent of the obligation contained in Section 4. Members do not comply with Section 3 merely by refraining from the use or threat of force. . . .

Obviously the obligation contained in Article 2 (3) of the Charter is one which falls short of a requirement that any particular method of settlement must be employed. . . .

The Procedures for Settling Disputes

The procedures actually available for the pacific settlement of disputes are rich in their variety. Apart from the International Court of Justice, with its contentious and advisory jurisdiction, there are many other established tribunals for the adjudication or conciliation of particular classes of dispute. There are of course the organs of regional political organizations: the inter-American system; the African Commission of Mediation, Conciliation and Arbitration; the European Communities Court; the European Commission of Human Rights and the Court of Human Rights. There is also the Permanent Court of Arbitration with its settled procedure and standing secretariat; and

70

the European Convention for the Settlement of International Disputes. There are also tribunals either standing or in some cases to be set up *ad hoc* attached to bilateral agreements for arbitration and conciliation. There are very many tribunals provided for in particular treaties. There are tribunals *ad hoc*, including Claims Tribunals which have been set up from time to time by governments for disposing of particular classes of case. There is the Convention of the International Bank of Reconstruction and Development for the Settlement of Investment Disputes, which at the time of writing has been signed by 52 States and ratified by 32. There are the specialist tribunals of various kinds which form part of the specialized agencies of the United Nations or other international organizations dealing with particular topics: the Council of the International Civil Aviation Organization, or the machinery for dealing with disputes which forms part of the General Agreement on Tariffs and Trade and so on. The specialized agencies of the United Nations have of course themselves the power, as a result of authorization by the General Assembly, of asking the International Court of Justice for an advisory opinion on a matter which falls within the competence of the Organization. Institutional machinery for dealing with disputes in the large sense is also a characteristic of some regional economic organizations which are themselves legion: e.g., the Organization for Economic Co-operation and Development, the Communist Council for Mutual Economic Aid, the Caribbean Organization, the Colombo Plan, the European Free Trade Organization, the European Economic Community, to mention only a few.

The position, then, is that the procedures for the pacific settlement of disputes of a legal kind are very well developed. There is a rich variety of procedures and tribunals available. There is also a clear obligation to settle if the dispute is of a kind likely to endanger peace. On the debit side, however, there is the fact that many of these procedures are remarkably little used by governments. There is also the near-failure of the attempt, through the Optional Clause, to build a compulsory jurisdiction for the International Court of Justice; and this is a pity in more ways than one, for the lack of compulsory jurisdiction inhibits the development of many important areas of substantive law which depend upon there being a court with compulsory jurisdiction. . . .

In assessing the place these procedures have in the ordinary life of States, it must never be forgotten that the most important, most used, and usually most effective, of the 'pacific means', are negotiations through the ordinary channels of diplomacy. This is as it should be. Busy law courts are not necessarily a symptom of a healthy society.

DOCUMENT 13. EXTRACTS FROM THE DAVID DAVIES MEMORIAL INSTITUTE'S *Report of a Study Group on the Peaceful Settlement of International Disputes*, 1966

The United Nations as an Organ of Conciliation

18. To-day, as indicated in the preceding paragraphs, the political organs of the United Nations are the hub of the machinery for the settlement of disputes which the parties cannot or will not settle either by agreement or by agreed procedures of their own choosing. Article 33 (1) of the Charter, by stating that the parties to a dispute 'shall *first of all* seek a solution by negotiation, etc.', implies that recourse to the political organs of the United Nations is a reserve rather than a primary means of settlement—that there is some obligation to try other means before referring to the Security Council or General Assembly. But it has not been interpreted as requiring a party to *exhaust* the various means mentioned in Article 33 (1) before taking the dispute to the United Nations and in practice a State sometimes takes a dispute to the United Nations after only the most perfunctory use of the diplomatic channel. If this may be understandable in urgent cases, in others it is more surprising, since the Charter provisions seem to give greater emphasis to the rôle of the Security Council in peace enforcement than in the peaceful settlement of disputes. . . .

Obstacles to the Settlement of Disputes

17. What factors militate against the settlement of disputes? In particular, in a world where points of friction and dispute arise constantly between States, why is it that the procedures which

invoke the assistance of third parties, such as good offices, mediation, arbitration and judicial settlement, are relatively so little used?

18. There are some major lines dividing the world giving rise to broad areas of dispute which, it must be recognized, are unlikely to be resolved by any procedural arrangements. Examples are the ideological debate between the Western and the Communist States and the economic differences between the developing and the developed countries. Only the gradual development of world society is likely to lead to a weakening and disappearance of these points of tension. But there are other less broad-based disputes where the procedures involving third parties have not even been tried.

19. States have as varied reasons for their failure to settle disputes as any other human disputants. But there are two specific factors in the community of states which are worth singling out both because they are characteristic of States and because they are especially relevant to any discussion of procedures for the settlement of disputes.

20. The first factor is the doctrine of state sovereignty held in an extreme form. The State has always wanted to have its way both internally and externally. The concept of sovereignty, originally developed to explain and justify unlimited internal freedom of action, was extended to justify unlimited external freedom of action—with unhappy results for the life of the international community. Doctrines which exalt the state's freedom of external action are of the greatest advantage to those states which wish to exercise this freedom of action at the expense of their neighbours. But it has never been found possible to reconcile the extreme doctrine of state sovereignty with the existence of international law; attempts to overcome the problem by the doctrine of auto limitation or of fundamental rights have carried no general conviction. 'Denial of a superior legal system cannot but lead to anarchy and hence to conflict'. Thus Soviet theorists, whose scriptures and dialectic derive from sources of the last century, at first rejected international law as a fully binding legal system; while they now recognize the binding force of international law, they still adhere to relatively extreme views of state sovereignty. In particular, they invoke sovereignty as a justification for never, or almost never,

accepting in advance any procedure involving third parties for the settlement of disputes; and for this reason they oppose arbitral and judicial procedures as generally appropriate to be adopted even for the settlement of questions of law.

21. States are vigilant in the defence of their independence, and rightly. But it can only be an exercise of sovereignty and no diminution to accept voluntarily an appropriate procedure for settlement of disputes. Furthermore, any state which values international law as a precondition of peace and sees the rôle of the independent State as one to be played in a community, must regard the strengthening of international law and international procedures as the best and highest exercise of its sovereignty.

22. But it is difficult to avoid the suspicion that extreme doctrines of state sovereignty may be no more than a rationalisation of the political reluctance of a State to risk losing its claim or its case. The best service of a lawyer is to establish that this position is illogical and is inconsistent with recognition of a legal community.

23. The second factor obstructing the settlement of disputes, which is worth mentioning at this point, is the influence on foreign policies of internal political forces. Foreigners have no votes and a political leader rarely gains internal political support by a generous or internationally minded external policy. This is equally true in a parliamentary regime with an open debate between Government and Opposition, and in a power struggle within the committees of a one-party or authoritarian regime. Similarly a political leader has often stilled internal criticism and won internal support by stimulating international tension, artificially if necessary, and adopting bellicose attitudes.

24. This factor is likely to operate until people have the judgment to realise that international strife benefits nobody in the long run. But its effect could to some extent be mitigated if one could be sure at least that these internal manoeuvres could less easily be based on false facts. A wider adoption of international procedures such as commissions of inquiry might help to make it more difficult to manipulate facts for internal reasons.

The Concept of Settlement of a Dispute

25. When is a dispute 'settled'? The word 'settlement' has

in it an element of ambiguity. In one sense, a dispute may be regarded as settled when it has been submitted to a procedure which leads to a binding decision; in another, it is only settled when the disputing parties accept, even reluctantly, a solution reached and cease to put forward opposed viewpoints. The latter sense is in part subjective and psychological. The interplay of these two factors must be constantly borne in mind. Thus, in general, a judicial settlement settles a dispute effectively in the psychological sense only insofar as the parties accept that the question is a question of law and that the system of law and the competence of the Court are in general adequate. And a territorial demarcation, however achieved, will in practice fail to settle the problem if a dissatisfied party encourages its nationals or ethnic kinsmen whether rightly or wrongly to regard it as unjust. It follows not only that procedures for the settlement of disputes must be such as to carry conviction to the parties but also that the States who have adopted them must show a certain loyalty to the institutions which they create or adopt and the solutions which result.

The Attitudes of States

26. The attitude of different states to the settlement of disputes and to procedures for this cover a wide range of views. . . .

27. The States of Africa and Asia, most of which attained independence only since the War of 1939–45, cannot properly be treated as a single unit since they hold widely differing political attitudes and views on subjects relating to the peaceful settlement of disputes. Nevertheless several of the new States show, in varying degrees, common attitudes of reserve to the judicial settlement of disputes and in particular to the International Court of Justice, and the grounds for this must be considered.

28. Their doubts in part arise from the substance of the law which the Court would apply. Most of the rules of international law were developed at a time before these States played an active role in the international community. And there is also much uncertainty as to their content. These States fear that in a specific case they might be held to be subject to obligations dating from their colonial pasts. . . .

75

29. Secondly, the present composition of the International Court does not in their view adequately reflect the African and Asian states, although there are now two African judges and three Asian judges out of fifteen in all. . . .

30. One must have considerable sympathy with the first of these objections. . . . The U.N. should continue its efforts in the field of the progressive development of international law and its codification in order to strengthen the legal basis of the judicial settlement of international disputes.

31. However, those who believe that tribunals are valuable instruments to develop the law—and this must be especially true of those who value the common law tradition, which include many of the new states— will be glad to see that the African and Asian states are not in principle opposed to the adoption of adjudication by tribunals. Thus in the *Temple of Preah Vihear Case* two Asian states sought the assistance of the International Court in a boundary dispute and in the *South West African Cases* (*Ethiopia v. S. Africa; Liberia v. South Africa*) two African states have taken proceedings there. . . .

32. Only the gradual development of the rules of international law will remove the criticism by the African and Asian states of the substance of the existing rules of international law, that they are uncertain or outmoded. But this criticism cannot in any case apply to the judicial interpretation of agreements, especially technical agreements, entered into since the independence of these states. In such agreements the provisions will be either uncertain or outdated. . . .

33. The attitude of the Soviet Union and other Communist States is more uncompromising. They give overwhelming primacy to negotiations as a means of settling disputes and say that other means of settlement need only be accepted if states choose to do so. They rely on the fact that most of the disputes which are settled are in practice settled by negotiation. They argue that the method of negotiation is flexible, that if it is pursued with goodwill and without pressure, it will lead to settlement, and that it pays most respect to sovereignty and equality.

34. It is true that many disputes have been settled by negotiation. Since the late World War alone many major disputes have been settled in this way if we may include international

conferences in this method, starting with the series of important agreements establishing international organisations and the Peace Treaties and leading up to the most dangerous dispute of all, the Cuba Crisis of 1962. The rôle of negotiations has been and will continue to be most important in international relations; nevertheless negotiations are not always successful and many disputes remain unsettled; the use of other procedures has not often been tried and this alone may be part of the reason why disputes have been settled by negotiation or not at all. In negotiation the absence of a third party deprives the parties in dispute of assistance in two important aspects; first, any disagreement of fact cannot be resolved; secondly, a party is not restrained by the moderating influence of a disinterested element from putting forward extreme or extravagant claims, in particular, where the bargaining power of states is unequal.

35. . . . . It is difficult to reconcile this attitude with the willingness of the Communist states to bring matters before political organs of the United Nations. This clearly results in the participation of third parties in action relating to the settlement of the disputes in question. And it can hardly be said that the political organs of the United Nations have exclusive competence when Article 33 clearly encourages the use of third party procedures not within the U.N. as well as negotiation and Article 36(3) advances the claim of the principal judicial organ of the United Nations, the International Court of Justice.

36. The overwhelming emphasis laid by these states on negotiation also ignores the course of history; for the very reason that negotiations are in many cases an inadequate means of solving disputes, other methods have been developed. Furthermore, it is agreed on all sides that the acceptance of procedures involving third parties involves no derogation from sovereignty. This is well established by the acceptance of the jurisdiction of the International Court of Justice by a large number of countries as well as in regional arrangements envisaging such procedures in the continents of Africa, America and Europe. It is difficult to see any good ground for carrying insistence on the priority of negotiations to the point where it hinders exploring fully and expanding as far as possible the use of other methods.

37. The Soviet Union and the Communist States of Eastern

Europe oppose in particular the extension of the jurisdiction of the International Court.

38. They argue that the forced acceptance of the compulsory jurisdiction of the Court is contrary to the U.N. Charter which foresees voluntary jurisdiction. In this they are overstating their opponents' case in order to destroy it. The Western States do not advocate that states should be forced to accept the compulsory jurisdiction of the Court but rather that they should be encouraged or urged to do so. . . .

39. These States support their position of hostility to the International Court by citing the general practice of states. The same argument might have been used in the past to justify war as an instrument of national policy. They argue that only a limited number of states have accepted the jurisdiction of the international Court under the Optional Clause, and many have made wide reservations which virtually, in the view of the States under discussion, nullify the acceptance. . . .

40. Nevertheless, these States admit that the existence of international law is consistent with the sovereignty of states, and are prepared to accept the jurisdiction in advance in certain instances. Thus the Soviet Union has done so, in particular, in connection with the U.N. Supplementary Convention on Slavery.

41. The attitude of a state to international law is likely to be influenced by its notion of law; and the notion of law held in the Soviet Union based on Marxist political analysis is directed primarily to the use of courts as instruments of political and social action for the repression of crime, including economic crime. By contrast, law in Western countries is seen, at least by lawyers, as primarily concerned with the regulation of competing individual liberties of action and the ordering of a complex system of property. Possibly international law, operating within and over a community of equal states, has a function more similar to that of law in the Western states.

42. A system of what is admitted to be law permanently lacking a system of courts is contrary to all the legal experience of mankind. Since the States under consideration concede that international law restricts in a binding effect the freedom of states and since they do not dispute that the use of procedures recognized by international law for the settlement of disputes

can in no way be regarded as incompatible with the principle of sovereign equality of states it may perhaps be hoped that they will come to be persuaded—and no one is attempting to compel them—that a greater readiness to accept judicial and arbitral procedures would be a step towards the strengthening of international law, an aim which they accept.

DOCUMENT 14. EXTRACT FROM 'THE PEACEFUL LIMITATION OF DISPUTES: POLICE POWERS AND SYSTEM PROBLEMS' BY WALTER GOLDSTEIN IN *Journal of Conflict Resolution*, VOL. 7 (1962), PP. 256–60

Contemporary Conflicts of the Cold War

A brief and 'ecological' (or environmental) classification of disputes in the last 17 years could usefully be arranged in order to demonstrate that every one of these disputes occurred within that loose, bipolar division of international security that has become known as the 'Cold War'. Given the general predominance (though not in *all* cases) of this bipolar division, the following pattern of international disputes can be discerned.

1. Tensions within the sphere of influence maintained by, and subjected to, the intervention of just one nuclear power (e.g., the unchallenged suppression of revolutions in Guatemala in 1954 or Hungary in 1956; or the repression by NATO members of nationalist insurrections in their African colonies).

2. Tensions in the no-man's-land between the spheres of influence or beyond the decisive influence of any nuclear power (e.g., the Indian assimilation of Goa, or the Chinese of Tibet; or the power 'vacuum' stresses in the Middle East after 1956).

3. Direct—but restrained—confrontations between the nuclear powers, where a boundary zone of tense friction is shared and cannot be disengaged (e.g., the no-shooting agreements in Berlin and Cuba; also, the tacitly limited and non-nuclear campaigns in Southeast Asia).

4. Disputes accessible to, or dependent upon, third-party mediation by the U.N. or by its neutralist majority (e.g., the

face-saving withdrawals from Suez, or from the Congo, and possibly from the health hazards of nuclear testing).

5. Unresolved but latent sources of tensions between the nuclear powers (e.g., the arms race, the rocket rivalry in outer space, or the competitive doctrines of economic and political coexistence).

6. The nuclear powers' covert subversion of, and ideological warfare upon, the neutralist and nonaligned majority in the General Assembly (e.g., the rival cultural and aid missions in India or Egypt, and the carefully controlled bestowal of military supplies).

This pattern of relationships has been termed, with some justice, a loose and bipolarized equilibrium maintained by the two predominant, competing, nuclear powers and by their attendant allies, satellites, clients, and proxies (Kaplan, 1962). It is remarkable how well this nuclear-dominated system has prevailed over 17 years. It has insured a permanent mechanism through which the Soviet Union and the United States have been able to control their own alliances and interests; it has maintained the ascendancy and the territorial integrity of the two great powers against all challengers; it has adjusted to the sweeping changes that have occurred in the excolonial world since 1945; and it has retained the two-headed, symbolic sway exercised by Washington and Moscow over the outcome of so much of the Conference-diplomacy at the United Nations. Despite the widespread revolutions of rising expectations, the crumbling of empires, and the technological progress of the nuclear arms race, it still remains true that the two great powers are able to maintain their decisive or veto authority over such key issues as:

1. The inclusion of summit agenda items (e.g., Berlin or Laos), which, therefore, will be precluded from any *effective* deliberation by the United Nations;

2. The secure maintenance of their own spheres of influence and collective alliances (e.g., the refusal to relieve or even discuss Hungary), while the loose groupings among the nonaligned frequently disintegrate (e.g., the Bandung powers never became a third force);

3. The preservation of a fairly widespread control over mili-

tary or diplomatic initiative outside, as well as inside, their own bloc (e.g., the United States influence over NATO missiles, or its 'presence' in the Organization of American States).

Sanctions and Adjustment Techniques Presently Available

It is hardly surprising to find that an international system that has preserved its bipolar hegemony despite 17 years of turmoil should have devised an impressive range of sanctions to conciliate or restrain the types of disputes listed above. . . . Until the bipolar pattern is broken—by the emergence of China or Western Europe as an independent nuclear force, for instance— it will still be appropriate to classify the available sanctions, diplomatic pressures, or political adjustment techniques within this two-pole system.

1. Unilateral sanctions of the nuclear powers, or collective security pressures exercised within just their own bloc (e.g., restrictions by the United States upon the army of South Korea, or the collective decision of NATO to support the United States quarantine of Cuba).

2. Bilateral and multilateral 'deals' between neutralists and one or both nuclear powers (e.g., 'awarding' West Irian to Indonesia, or the agreed neutralization of Finland and Austria).

3. Summit compromises and the trading of mutual concessions between the nuclear powers (e.g., the 'climb-down' on Cuban missiles, postponing an East German peace treaty, or desisting from U-2 overflights).

4. The diplomatic gambit at the United Nations of succumbing to a majority vote in order to save face, but only on a few issues (e.g., the obeying of General Assembly votes when it is expedient to pretend to morality; as in the abortive British and French withdrawal from Suez, or the abandoning of the Soviets' insistence upon a 'troika' in U.N. offices).

5. *De facto*, tacit, quietly contrived, and other forms of essentially diplomatic *détentes* between the nuclear 'camps' (e.g., the procedural development of 'parliamentary democracy' within the councils of the United Nations, as seen in the package deals for the seating of U.N. members). These diplomatic adjustments also include the delaying tactics and collective

bargaining exercised subtly within each bloc and between the bloc leaders at summit conferences.

6. The transcending deterrence of the balance of terror: a multilevel attempt to freeze the fundamental status quo, while allowing—within agreed limits—carefully controlled encroachments with the use of tactical weapons, paramilitary infiltration, and guerrilla subversion (e.g., the 'nuclear abstinence' pact tacitly agreed between the great powers, especially during their hegemony disputes in Korea, Laos, Cuba, and the Congo).

It is immediately apparent that these sanctions and limitations are far less than universal in their efficacy. Many small nations have been able to elude these sanctions by aggressively defying their bloc leader (e.g., France or Albania) or by indulging in unilateral actions (e.g., India or Indonesia). The lack of control over—or between—the actions of the great powers has been far more serious, and hence the urgent need to devise new methods of limiting their disputes. To put the choice baldly: the nuclear powers must either establish a more powerful and a more reliable form of bipolar equilibrium, or they must mutually agree to subjugate their authority to an international rule of law. To reformulate this in conventional terms, it could be said that the great powers either must learn to share the powers and responsibility of coexistence more effectively or they must submit to the powerful and centralized authority of a supranational organization, such as a world court and police force. Any other alternative is unrealistic.

Feasible and Desirable Limitations, Currently Absent

The primary and indispensable prerequisite of any international system is that it should contain a sufficient number of stabilizing factors to insure that the relations among nations can be conducted with predictably peaceful means. . . . Peace with justice has long stood as the ideal goal for civilized societies; peace as a stable but inequitable compromise has been achieved, in fact, on the rarest of occasions—if at all—during any one generation. Faced with this pessimistic expectation, the ability of the contemporary, bipolar system to 'keep the peace' must be firmly questioned. . . . If it is, then attention must be focused upon this key choice: whether it is better to patch and repair the faulty equilibrium system of today, or if it would be wiser to boldly replace it with a new revolutionary pattern of international authority?

One way to handle this is to examine the feasibility of instituting an utterly novel, untried process of international security restraints and adjudicating procedures. Another method can be achieved by simply listing the inadequacies of the present system in order to determine whether a series of modifications of the U.N. and of the bipolar balance of today can still be effected. Among the inadequate stabilizing functions of the contemporary equilibrium, then, the following can be briefly noted.

1. While the nuclear powers are compelled to compete for military or ideological prestige, their political intolerance and exaggerated fears of the other tend strongly to reinforce the international climate of distrust. . . .

2. In such an ethos of distrust it is impossible to promote confidence in formal agreements, inspection schemes, independent adjudication (e.g., the United Nations or a revitalized International Court), informal exchanges of military intelligence, flexible *détentes*, or reciprocal measures to limit interstate disputes. . . .

3. Since an increment in the security of one nation or alliance tends to jeopardize that of another, each seeks to 'buy time', to 'negotiate from strength', and to score zero-sum victories through superior manoeuvrability. . . .

4. The irrational and inconclusive pattern of package deals and countervailing gambits has left many, urgent problems unresolved. It has maximized the ambiguities of Cold War diplomacy, instead of promoting co-operative methods to cope with them, and it has created an ethos that is inimical to the secure and long-range planning of a stable equilibrium. Among the imperative needs that this hit-and-run form of equilibration has failed to accommodate are:

(a) An effective and/or inspected method of arms control and disarmament.

(b) Banning nuclear weapons from space satellites.

(c) Terminating nuclear testing under valid controls.

(d) Disengaging military forces from zones of latent friction.

(e) Negotiating spheres of influence or standoff margins to curb disruptive misunderstandings.

(f) Anticipating the future threats posed by the widespread diffusion of thermonuclear knowledge and its military application.

(g) Strengthening the United Nations, its police capabilities, and the International Court, so that speedy and collective mediation can be decided and enforced *before* an acute crisis erupts.

(h) Establishing common 'codes' to govern limited or retaliatory wars, or wars of national independence, since they are very likely to occur—and very likely to escalate rapidly.

(i) Establishing common procedures to cope with the ambiguities of accidental war, pre-emptive miscalculations, or an unintended nuclear escalation.

(j) Joint agreements to curb revolutionary (or *n*th country) powers from territorial aggrandizement or infiltrative techniques.

(k) Employing the vast but ill-distributed benefits of technological research and economic abundance to promote the nutrition and prosperity of the 'hungry bloc'.

(l) Effectuating an exchange of scientific, academic, and cultural personnel (e.g. in joint projects, such as the moon shot), so that sympathetic traits and not hostility or insecure rivalries should be fostered.

Again, this listing seeks to be illustrative rather than exhaustive. Irrespective of its omissions, however, the list should suggest the many possibilities of upheaval that currently persist, and also the multitude of dysfunctional challenges (such as the emergence of China as a nuclear power) that the present system might be unable to handle during the next decade. . . .

A Revolutionary System Change?

Ideally, the international blueprint for a totally new and maximally rational system should be capable of fulfilling all those tasks—and more—in which the present balance falters. . . . In its optimum operation, the new system should depend neither upon the stalemate of the great powers nor upon the temporary triumph of one over the other. Preferably, it should depend upon a restructured equilibrium that required a minimum of intervention and institutional prodding by supranational authorities; in case of failure, though, the authority would have to be entrusted with considerable centralized power so that sanctions could be imposed upon any deviant member-nation or group of nations. Like any realistic proposal for a system of world government, therefore, its success will hinge exclusively upon its ability to demonstrate to each member-state that a truly enlightened calculation of self-interest would induce the surrender of a certain segment of the nation's sovereignty to the collective power of the supranational authorities.

SUGGESTED STUDY QUESTIONS

1. Consider the role of diplomacy both in avoiding and in settling international disputes.
2. How do states negotiate?
3. What aids to the settlement of disputes does the United Nations offer?
4. In what respects does international law differ from municipal law in the methods it provides for the settlement of legal disputes?
5. Lacking an international Parliament, how does international society achieve peaceful change?

FURTHER READING

CLARK, GRENVILLE and SOHN, LOUIS B., *World Peace through World Law*, 3rd ed., esp. Annex III, Cambridge, Mass.; Harvard University Press, 1966.

HALL, A., *Modern International Negotiation: Principles and Practice*, New York: Columbia University Press, 1966.

ILKÉ, F. C., *How Nations Negotiate*, New York: Harper & Row, 1964.

KERTESZ, S. D., *The Quest for Peace through Diplomacy*, London: Prentice-Hall, 1967.

NICHOLAS, H. G., *The United Nations as a Political Institution*, London: Oxford University Press, 1966.

NICHOLSON, H., *The Evolution of a Diplomatic Method*, Glasgow: Glasgow University Press, 1954.

Report of a Study Group on the Peaceful Settlement of International Disputes, David Davies Memorial Institute, Thorney House, Smith Square, London, S.W.1.

PART III

Peace-Keeping by the United Nations

The United Nations is essentially an organization for collective security, and its primary aim is the maintenance of international peace and security. This aim may be pursued by ensuring the peaceful settlement of disputes or, where the parties resort to force, by the employment of a countervailing force in the name of the United Nations with the purpose of dissuading the parties from recourse to violence: in this section we are concerned with this second alternative means.

The Charter had intended that the Security Council should assume the role of authorization and control of such 'preventive or enforcement' action as might be taken under UN auspices, and Chapter VII sets out in some detail the scheme of things which had seemed eminently practicable in the optimistic days of San Francisco in 1945. That scheme contained certain assumptions: first, that great-power unanimity was required to authorize such measures; second, that no such measure would be taken against a great power; and, third, that military contingents would be provided under specific agreements concluded between the Council and individual member States.

The political impasse—the 'Cold War'—rapidly developed and prevented the implementation of that scheme, so that the Security Council was never provided with the military forces it was intended to have. Far from reaching a military potential which the USA calculated should be of the order of 20 ground divisions, 1,250 bombers, 2,250 fighters, 3 battleships, 6 carriers, 15 cruisers, 84 destroyers and 90 submarines, to this day not a single member State of the UN is legally committed to provide a single soldier.

There remained, however, sufficient of a political will within the veto-bound organization to develop *ad hoc* machinery, very

87

much different from the Chapter VII scheme, which has to a limited extent fulfilled the organization's aims. If we set aside the Korean action in 1950[1] (explicable only by the absence of the USSR from the Council), the Security Council has developed a role of 'peace-keeping' quite different from its role under Chapter VII. Using forces of very limited size provided by member States on a purely voluntary and *ad hoc* basis, it has undertaken military operations not for fighting off aggression, but for operating with the parties to a conflict, on the basis of their consent. Thus, military observer groups were established in the Balkans (1946), in Indonesia (1947), in Palestine (1948), in Kashmir (1948), in the Lebanon (1958) and in the Yemen (1963). More sizeable forces were used by the Council in the Congo (1960) and in Cyprus (1964), in situations where a breakdown of internal order within a state seemed likely to produce international conflict: in the Congo, more than 20,000 troops were employed. In all these cases, other than Korea, great power unanimity existed for the authorization of these operations.

The factor which complicated this development was the assertion by the General Assembly of a similar power. First evidenced in the Resolution on Uniting for Peace of 3 November 1950, the General Assembly's wish to avoid the stultifying effect of the veto became manifest in the Assembly's authorization of UNEF—as an 'interposition force' between Egypt and Israel—in 1956. By a curious paradox, the veto which had on that occasion frustrated the Security Council came from Britain and France, not the USSR. It was at this stage that the UN ran into a debate of far-reaching consequences, a debate which still continues and which affects the whole future of the Organization. In essence, it involves questions of authorization of such operations, of control and of financing.

AUTHORIZATION OF PEACE-KEEPING OPERATIONS

The USSR has consistently maintained that the Security

---

[1] In June 1950, following an attack by armed forces from North Korea against South Korea, the Security Council did pass a resolution recommending member States to provide armed assistance to South Korea and, in due course, some sixteen member States provided military contingents which comprised a United Nations Command.

Council alone can authorize military operations by the UN,[1] and on this basis contested the constitutionality of both 'Uniting for Peace' and the UNEF operation. The majority of member States have rejected this thesis of a Security Council 'monopoly' and asserted a 'secondary' responsibility for the Assembly, acting by way of recommendation to member States. Clearly the basic issue here is political, despite its constitutional form, for the evasion of the veto is an evasion of Soviet control and an expression of confidence in the political wisdom of the Assembly. The issue has become increasingly complicated due to the vastly increased participation of new Afro-Asian powers within the Assembly, for the western powers could no longer, in 1969, control a two-thirds majority vote in the Assembly as they could in 1950 or even 1956. Loss of control has been accompanied by increasing doubts as to the Assembly's political wisdom. However, this majority view now has the backing of the International Court of Justice which, in 1962 in the *Expenses Case*, handed down an opinion affirming the constitutionality of the General Assembly's peace-keeping powers.

CONTINUING POLITICAL CONTROL OVER SUCH OPERATIONS

The Congo operations highlighted a second major issue. Assuming a valid authorization of an operation by the Council, can a great power use its veto thereafter as a means of controlling the directives to be given to the forces in the field? It may be recalled that the question of forceful intervention to end secession of Katanga from the Congo split the Council, destroyed any working relationship between Hammarskjöld and Prime Minister Lumumba, and led to the USSR refusing to bear any further responsibility for the military operations. Nor is this issue confined to the Council, for even in an operation authorized by the Assembly, the question could arise there of

[1] The Soviet Union's position is stated in UN Doc. S/7841 dated 5 April 1967: essentially, she argues that if power to authorize such operations were transferred to the Assembly the western powers would abuse this power by using it for their 'colonial' ends. The argument lacks conviction when we recall that the Afro-Asian powers wield the majority in the Assembly.

the form in which such control should be exercised. In practice, the Secretary-General has tended to assume control,[1] for the very existence of any radical disagreement prevented new directives from emerging from the political organs. The end result has been to place on the holder of that office a burden of responsibility which is too great, and which exposes him to the loss of confidence of those States which disagree with his interpretation of the original mandate given to the UN Force.

FINANCING

The earlier attempts by the Assembly to assess the costs of financing a UN Force as part of the annual, compulsory assessment of all member States (and in the same ratio of assessment) have given rise to acute difficulties. For the USSR, any operation authorized by the Assembly (such as UNEF) was *ultra vires*, and therefore she refused to pay any contribution: moreover, even where (as in the Congo) the Council itself authorized the operations the USSR has contended that authority over financing rests with the Council and not the Assembly. This is a minority view, rejected both by the International Court and the majority of the membership. A considerable number of States have argued that costs should be apportioned by the Assembly, but on a different scale to the normal budgetary appropriations and on different criteria—so as to minimize the burden of the poorer States, increase the burden of the great powers, penalize the States 'responsible' for the threat to peace, etc. Some States, including France, have argued that the General Assembly cannot impose compulsory assessments, so that financing must rest on voluntary contributions. The combination of these differences of view led to a financial crisis of the organization, with a deficit for the organization which, at the height of the crisis in March 1963, stood at $93·9 million.

---

[1] The Soviet Union's misgivings on this point are revealed in UN Doc. S/7841, particularly in the references to the 'Congo Club', the group of senior Secretariat members in charge of the Congo operation.

These are not hopeful within the immediate future. It is unlikely that the Assembly will abandon its assertion of a 'secondary' responsibility, at least to maintain a peace-keeping operation as opposed to forceful action against an aggressor State: the Soviet Union has now lived with this position for nearly twenty years and in due course may come to accept it. There are hopes that greater unanimity in the Council will be achieved, thus rendering the need for assertion of this secondary responsibility minimal: but even these hopes may founder if Communist China assumes the Chinese seat in the Council and proves more obstructionist than even the USSR. The case for a greater degree of responsibility over the continuing political control of a UN Force by the member States themselves is clear, and it may be expected that the Council, or a Committee of the Assembly comprising States actually contributing contingents, or even a joint Committee of both organs, could be established, provided the operation as such had general political support. It seems abundantly clear that the veto ought to have no application in questions of continuing control, for it would be intolerable for a military operation, once begun, to be hamstrung in this way.

The issue of finance is, of course, inextricably linked to these two preceding issues. Ultimately, authority over finance will probably have to rest with the Assembly, but the case for different criteria of apportionment is generally accepted and the application of these criteria to any particular operation will have to be *ad hoc* and, for the foreseeable future, the greater part of the costs is likely to be raised on a voluntary basis. Authorization of finance will, of course, be one means of controlling both the question of authorizing an operation in the first case and of ensuring continuing control, so that the powers and composition of any body controlling finance will be crucial. It would be tragic if the organization completely abandoned the notion of compulsory assessments for carrying out what is a primary aim of the organization. Indeed, for operations decided upon by the Council, there seems no need to abandon it. Even with an operation commenced on the basis of a mere recommendation of the Council, or of the Assembly, it is possible that some element of obligatory assessment could be retained, perhaps by the institution of a Peace-keeping Fund into which an annual contribution from every member could be paid. This would then provide a reserve upon which the organization could draw in any particular operation, supplemented by voluntary contributions.

LONG-TERM PROSPECTS

If, indeed, these extraordinarily difficult issues can be solved by some compromise, the prospects for longer-term development of a UN peace-keeping capacity would seem to be good. The argument that minimal, peace-keeping forces are so small as to be useless against any powerful State—and therefore are not worth the effort—misses the point. The essence of the peace-keeping force is not its fighting capacity but its deterrent function. It has been likened to a 'trip-wire', although the simile of a wedge, a small block whose effectiveness depends upon the counter-balancing of greater, external forces, is the more apt. A force of 6,000 men in UNEF for some time contributed to the separation of vastly superior Arab and Israeli armies,[1] and the deterrent to Greek or Turkish invasion of Cyprus of a mere 7,000 men cannot be estimated. Moreover, in the long-term, if the problems involved in peace-keeping can be solved, we may yet see a move towards the establishment of the larger forces which Chapter VII of the Charter envisaged and which will be absolutely indispensable to any agreement on disarmament.

The steps necessary for long-term development would seem to be the following. First, the UN must have its own Military Planning Staff, a group of highly competent military officers who could plan military operations in advance, provide the nucleus of a command in the field once an operation began, and also provide continuing liaison with States prepared to maintain standby units. Second, States should be encouraged to follow the Canadian and Scandinavian practice of main-

[1] The withdrawal of the Force by Secretary-General U Thant, upon Egypt's request, shortly before the Arab-Israeli war of June 1967 of course weakens this argument of effectiveness: U Thant's action met with a good deal of criticism.

taining within their armed forces units available immediately for UN use, so that there would exist a substantial reserve of men, materials and supplies. Third, these arrangements for voluntary help should gradually be transformed, as the Charter envisaged, into specific legal agreements containing obligations of assistance.

If, indeed, the immediate political problems can be solved, then, in addition to the steps indicated above, it is clear that considerable thought will have to be given to the nature of peace-keeping operations and the limiting conditions which have so far been assumed to apply to them.

For example, the notion that such operations must necessarily rest on the consent of all parties affected by them is extra-ordinarily limiting, and does not arise by necessary legal implication from the Charter. Clearly in practice a peace-keeping force of minimal size cannot operate in a State's territory without its consent. But does this extend even to rights of transit through, or overflight across, a neighbouring State? Is the operation of the force to be suspended if, in a situation of complete breakdown of law and order, there appears to be no established government competent to give consent? Is it right to assume, as U Thant did over UNEF, that by simply terminating its consent a State can require the with-drawal of the UN Force or should the State be committed to allowing the Force to remain until its task is completed?

Again, one may question the desirability of using a UN Force in a situation which is essentially one of internal, domestic strife. Can this be done without involving intervention and possible interference with the right of self-determination of the people? Ought the mandate of the Force to be limited to the preservation of human life and the avoidance of interference in the internal conflict by outside States?

In respect of the powers of the Force itself, the traditional limitation of the contingents to a right of self-defence has proved extraordinarily restrictive, and, indeed, was abandoned in the Congo and adopted only with considerable 'glosses' in Cyprus. Where, basically, disorder arises from armed, dis-orderly bands, should not the Force be entitled to go beyond self-defence and actually disarm, by force if necessary, these dangerous and undisciplined elements? These are but a few examples of the kinds of question which, in a more favourable political climate, will need to be examined within the United Nations.

If, as will doubtless seem to many, this approach appears to be based on a misguided optimism which ignores the cold realities of the present world, it may be useful to re-state one or two basic propositions. The first is simply that the political realities are never fixed. The UN has seen such extraordinary shifts of attitudes and powers that it is unwise in the extreme to predict failure in advance. Moreover, if the basic aims are right, as this writer is convinced they are, it is part of the responsibility of right-thinking people to seek to contribute to that end. The politicians have no monopoly of the right to develop ideas for the preservation of the peace of the world—indeed they are often too busy. If this really is at stake, and with it the future of mankind, and if this fairly minor development within the UN can make any contribution to securing peace, then it is high time people began to develop an attitude of active optimism, and not settle into passive pessimism.

It is also clear that, unless the UN can effectively equip itself with peace-keeping forces, this task will be assumed by regional organizations: the UK tried to establish a NATO or Commonwealth force in Cyprus before resorting to the UN and the USA did establish, via the Organization of American States, an Inter-American Peace Force in the Dominican Republic in 1965. Regional peace-keeping is not, intrinsically, a bad thing, but it is likely to widen the gulf between East and West and to lack the guarantees of objectivity which the UN might afford. All the regional groups are in a sense biased: they are 'against' communism, or capitalism, or colonialism. There is no sure guarantee that they will always act only with the interests of international peace in mind.

In the extracts of documents which follow one finds Hammarskjöld's summary of the principles derived from the experience of UNEF and assumed to be of general application to any peace-keeping operation. This, written in 1958, appears over-confident. The UNEF was an 'interposition' force, placed between Israel and Egypt. Not only were Hammarskjöld's assumptions about the situation in which Egypt might ask for withdrawal of the Force proved wrong (for U Thant treated the

Egyptian request in 1967 not as a matter calling for consultation but as a termination of the basic consent required for the presence of the Force) but he had failed to appreciate the more difficult problems likely to arise when the UN intervened in a civil war. The Congo and Cyprus operations both brought new dilemmas and it was soon found that strict 'non-intervention' in the internal dispute was in practice not possible. Moreover, the narrow restriction of the UN Force to self-defence was scarcely practicable and, finally, his assumptions about financing proved unacceptable to the UN members.

The extract from U Thant's speech in 1963 shows all the fruits of these later, and rather bitter, UN experiences. Although he has no doubt that the world will need a permanent UN Force, in due course, he is obsessed by the then acute financial crisis and the present inability of both States and people to shift their thinking from national to international terms: thus, his views are pessimistic, realistic and almost entirely unconstructive.

The next extract is from Professor Louis Sohn who examines some of the very difficult issues arising from UN intervention in situations of civil strife. This is a crucial problem because, on balance, it looks as though the threats to international peace will in the future arise more frequently from internal conflicts than from the traditional, inter-State, 'across-the-frontier' military conflict. The UN has somehow got to find the means and guiding principles which will enable its intervention to safeguard world peace without taking sides and dictating to a people their choice of government.

Lastly, since in the long-term the question of a permanent UN Force is bound to arise, an extract from my own writing summarizes the arguments for and against such a permanent Force.

DOCUMENT 15. EXTRACTS FROM SECRETARY-GENERAL HAMMAR-SKJÖLD'S SUMMARY STUDY OF THE EXPERIENCE DERIVED FROM THE ESTABLISHMENT AND OPERATION OF UNEF, UN DOC. A/3943, 9 OCTOBER 1958

B. Basic Principles

154. In view of the impossibility of determining beforehand

the specific form of a United Nations presence of the type considered in this report, which would be necessary to meet adequately the requirements of a given situation, a broad decision by the General Assembly should attempt to do no more than endorse certain basic principles and rules which would provide an adaptable framework for later operations that might be found necessary. In a practical sense, it is not feasible in advance of a known situation to do more than to provide for some helpful stand-by arrangements for a force or similar forms of a United Nations presence. In the following paragraphs, certain principles and rules are laid down in the light of the experience gathered in the past years, which, if they were to meet with the approval of the General Assembly, would provide a continuing basis on which useful contacts in a stand-by context might be established with interested Governments, with the aim of being prepared for any requests which might arise from future decisions by the Assembly on a force or similar arrangement to deal with a specific case.

155. As the arrangements discussed in this report do not cover the type of force envisaged under Chapter VII of the Charter, it follows from international law and the Charter that the United Nations cannot undertake to implement them by stationing units on the territory of a Member State without the consent of the Government concerned. It similarly follows from the Charter that the consent of a Member nation is necessary for the United Nations to use its military personnel or matériel. These basic rules have been observed in the recent United Nations operations in the Middle East. They naturally hold valid for all similar operations in the future.

156. The fact that a United Nations operation of the type envisaged requires the consent of the Government on whose territory it takes place creates a problem, as it is normally difficult for the United Nations to engage in such an operation without guarantees against unilateral actions by the host Government which might put the United Nations in a questionable position, either administratively or in relation to contributing Governments.

157. The formula employed in relation to the Government of Egypt for UNEF seems, in the light of experience, to provide an adequate solution to this problem. The Government of

Egypt declared that, when exercising its sovereign right with regard to the presence of the Force, it would be guided by good faith in the interpretation of the purposes of the Force. This declaration was balanced by a declaration by the United Nations to the effect that the maintenance of the Force by the United Nations would be determined by similar good faith in the interpretation of the purposes.

158. The consequence of such a bilateral declaration is that, were either side to act unilaterally in refusing continued presence or deciding on withdrawal, and were the other side to find that such action was contrary to a good faith interpretation of the purposes of the operation, an exchange of views would be called for towards harmonizing the positions. This does not imply any infringement on the sovereign right of the host Government, nor any restriction of the right of the United Nations to decide on termination of its own operation whenever it might see fit to do so. But it does mean a mutual recognition of the fact that the operation, being based on collaboration between the host Government and the United Nations, should be carried on in forms natural to such collaboration, and especially so with regard to the questions of presence and maintenance.

159. It is unlikely that any Government in the future would be willing to go beyond the declaration of the Government of Egypt with regard to UNEF. Nor, in my view, should the United Nations commit itself beyond the point established for UNEF in relation to the Government of Egypt. In these circumstances, I consider it reasonable to regard the formula mentioned in paragraph 158 above as a valid basis for future arrangements of a similar kind.

160. Another point of principle which arises in relation to the question of consent refers to the composition of United Nations military elements stationed on the territory of a member country. While the United Nations must reserve for itself the authority to decide on the composition of such elements, it is obvious that the host country, in giving its consent, cannot be indifferent to the composition of those elements. In order to limit the scope of possible difference of opinion, the United Nations in recent operations has followed two principles: not to include units from any of the permanent

members of the Security Council; and not to include units from any country which, because of its geographical position or for other reasons, might be considered as possibly having a special interest in the situation which has called for the operation. I believe that these two principles also should be considered as essential to any stand-by arrangements.

161. . . . It would seem desirable to accept the formula applied in the case of UNEF, which is to the effect that, while it is for the United Nations alone to decide on the composition of military elements sent to a country, the United Nations should, in deciding on composition, take fully into account the viewpoint of the host Government as one of the most serious factors which should guide the recruitment of the personnel. . . .

162. The principles indicated in the four points discussed above (paragraphs 155–161 inclusive) were either established by the General Assembly itself, elaborated in practice or in negotiations with the Government of Egypt. They have served as the basis for a status Agreement which applies to the United Nations personnel in the Force in Egypt. . . .

163. The most important principle in the status Agreement ensures that UNEF personnel, when involved in criminal actions, come under the jurisdiction of the criminal courts of their home countries. The establishment of this principle for UNEF, in relation to Egypt, has set a most valuable precedent. Experience shows that this principle is essential to the successful recruitment by the United Nations of military personnel not otherwise under immunity rules, from its member countries. The position established for UNEF should be maintained in future arrangements.

164. Another principle involved in the UNEF status Agreement, and which should be retained, is that the United Nations activity should have freedom of movement within its area of operations and all such facilities regarding access to that area and communications as are necessary for successful completion of the task. This also obviously involves certain rights of over-flight over the territory of the host country. . . .

165. Apart from the principles thus established in negotiated agreements or formal decisions, a series of basic rules has been developed in practice. Some of these rules would appear to merit general application. This is true especially of the precept

that authority granted to the United Nations group cannot be exercised within a given territory either in competition with representatives of the host Government or in co-operation with them on the basis of any joint operation. Thus, a United Nations operation must be separate and distinct from activities by national authorities. . . .

166. A rule closely related to the one last-mentioned, and reflecting a basic Charter principle, precludes the employment of United Nations elements in situations of an essentially internal nature. As a matter of course, the United Nations personnel cannot be permitted in any sense to be a party to internal conflicts. Their role must be limited to external aspects of the political situation as, for example, infiltration or other activities affecting international boundaries.

167. Even in the case of UNEF, where the United Nations itself had taken a stand on decisive elements in the situation which gave rise to the creation of the Force, it was explicitly stated that the Force should not be used to enforce any specific political solution of pending problems or to influence the political balance decisive to such a solution. This precept clearly imposes a serious limitation on the possible use of United Nations elements, were it to be given general application to them whenever they are not created under Chapter VII of the Charter. However, I believe its acceptance to be necessary, if the United Nations is to be in a position to draw on Member countries for contributions in men and matériel to United Nations operations of this kind. . . .

172. In full recognition of the wide variety of forms which decisions on a United Nations operation may take in seeking to fit differing situations calling for such an operation, the underlying rule concerning command and authority which has been consistently applied in recent years, as set out above, should, in my view, be maintained for the future. Thus, a United Nations operation should always be under a leadership established by the General Assembly or the Security Council, or on the basis of delegated authority by the Secretary-General, so as to make it directly responsible to one of the main organs of the United Nations, while integrated with the Secretariat in an appropriate form. . . .

179. . . . I have touched upon the extent to which a right of

self-defence may be exercised by United Nations units of the type envisaged. It should be generally recognized that such a right exists. However, in certain cases this right should be exercised only under strictly defined conditions. A problem arises in this context because of the fact that a wide interpretation of the right of self-defence might well blur the distinction between operations of the character discussed in this report and combat operations, which would require a decision under Chapter VII of the Charter and an explicit, more far-reaching delegation of authority to the Secretary-General than would be required for any of the operations discussed here. A reasonable definition seems to have been established in the case of UNEF, where the rule is applied that men engaged in the operation may never take the initiative in the use of armed force, but are entitled to respond with force to an attack with arms, including attempts to use force to make them withdraw from positions which they occupy under orders from the Commander, acting under the authority of the Assembly and within the scope of its resolutions. The basic element involved is clearly the prohibition against any initiative in the use of armed force. This definition of the limit between self-defence, as permissible for United Nations elements of the kind discussed, and offensive action, which is beyond the competence of such elements, should be approved for future guidance. . . .

181. In the case of UNEF, the General Assembly decided to organize an Advisory Committee under the chairmanship of the Secretary-General, to assist the operation. In practice, this arrangement has proved highly useful. In principle, it should be accepted as a precedent for the future. Extensive operations with serious political implications, regarding which, for practical reasons, executive authority would need to be delegated to the Secretary-General, require close collaboration with authorized representatives of the General Assembly. However, it would be undesirable for this collaboration to be given such a form as to lead to divided responsibilities or to diminished efficiency in the operation. The method chosen by the General Assembly in the case of UNEF seems the most appropriate one if such risks are to be avoided. The Committee is fully informed by the Secretary-General and his associates. There is a free exchange of views in closed meetings where advice can be

sought and given. But ultimate decisions rest with the Secretary-General, as the executive in charge of carrying out the operation. Dissenting views are not registered by vote, but are put on record in the proceedings of the Committee. It is useful for contributing countries to be represented on such an advisory committee, but if the contributing States are numerous the size of the committee might become so large as to make it ineffective. On the other hand, it is obviously excluded that any party to the conflict should be a member. Normally, I believe that the same basic rule regarding permanent members of the Security Council which has been applied to units and men in the recent operations should be applied also in the selection of members for a relevant advisory committee. . . .

185. . . . At some stage, a standing group of a few military experts might be useful in order to keep under review such arrangements as may be made by Member Governments in preparation for meeting possible appeals for an operation. I would consider it premature, however, to take any decision of this kind at the present time, since the foreseeable tasks that might evolve for the Secretariat do not go beyond what it is now able to cope with unassisted by such special measures. Were a more far-reaching understanding than I have indicated to prove possible, the matter obviously would have to be reconsidered and submitted again in appropriate form to the General Assembly, which then might consider the organizational problem. . . .

187. The financial obligations of Member countries to the United Nations are of two kinds. On the one hand, there are such obligations as are covered by the scale of contributions established by the General Assembly; on the other, there are certain voluntary commitments outside that scale. . . .

189. I believe that, as part of the stand-by arrangements, it should be established that the costs for United Nations operations of the type in question, based on decisions of the General Assembly or the Security Council, should be allocated in accordance with the normal scale of contributions. The United Nations in this way should assume responsibility for all additional costs incurred by a contributing country because of its participation in the operation, on the basis of a cost assessment which, on the other hand, would not transfer to the United

Nations any costs which would otherwise have been incurred by a contributing Government under its regular national policy. . . .

193. The approach indicated in this chapter suggests a way in which the United Nations, within the limits of the Charter, may seek the most practical method of mustering and using, as necessary, the resources—both of nations and its own— required for operations involving military personnel which may be conceived in response to the needs of specific conflict situations. The national resources likely to be available for such purposes, if our limited experience is a gauge, are no doubt substantial, but they cannot now be calculated or even esti- mated, and even their availability at any particular time would probably be subject to considerable fluctuation, for political and other reasons. Formalizing the principles and rules out- lined above, however, would afford a strengthened basis on which to expedite the mobilization of voluntary aid towards meeting urgent need. Their approval by the Assembly, thus clarifying and regularizing important legal and practical issues, would also ensure a more efficient use of any aid extended to the Organization, were it again to have to appeal to member nations for such assistance.

DOCUMENT 16. EXTRACT FROM SECRETARY-GENERAL U THANT'S ADDRESS AT HARVARD UNIVERSITY ON 13 JUNE 1963 ENTITLED 'UNITED NATIONS PEACE FORCE'

In my opinion, a permanent United Nations force is not a practical proposition at the present time. I know that many serious people in many countries are enthusiastic about the idea, and I welcome their enthusiasm and the thought they are putting into the evolution of the institution which will eventually and surely emerge. Many difficulties still stand in the way of its evolution.

Personally, I have no doubt that the world should eventually have an international police force which will be accepted as an integral and essential part of life in the same way as national police forces are accepted. Meanwhile, we must be sure that developments are in the right direction and that we can also meet critical situations as and when they occur.

There are a number of reasons why it seems to me that the establishment of a permanent United Nations force would be premature at the present time. I doubt whether many Governments in the world would yet be prepared to accept the political implications of such an institution and, in the light of our current experience with financial problems, I am sure that they would have very serious difficulties in accepting the financial implications.

I believe that we need a number of parallel developments before we can evolve such an institution. We have to go further along the road of codification and acceptance of a workable body of international law. We have to develop a more sophisticated public opinion in the world, which can accept the transition from predominantly national thinking to international thinking.

We shall have to develop a deeper faith in international institutions as such, and a greater confidence in the possibility of a United Nations civil service whose international loyalty and objectivity are generally accepted and above suspicion. We shall have to improve the method of financing international organization. Until these conditions are met, a permanent United Nations force may not be a practical proposition.

But we have already shown that, when the situation demands it, it is possible to use the soldiers of many countries for objectives which are not national ones and that the soldiers respond magnificently to this new challenge. We have also seen that, when the situation is serious enough, Governments are prepared to waive certain of the attributes of national sovereignty in the interest of keeping the peace through the United Nations. We have demonstrated that a loyalty to international service can exist side by side with legitimate national pride.

And, perhaps most important of all, we have shown that there *can* be a practical alternative to the deadly ultimate struggle and that it is an alternative which brings out the good and generous qualities in men rather than their destructive and selfish qualities.

Although it is perhaps too early, for the reasons I have already given, to consider the establishment of a permanent United Nations force, I believe there are a number of measures which could be taken even now to improve on our present capacity for meeting dangerous situations. It would be extremely desirable, for example, if countries would, in their national military planning, make provision for suitable units which could be made available at short notice for United Nations service and thereby decrease the degree of improvisation necessary in an emergency.

I take this opportunity publicly to welcome and express my appreciation for the efforts of the Scandinavian countries in this direction. Denmark, Norway and Sweden have for some time now engaged in joint planning of a stand-by force compromising various essential components to be put at the disposal of the United Nations when necessary. It would be a very welcome development if other countries would consider following the lead of the Scandinavian countries in this matter.

At present, the activities of the United Nations are overshadowed by a very serious financial crisis, a crisis which stems directly from the costs of the special peace-keeping operations in the Middle East and the Congo and from the failure of some members to pay their assessments for those operations. Although the sums of money involved are small in comparison to the sums spent by many countries on military budgets, they do, nonetheless, present a very serious financial and political challenge to the stability of the United Nations.

The United Nations is the sum of all its members and, to develop in the right direction, it must maintain and develop its active role in keeping the peace. I therefore view with the gravest concern the prolongation of the financial crisis of the United Nations with its very serious political overtones, and I trust that we may see a solution of the problem before too long.

I am concerned at this financial crisis more particularly because I see, in the long run, no acceptable alternative method of keeping peace in the world to the steady and sound development of the peace-keeping functions of the United Nations. It is no longer possible to think rationally in terms of countering aggression or keeping the peace by the use of the ultimate weapons.

However improvised and fumbling the United Nations approach may be, we have to develop it to deal with the sudden antagonisms and dangers of our world, until we can evolve more permanent institutions. There has been already a great

advance in the world towards co-operation, mutual responsibility and common interest. I have described some of the
proneering co-operative efforts made by the United Nations to
keep the peace.

I believe that these efforts constitute vital steps towards a
more mature, more acceptable, and more balanced world order.
We must have the confidence and the means to sustain them
and the determination to develop out of them a reliable and
workable system for the future.

I am a firm believer in the organic development of institutions. I also firmly believe that, if the United Nations is to
justify the hopes of its founders and of the peoples of the world,
it must develop into an active and effective agency for peace
and international conciliation by responding to the challenges
which face it. May we have the courage, the faith, and the
wisdom to make it so.

DOCUMENT 17. EXTRACT FROM 'THE ROLE OF THE UNITED
NATIONS IN CIVIL WARS' BY LOUIS B. SOHN, IN PROCEEDINGS OF
THE AMERICAN SOCIETY OF INTERNATIONAL LAW, 1963

[T]he United Nations has developed a constant practice of condemning and, when possible, preventing, the rendering of
support to rebel forces against an established government. In
the Congo Question the additional precedent was established
that assistance to the government itself should be provided
only through United Nations channels. This is quite contrary
to prior precedents. During the early years of the United
Nations the Security Council refused to condemn assistance
rendered by the United Kingdom in Greece and Indonesia.
When the United States proclaimed the Truman Doctrine and
agreed to send military assistance to Greece and Turkey, these
agreements were made subject to the condition that such
assistance will be withdrawn if 'the Security Council of the
United Nations finds (with respect to which finding the United
States waives the exercise of any veto) or the General Assembly
of the United Nations finds that action taken or assistance fur-
nished by the United Nations makes the continuance of
assistance by the Government of the United States pursuant to
[these agreements] unnecessary or undesirable'; but no such

finding was ever made by the United Nations. Similarly in later years, while complaints were sometimes made to the United Nations with respect to military assistance rendered by one government to another, no resolutions condemning such assistance were ever adopted, except in the Hungarian Case, where the government supported by the Soviet Union was not considered by the United Nations as a real government of Hungary but merely as a puppet.

The final question is whether the United Nations itself should assist any member government which is in trouble because of a dangerous rebellion and whether it should, whenever it deems it desirable, try to encourage a change in government either by itself taking action against that government or assisting an insurrection against it. In the Spanish Case, the General Assembly adopted a far-reaching resolution, in which it expressed its conviction that 'the Franco Fascist Government of Spain, which was imposed by force upon the Spanish people with the aid of the Axis Powers . . . does not represent the Spanish people,' and recommended that

> if, within a reasonable time, there is not established a government which derives its authority from the consent of the governed, committed to respect freedom of speech, religion and assembly and to the prompt holding of an election in which the Spanish people, free from force and intimidation and regardless of party, may express their will, the Security Council consider the adequate measures to be taken in order to remedy the situation.

At the same time, the General Assembly debarred Spain from membership in the specialized agencies of the United Nations and recommended that all members of the United Nations recall their ambassadors from Madrid. Though the regime in Spain did not change, the General Assembly revoked its recommendations in 1950, and in 1955 Spain was admitted to the United Nations as part of an arrangement involving simultaneous admission of sixteen states. As already mentioned, the General Assembly has repeatedly called for the holding of free elections in Hungary under United Nations auspices, but here also no effect was given to these resolutions.

But if there is a civil war raging in a country, should not the

United Nations take vigorous steps to support one side or another, depending on the 'justness' of their cause, even if no threat to the peace is directly involved? Is not the establishment by force of a totalitarian government contrary to the basic principles of the United Nations Charter, and should not the United Nations do something about it? Should the United Nations, to paraphrase the Constitution of the United States, try to maintain a 'democratic form of government' in each member State, or at least in those member States in which an attempt is made, through civil war, to establish democracy or to destroy it? If a civil war should be waged in a country on the scale of the Spanish Civil War, should the United Nations try at least to stop it, even if there is no foreign intervention? What is the paramount interest of the world community in a civil strife?

There is clearly a conflict here between the interest of the United Nations in the maintenance of international peace and the right of a people to self-determination and enjoyment of fundamental freedoms. In the interest of peace, the United Nations should either support the legitimate government or the stronger party in order to bring the conflict quickly to an end, before other nations become involved. The right of self-determination seems to imply that the matter should be left to the people itself, even if a prolonged conflict would result therefrom. But the right of self-determination could also form the basis of United Nations intervention on the side which is more likely to grant a greater measure of freedom to the people.

Judge Jessup[1] once answered firmly 'yes' to the question: 'Shall the preservation of the world's peace be exalted over the attainment of a "republican form of government" in every country of the world?' He added that:

> if we allow a civil strife to broaden and degenerate into a general international war between the advocates of two opposing factions, representing two opposing theories of government, we settle nothing.

On another occasion, Judge Jessup said that:

[1] Judge Jessup is a distinguished American international lawyer, a former professor of international law and judge on the International Court of Justice.

the interest of the world community in peace is greater than the assertion of an individual or group of individuals that his or their rights are being disregarded. If the state has relinquished its right to resort to war, so the individual must relinquish any right to overthrow his own government by force.

The international community would have to be prepared 'to render assistance to any of its members whose local forces are inadequate to preserve domestic peace and tranquillity'. In some cases an international police force might be dispatched to restore peace, in others there might be 'resort to collective blockade or quarantine of the state in which the civil war has broken out'. While this might result in sustaining sometimes the 'right' and sometimes the 'wrong' side, this is preferable—according to Judge Jessup—to the situation in the past when 'each outside state or each group of individuals in such outside states' was 'free to reach its own conclusion and to intervene on one side or the other'.

Judge Jessup's injunction was not followed in the Congo Question. While some United Nations activities in that case were directed against foreign intervention and the prevention of shipment of foreign arms into the Congo, other actions went much further. Thus, the Security Council, taking into account that a threat to international peace and security was involved, urged that:

> the United Nations take immediately all appropriate measures to prevent the occurrence of civil war in the Congo, including arrangements for the cease-fire, the halting of all military operations, the prevention of clashes, and the use of force, if necessary, in the last resort.

Later, the Council, deploring 'all armed action in opposition to the authority of the Government of the Republic of the Congo,' declared that 'all secessionist activities against the Republic of the Congo are contrary to the *loi fondamentale* and Security Council decisions,' and demanded that 'such activities which are now taking place in Katanga shall cease forthwith'. The Council also declared 'full and firm support for the Central Government of the Congo, and the determination to assist that

Government in accordance with the decisions of the United Nations to maintain law and order and national integrity'.

The answer thus to our original question seems to be that every civil war, if not ended quickly, is likely to become a threat to the peace, and the United Nations would be entitled to step in to remove such a threat. As a minimum, the United Nations would have the authority to establish a blockade on land and sea of the territory in which the civil war is waged in order to ensure that no foreign assistance would be given to either side. If invited by the government concerned, and perhaps even if invited by the rebels, it might send a peace force to assist in a cease-fire and to police the truce line. But should the United Nations force also be entitled to disarm the rebels, if so requested by the government? Or, even more drastically, should it arrest the government and disarm its forces, if its investigation should show that the rebels and not the government have the confidence of the population? Or, if it is not clear who should rule the country in accordance with the wishes of the people, should the United Nations establish a temporary government drawn from groups not involved on either side of the civil war, and arrange for an internationally supervised election? At present, the answer seems to be 'no' to these three questions, except when a secessionist movement threatens the integrity of the country which, because of particular circumstances, is entitled to special protection by the United Nations, as in the Congo Question. It might even be doubtful that a different answer would be desirable in the near future. If the United Nations could effectively maintain international peace and, in addition, prevent civil wars from becoming threats to the peace, it would have done enough to improve our present situation; we should not burden it with more until better means are devised to cope with the problem of peaceful change on the international and domestic level.

DOCUMENT 18. EXTRACT FROM *United Nations Forces* BY D. W. BOWETT, PP. 600–5 (STEVENS & SONS LTD, LONDON, 1964)

(a) *The Arguments for a Permanent Force*

These have been put by various people, in various forms, at different times. Essentially they are the following:

1. The improvisation inherent in an *ad hoc* Force leads to inefficient use of resources, uncertainty as to whether a suitable Force can be collected together, and delay in the use of the Force, which could have serious consequences for international peace.

2. With the dissipation of an *ad hoc* Force, and with no permanent Force remaining in being, much of the experience gained is lost. It is not enough to commit experience to paper for future reference: experience means also the experience of people in handling a given set of problems, so that permanent personnel become more important than permanent records.

3. The decision to use the Force must always remain a political decision, but the additional decision of how to constitute a Force—which is necessary when reliance is placed on *ad hoc* Forces—adds further complicating factors which could be avoided if a permanent Force were established.

4. Personnel of a permanent Force recruited as individuals would not remain members of national forces and would therefore be able to assume the international loyalty and *esprit de corps* which Secretariat members assume, and would become subject to rights and obligations under Article 100 of the Charter.

5. The possibility of recruitment of individuals in a permanent Force secures, in addition to the advantages in (4) above, a Force which cannot be dissipated by the withdrawal of national contingents.

6. In operations of an indefinite nature States are unwilling to see contingents of their national forces committed indefinitely.

7. Member States might be more prepared to finance a permanent international Force, than a Force comprised of relatively few national contingents.

8. Service with a United Nations Force requires special skills which cannot be readily imparted to an *ad hoc* Force, and which should be retained.

9. Consent to the presence of the Force would be more readily forthcoming.

10. Unity of command and better control over the Force could be achieved.

11. The permanent Force could become a nucleus around

which a larger Force could be constituted, by the contribution of national contingents, for the larger peace-keeping operations (like the Congo) or even enforcement action.

12. The permanent Force would constitute a 'pilot scheme' so as to build up the experience and confidence necessary for the progression to general disarmament, in which a larger United Nations Force would be necessary.

(b) The Arguments against a Permanent Force

1. The type of Force required for a particular operation will vary according to the situation, and *ad hoc* Forces give the necessary flexibility to meet different situations.

This was very much the argument used by Hammarskjöld in his *Summary Study of the Experience derived from the establishment and operation of the Force* (UNEF). Interestingly enough, U Thant, speaking on 13 June 1963, continued the Secretary-General's traditional opposition. He stated that:

> In my opinion, a permanent United Nations Force is not a practical proposition at the present time . . . Many difficulties still stand in the way of its evolution. Personally, I have no doubt that the world should eventually have an international police Force which will be accepted as an integral and essential part of life in the same way as national police forces are accepted.

However, the reasons against a permanent Force given by U Thant are not the variety of situations to be encountered, and the flexibility of the *ad hoc* system, but rather doubts 'whether many governments in the world would yet be prepared to accept the political implications of such an institution and, in the light of our current experience with financial problems, I am sure that they would have very serious difficulties in accepting the financial implications'. Hence, the Secretary-General advanced no more reasons of an intrinsically persuasive character against a permanent Force, but rather the simple political fact that governments are not prepared to accept the idea.

2. The selection of personnel for a permanent Force would be difficult.

This argument has never seemed particularly persuasive to the present writer. Whether secondment from national forces or individual recruitment is chosen, the problems are much the same as in recruiting the United Nations Secretariat—and this has never seemed insurmountable! Clearly some kind of quota system could be devised to prevent over-reliance on a few nationalities, and, even though exclusion of nationals from the permanent members might be desirable, there would still be plenty of available and sufficiently expert personnel of the right calibre and qualifications.

3. The financial implications.

This is, in a relative sense, an extremely strong objection and it is, as we have seen, still the objection which U Thant is raising. No one with any knowledge of the financial difficulties which the United Nations has experienced over UNEF and ONUC would deny the seriousness of this objection. However, it has to be placed in perspective, and it must first be said that, as one conceives of a peace-keeping Force or even a permanent Military Staff, and not a Force capable of enforcement action, so does one's conception of the cost involved alter, and the validity of the objection diminish. It may be recalled that the Secretary-General's estimate for his 800-man Guard Force in 1949 was $4m. per annum. Frye's estimate for a force of 7,000 men was $25m. per annum when not in action. UNEF, of 6,000 strong in 1958, was costing approximately $20m., and ONUC, of 16,000, approximately $120m.; in both cases, however, large parts of the upkeep was the burden of the participating States and not the United Nations. Astronomic though these sums might be, viewed relatively they are reduced to their proper perspective, and they make a rather favourable comparison to the sums States are prepared to spend on their defence budgets or even single items in those budgets.* More-

---

* The cost of a Forrestal aircraft-carrier is $200m. In *NATO, Facts about the North Atlantic Treaty Organisation* (1962) at p. 105 the total defence expenditures for the NATO countries are given, and the following figures are taken from the table there produced:

	Currency Unit	1958	1959	1960	1961 (Forecast)
Canada	Million Can. $	1,740	1,642	1,654	1,703
France	Million New Frs.	16,569	17,926	18,940	19,800
U.K.	Million £s Strlg.	1,591	1,589	1,652	1,701
U.S.A.	Million U.S. $	45,503	46,614	46,545	51,093

It is believed that the Soviet Union's defence expenditure in 1961 was £4,960 million. [Footnote in original.]

over, as the recent examples of UNTEA and the Yemen Group show, on some occasions the States directly concerned may be prepared to assume the entire cost of the operations.

Basically, the objection of finance is an objection to the assessment of a permanent Force as an institution of high priority in the maintenance of peace and security. The moment that one accepts that such a Force would make a contribution to the maintenance of international peace and security of the same order as the vast standing armies of the member States, the objection of finance loses a great deal of its force.

Finally, it may be said that what is proposed above is not even, as a first step, a standing, permanent Force but rather a permanent Headquarters Military Staff. If one visualises a Staff of, say, fifty experienced officers, the cost may well be in the order of $500,000 per annum: by any standards a not oppressive sum for more than a hundred member States.

4. Political unacceptance of the idea.

There is little doubt that the majority of member States, as represented by their governments, show relatively little enthusiasm for the idea. Quite apart from the question of cost, there are many who distrust the idea because of a fear that the Force may be used to interfere with State sovereignty, or may be used to augment the Secretary-General's power in an improper way, or used by a group or *bloc* of States in a way designed to further their regional interests rather than the purposes and principles of the Charter and the interests of the members as a whole. There is a certain validity in these objections, but they go to the desirability of establishing a proper system of political control rather than to the establishment of a permanent Force as such. Moreover, since we are for the present talking in terms of a permanent United Nations Military Staff, and in the more remote future perhaps a permanent Force of 5–10,000 men, the very limited size of the Force is such that it can scarcely be regarded as a potential aggressor against States.

It may be that governments also instinctively dislike proposals which imply some restraint on their freedom of action—and certainly a permanent United Nations Force will be utilized to curb certain forms of action—but this is scarcely an objection which ought to carry much weight once the Force is conceived as an instrument designed to ensure that governments abide by the obligations they have already assumed under the Charter with regard to the limitation of the use of force. The other comment which must be made on the objection of 'political unacceptance' is that governments may be becoming divorced from the opinions of their people. Ill-informed as the general public may be, gallup polls in the United States have revealed a majority view in favour of a permanent Force for the United Nations, and one suspects that a good many States would find a similar view amongst their people.

A final, and perhaps the most important, comment is that unless a beginning is made in this modest way it is difficult to see how the long-term plans for general disarmament which (at least from the standpoint of the proposals of the United States) envisage a United Nations Force of a permanent kind can ever be found acceptable. An experiment to build up confidence must be begun soon.

5. The unconstitutionality of the proposal in terms of the United Nations Charter.

The objection has been made[1] that, since the Charter envisages a Force constituted by means of national contingents provided by States pursuant to agreements under Article 43, to establish a permanent Force would be to act *ultra vires*. This is an objection which has, in one sense, already been rejected by Member States generally and by the International Court of Justice in the *Expenses Case*, for it rests on the premise that the only type of Force permissible for the United Nations is the Article 43 type of Force: not one of the Forces so far established has been of this type and the different constitutional bases for United Nations Forces have already been examined to demonstrate the invalidity of this premise.

SUGGESTED STUDY QUESTIONS

1. How has military 'peace-keeping' developed under the United Nations as contrasted with the scheme for maintaining peace envisaged in Chapter VII of the Charter?
2. What are the guiding principles for UN military peace-keeping?
3. Assuming agreement by the Soviet bloc to the establishment of

[1] Principally by the Soviet bloc.

a permanent UN peace-keeping machinery, how would you envisage this being established and operated?

4. Does military peace-keeping by limited military forces really make any substantial contribution to the maintenance of peace?

FURTHER READING

BLOOMFIELD, P., *International Military Forces*, Boston: Brown, Little and Co., 1964.

BOWETT, D. W., *United Nations Forces*, esp. conclusions, London: Stevens, 1964.

BOYD, F., *The Peace-Keeping Experiment*, London: UNA publications, 1968.

BURNS, A. L. and HEATHCOTE, N., *Peace-Keeping by U.N. Forces*, London: Pall Mall Press, 1963.

The Functioning of Ad Hoc UN Emergency Forces, Report by World Veterans Federation, Paris, 1963.

PART IV

The Great Powers and 'Brinkmanship'

The United Nations machinery for maintaining world peace, set out in Chapter VII of the Charter, was never intended to be used against the great powers: this was ensured by the veto. Obviously, therefore, an active peace-keeping role for UN military forces cannot be envisaged in any war between the great powers and, in the realm of 'primary' peace, the UN must be accepted to have little or no role. It will operate, if at all, in the realm of 'secondary' peace, the area of conflicts between smaller powers or, possibly, between a great power and smaller powers[1] but *not* between two or more great powers.

If we are primarily concerned with the threat of world war, of conflicts between the great powers, we must accept that mutual restraint depends on a balance of power—principally the balance between the USSR and the USA. Since this 'power' is now reflected in nuclear armaments of unprecedented destructive potential, the phrase 'balance of terror' may seem more apposite.

The question which should exercise the minds of all intelligent people is whether this balance is sufficiently stable to ensure peace. Many would doubt this. Not only does such a balance depend upon both sides exercising mutual restraint and judgment—and we have no absolute guarantee of their judgment or sanity—but, in addition, it is subject to the vagaries of miscalculation, accident, error (see the film *Dr Strangelove* for a plot based upon this happening) and of a change in the balance. This change in the balance of power

[1] Just as UNEF was established as a means of terminating the hostilities between France and UK on the one hand and Egypt on the other, in the 1956 Anglo–French invasion of Suez. However, both the great powers consented to this use of a UN Force. It would not have been possible to establish a UN Force actively to fight against Britain and France.

could emerge either as the result of one side suddenly acquiring an overwhelming technical superiority in nuclear weaponry or even as the result of new powers emerging to upset the 'bi-polarized' system. The advent of China as a nuclear power, or of an independent, united western Europe, or even of Japan could well operate so as to enlarge the number of players in the highly dangerous contest. And a game of chance in which the number of players is increased makes the game that much more unpredictable, especially if some players (China?) choose not to abide by the same rules of restraint.

Moreover, this 'game' is one in which, from time to time, the essentially antagonistic players push their opponent to the limit of tolerance in order to pursue an immediate advantage: hence the art of 'brinkmanship', the policy of pushing the opponent to the brink of war but stopping short of initiating a world war.

Successive crises have demonstrated the reality of the threat to 'primary' peace. The Berlin Crisis of 1948 might well have resulted in war had not the Allies been able to support West Berlin by an airlift. The Korean War of 1950 saw China enter the conflict against the USA, although the USSR abstained. The Middle East Crisis of 1956 saw Britain and France engaged in hostilities against Egypt, although general conflict was avoided by both the USSR and the USA agreeing to oppose the venture. The invasion of Hungary in 1956 by the USSR met with no military response by the USA. The Cuban Missile Crisis of 1962 brought the USSR and the USA to the verge of conflict, saved only by the USSR's agreement to withdraw the missiles delivered to Cuba.

The American involvement in Vietnam has brought no direct military involvement of the USSR and, more surprisingly perhaps, none from China. The Middle East War of June 1967 saw both the USSR and the USA abstain, and the USSR's invasion of Czechoslovakia in 1968 saw the abstention of the USA. In each crisis a challenge was made and the risk of war accepted but, happily, the policy of restraint prevailed. For how long this triumph of restraint will continue is anybody's guess.

However, it does appear as though certain basic rules of restraint are currently accepted. These appear to be:

1. That the USA will not intervene militarily in Soviet actions, however reprehensible, in eastern Europe (Hungary, 1956; Czechoslovakia, 1968).

2. That the Soviet Union will not intervene militarily in the Americas (Cuba, 1962; Dominican Republic, 1965).

3. That the Soviet Union will not intervene in South East Asia or the Far East to counteract US action but will leave this area to China to act as she deems best (Korea, 1950; Vietnam, 1960–9).

This may smack of 'zones of influence', tacitly accepted by both sides, although the USA rejects this (Document 19). But there are other highly questionable zones in which it is difficult to predict any mutual tolerance. It may be doubted whether in the Middle East, or in Africa, or in the Indian Continent either side will concede a free hand to the other. Certainly in western Europe it is likely that the USA will not tolerate Soviet military action: this is really the whole basis of NATO. Moreover, it is not simply a question of geographical area but of methods: thus, military intervention may not be tolerated whilst political influence, economic aid or subversion will. Space does not permit more than a few examples or 'case-studies' of brinkmanship and, in the documents that follow, some light is cast on the respective attitudes on the Cuban Missile Crisis of 1962, Vietnam and the invasion of Czechoslovakia in 1968. All of these demonstrate an attempt by the parties to justify, in legal terms, the action taken. This is perhaps surprising in the context of a blatant struggle either to extend control or maintain control and, clearly, the legal restraints are rather marginal in effect. In many cases the difficulty is not so much that the propositions of law are unsound but rather that the facts do not support them. For example, did the North Vietnamese really invade South Vietnam *before* the USA intervened? Or did the West really attempt to subvert the Czechoslovakian system before the Soviet Union invaded?

Two conclusions emerge. The first is that the conduct of virtually all the great powers scarcely allows them to adopt an attitude of moral superiority towards the lesser powers whose belligerent habits are so frequently condemned. The second is that, in the realm of 'primary' peace, the future of the world is by no means guaranteed by this present, highly precarious balance of power. It is for this very reason that, as we shall see in Part VI, an effort is being made to arrive at an agreement on general and complete disarmament. If the antagonisms cannot be lessened, then at least one can diminish the risk to the world at large if the destructive power available to the protagonists is minimized.

DOCUMENT 19. UNITED STATES' STATEMENT ON SPHERES OF INFLUENCE, PRESS RELEASE NO. 196, 23 AUGUST 1968

The United States Government has never entered into any 'sphere of influence' agreements or understandings with anyone anywhere in the world. There has been no discussion of any such idea in connection with recent developments in Czecho-slovakia nor has any government attempted to elicit from the United States Government any such understanding.

Any suggestion that the United States, tacitly or otherwise, gave the Soviet Union to understand that the United States would be indifferent to the action which the Soviet Union and other Warsaw Pact countries have now taken in Czecho-slovakia is malicious and totally without foundation.

It has been intimated that the Yalta Conference led to the creation of 'spheres of influence' in Europe. In fact the Yalta Conference, held from February 1–11, 1945, between the U.S., Great Britain and the Soviet Union, did not in any manner either directly or indirectly deal with any questions of spheres of influence. The entire record of the conference, without exception, was published by the U.S. Government in 1955 in the series 'Foreign Relations of the United States Diplomatic Papers—The Conferences of Malta and Yalta'. The U.S. attitude towards spheres of influence is set forth in a pre-conference paper on pages 103–108.

The zonal agreements, which merely delimited the zones of military occupation of Germany and Austria, were officially and finally confirmed at Yalta. The zonal limits were actually negotiated in the meetings of the European Advisory Council and were submitted to governments in November 1944. The only substantial change affecting the zones was the final Soviet consent, under British and American urgings, to agree to granting a zone to France and a place for her on the Control Council for Germany.

The document adopted by the conference, entitled 'Declaration of Liberated Europe', a document of American origin, had as its purpose the exact opposite of spheres of influence in Eastern Europe, since it provided for tripartite participation in the Control Councils and administration of former enemy states in Europe.

DOCUMENT 20. EXTRACTS FROM THE FINAL DECLARATION OF THE GENEVA CONFERENCE ON THE PROBLEM OF RESTORING PEACE IN INDO-CHINA, GENEVA, 21 JULY 1954

1. The Conference takes note of the Agreements ending hostilities in Cambodia, Laos and Viet Nam and organising international control and the supervision of the execution of the provisions of these Agreements.

2. The Conference expresses satisfaction at the ending of hostilities in Cambodia, Laos and Viet Nam; the Conference expresses its conviction that the execution of the provisions set out in the present declaration and in the Agreements on the cessation of hostilities will permit Cambodia, Laos and Viet Nam henceforth to play their part, in full independence and sovereignty, in the peaceful community of nations. . . .

4. The Conference takes note of the clauses in the Agreement on the cessation of hostilities in Viet Nam prohibiting the introduction into Viet Nam of foreign troops and military personnel as well as of all kinds of arms and munitions. The Conference also takes note of the declarations made by the Governments of Cambodia and Laos of their resolution not to request foreign aid, whether in war material, in personnel or in instructors except for the purpose of the effective defence of their territory and, in the case of Laos, to the extent defined by the agreements on the cessation of hostilities in Laos.

5. The Conference takes note of the clauses in the Agreement on the cessation of hostilities in Viet Nam to the effect that no military base under the control of a foreign state may be established in the regrouping zones of the two parties, the latter having the obligation to see that the zones allotted to them

shall not constitute part of any military alliance and shall not be utilised for the resumption of hostilities or in the service of an aggressive policy. . . .

6. The Conference recognises that the essential purpose of the Agreement relating to Viet Nam is to settle military questions with a view to ending hostilities and that the military demarcation line is provisional and should not in any way be interpreted as constituting a political or territorial boundary. The Conference expresses its conviction that the execution of the provisions set out in the present declaration and in the Agreement on the cessation of hostilities creates the necessary basis for the achievement in the near future of a political settlement in Viet Nam.

7. The Conference declares that, so far as Viet Nam is concerned, the settlement of political problems, effected on the basis of respect for the principles of independence, unity and territorial integrity, shall permit the Vietnamese people to enjoy the fundamental freedoms, guaranteed by democratic institutions established as a result of free general elections by secret ballot. In order to ensure that sufficient progress in the restoration of peace has been made, and that all the necessary conditions obtain for free expression of the national will, general elections shall be held in July 1956 under the supervision of an international commission composed of representatives of the member states of the International Supervisory Commission, referred to in the Agreement on the cessation of hostilities. Consultations will be held on this subject between the competent representative authorities of the two zones from 20 July 1955, onwards.[1]

8. The provisions of the Agreement on the cessation of hostilities intended to ensure the protection of individuals and of property must be most strictly applied and must, in particular, allow everyone in Viet Nam to decide freely in which zone he wishes to live.

DOCUMENT 21. EXTRACTS FROM 'THE LEGALITY OF UNITED STATES PARTICIPATION IN THE DEFENSE OF VIET NAM', MEMORANDUM OF US DEPARTMENT OF STATE, 4 MARCH 1966

[1] These the Saigon Government refused to hold.

1. *The United States and South Viet-Nam have the Right under International Law to Participate in the Collective Defense of South Viet-Nam against Armed Attack*

In response to requests from the Government of South Viet-Nam, the United States has been assisting that country in defending itself against armed attack from the Communist North. This attack has taken the forms of externally supported subversion, clandestine supply of arms, infiltration of armed personnel, and most recently the sending of regular units of the North Viet-namese army into the South.

International law has long recognized the right of individual and collective self-defense against armed attack. South Viet-Nam and the United States are engaging in such collective defense consistently with international law and with United States obligations under the United Nations Charter.

A. South Viet-Nam is being subjected to armed attack by Communist North Viet-Nam

The Geneva accords of 1954 established a demarcation line between North Vietnam and South Vietnam. They provided for withdrawals of military forces into the respective zones north and south of this line. The accords prohibited the use of either zone for the resumption of hostilities or to 'further an aggressive policy'.

During the 5 years following the Geneva conference of 1954, the Hanoi regime developed a covert political-military organization in South Viet-Nam based on Communist cadres it had ordered to stay in the South, contrary to the provisions of the Geneva accords. The activities of this covert organization were directed towards the kidnaping and assassination of civilian officials—acts of terrorism that were perpetrated in increasing numbers.

In the 3-year period from 1959 to 1961, the North Viet-Nam regime infiltrated an estimated 10,000 men into the South. It is estimated that 13,000 additional personnel were infiltrated in 1962, and, by the end of 1964, North Viet-Nam may well have moved over 40,000 armed and unarmed guerrillas into South Viet-Nam.

The International Control Commission reported in 1962 the findings of its Legal Committee:

there is evidence to show that arms, armed and unarmed personnel, munitions and other supplies have been sent from the Zone in the North to the Zone in the South with the objective of supporting, organizing and carrying out hostile activities, including armed attacks, directed against the Armed Forces and Administration of the Zone in the South.

. . . there is evidence that the PAVN [People's Army of Viet Nam] has allowed the Zone in the North to be used for inciting, encouraging and supporting hostile activities in the Zone in the South, aimed at the overthrow of the Administration in the South.[1]

Beginning in 1964, the Communists apparently exhausted their reservoir of Southerners who had gone North. Since then the greater number of men infiltrated into the South have been native-born North Vietnamese. Most recently, Hanoi has begun to infiltrate elements of the North Vietnamese army in increasingly large numbers. Today, there is evidence that nine regiments of regular North Vietnamese forces are fighting in organized units in the South.

In the guerrilla war in Viet-Nam, the external aggression from the North is the critical military element of the insurgency, although it is unacknowledged by North Viet-Nam. In these circumstances, an 'armed attack' is not as easily fixed by date and hour as in the case of traditional warfare. However, the infiltration of thousands of armed men clearly constitutes an 'armed attack' under any reasonable definition. There may be some question as to the exact date at which North Viet-Nam's aggression grew into an 'armed attack,' but there can be no doubt that it had occurred before February 1965.[2]

[1] The International Control Commission, composed of representatives of Canada, India and Poland, also found that the USA had violated Articles 16 and 17 of the Geneva Accords by introducing military personnel and equipment into South Vietnam.

[2] This is the crucial question of fact which is much disputed. February 1965 was the date of the commencement of the bombing of the North, but the real question is whether an armed attack from the North preceded the US intervention, which came much earlier. For demonstrations that the US intervention preceded any direct military intervention from the North see Theodore Draper, *Abuse of Power*, Viking Press, New York, 1966, Ch. IV and Richard A. Falk, *The Vietnam War and International Law*, Princeton University Press, Princeton, 1968, pp. 271, 445.

B. International Law recognizes the right of individual and collective self-defense against armed attack

International law has traditionally recognized the right of self-defense against armed attack. This proposition has been asserted by writers on international law through the several centuries in which the modern law of nations has developed. The proposition has been acted on numerous times by governments throughout modern history. Today the principle of self-defense against armed attack is universally recognized and accepted.

The Charter of the United Nations, concluded at the end of World War II, imposed an important limitation on the use of force by United Nations members. Article 2, paragraph 4, provides:

> All members shall refrain in their international relations from the threat or use of force against the territorial integrity or political independence of any State, or in any other manner inconsistent with the Purposes of the United Nations.

In addition, the charter embodied a system of international peacekeeping through the organs of the United Nations. Article 24 summarizes these structural arrangements in stating that the United Nations members:

> confer on the Security Council primary responsibility for the maintenance of international peace and security, and agree that in carrying out its duties under this responsibility the Security Council acts on their behalf.

However, the charter expressly states in article 51 that the remaining provisions of the charter—including the limitation of article 2, paragraph 4, and the creation of United Nations machinery to keep the peace—in no way diminish the inherent right of self-defense against armed attack. Article 51 provides:

> Nothing in the present Charter shall impair the inherent right of individual or collective self-defense if an armed attack occurs against a member of the United Nations, until the Security Council has taken the measures necessary to maintain international peace and security. Measures taken by members in the exercise of this right of self-defense shall

be immediately reported to the Security Council and shall not in any way affect the authority and responsibility of the Security Council under the present Charter to take at any time such action as it deems necessary in order to maintain or restore international peace and security.

Thus, article 51 restates and preserves, for member States in the situations covered by the article, a long-recognized principle of international law. The article is a 'saving clause' designed to make clear that no other provision in the charter shall be interpreted to impair the inherent right of self-defense referred to in article 51.

Three principal objections have been raised against the availability of the right of individual and collective self-defense in the case of Viet-Nam: (1) that this right applies only in the case of an armed attack on a United Nations member; (2) that it does not apply in the case of South Viet-Nam because the latter is not an independent sovereign state; and (3) that collective self-defense may be undertaken only by a regional organization operating under chapter VIII of the United Nations Charter. These objections will now be considered in turn.[1] . . .

III. Actions by the United States and South Viet-Nam are Justified under the Geneva Accords of 1954

A. Description of the Accords

The Geneva accords of 1954* established the date and hour for

---

[1] These are not the real objections. The real objection is that the US intervened in what was essentially an internal conflict between the Saigon Government and the Viet Cong. If this was the true nature of the conflict (and we therefore exclude the argument that the North had already intervened so as to commit an armed attack on the South) there could be no right of collective self-defence for an outside Power like the US.

* These accords were composed of a bilateral cease-fire agreement between the 'Commander-in-Chief of the People's Army of Viet-Nam' and the 'Commander-in-Chief of the French Union forces in Indo-China', together with a Final Declaration of the Conference, to which France adhered. However, it is to be noted that the South Vietnamese Government was not a signatory of the cease-fire agreement and did not adhere to the Final Declaration. South Viet-Nam entered a series of reservations in a statement to the conference. This statement was noted by the conference, but by decision of the conference chairman it was not included or referred to in the Final Declaration. [Footnote in original.]

a cease-fire in Viet-Nam, drew a 'provisional military demarcation line' with a demilitarized zone on both sides, and required an exchange of prisoners and the phased regroupment of Viet Minh forces from the south to the north and of French Union forces from the north to the south. The introduction into Viet-Nam of troop reinforcements and new military equipment (except for replacement and repair) was prohibited. The armed forces of each party were required to respect the demilitarized zone and the territory of the other zone. The adherence of either zone to any military alliance, and the use of either zone for the resumption of hostilities or to 'further an aggressive policy', were prohibited. The International Control Commission was established, composed of India, Canada and Poland, with India as chairman. The task of the Commission was to supervise the proper execution of the provisions of the cease-fire agreement. General elections that would result in reunification were required to be held in July 1956 under the supervision of the ICC.

B. *North Viet-Nam violated the accords from the beginning*

From the very beginning, the North Vietnamese violated the 1954 Geneva accords. Communist military forces and supplies were left in the South in violation of the accords. Other communist guerrillas were moved north for further training and then were infiltrated into the South in violation of the accords.

C. *The introduction of United States military personnel and equipment was justified*

The accords prohibited the reinforcement of foreign military forces in Viet-Nam and the introduction of new military equipment, but they allowed replacement of existing military personnel and equipment. Prior to late 1961 South Viet-Nam had received considerable military equipment and supplies from the United States, and the United States had gradually enlarged its Military Assistance Advisory Group to slightly less than 900 men. These actions were reported to the ICC and were justified as replacements for equipment in Viet-Nam in 1954 and for French training and advisory personnel who had been withdrawn after 1954.

As the Communist aggression intensified during 1961, with increased infiltration and a marked stepping up of Communist terrorism in the South, the United States found it necessary in late 1961 to increase substantially the numbers of our military personnel and the amounts and types of equipment introduced by this country into South Viet-Nam. These increases were justified by the international law principle that a material breach of an agreement by one party entitles the other at least to withhold compliance with an equivalent, corresponding, or related provision until the defaulting party is prepared to honor its obligations.[1]

In accordance with this principle, the systematic violation of the Geneva accords by North Viet-Nam justified South Viet-Nam in suspending compliance with the provision controlling entry of foreign military personnel and military equipment.

D. South Viet-Nam was justified in refusing to implement the election provisions of the Geneva accords

The Geneva accords contemplated the reunification of the two parts of Viet-Nam. They contained a provision for general elections to be held in July 1956 in order to obtain a 'free expression of the national will'. The accords stated that 'consultations will be held on this subject between the competent representative authorities of the two zones from 20 July 1955 onwards'.

There may be some question whether South Viet-Nam was bound by these election provisions. As indicated earlier, South Viet-Nam did not sign the cease-fire agreement of 1954, nor did it adhere to the Final Declaration of the Geneva conference. The South Vietnamese Government at that time gave notice of its objection in particular to the election provisions of the accords.

However, even on the premise that these provisions were binding on South Viet-Nam, the South Vietnamese Government's failure to engage in consultations in 1955, with a view to holding elections in 1956, involved no breach of obligation. The conditions in North Viet-Nam during that period were such as

---

[1] This proposition assumes that the North had already committed a 'material breach' by its armed attack on the South: but this is the very fact in dispute.

to make impossible any free and meaningful expression of popular will.

Some of the facts about conditions in the North were admitted even by the Communist leadership in Hanoi. General Giap, currently Defense Minister of North Viet-Nam, in addressing the Tenth Congress of the North Vietnamese Communist Party in October 1956, publicly acknowledged that the Communist leaders were running a police state where executions, terror, and torture were commonplace. A nationwide election in these circumstances would have been a travesty. No one in the North would have dared to vote except as directed. With a substantial majority of the Vietnamese people living north of the 17th parallel, such an election would have meant turning the country over to the Communists without regard to the will of the people. The South Vietnamese Government realized these facts and quite properly took the position that consultations for elections in 1956 as contemplated by the accords would be a useless formality.[1]

DOCUMENT 22. PRESIDENT HO CHI-MINH'S REPLY TO PRESIDENT LYNDON B. JOHNSON, FEBRUARY 1967, FROM *Against the US Aggression for National Salvation* (FOREIGN LANGUAGES PUBLISHING HOUSE, HANOI, 1967)

Your Excellency,
On 10 February 1967 I received your message. This is my reply.

Vietnam is thousands of miles away from the United States. The Vietnamese people have never done any harm to the United States. But contrary to the pledges made by its representative at the 1954 Geneva Conference, the U.S. Government has ceaselessly intervened in Vietnam, it has unleashed and intensified the war of aggression in South Vietnam with a view to prolonging the partition of Vietnam and turning South Vietnam into a neo-colony and military base of the United

[1] Possibly the Saigon Government were correct in assuming that the communists would not permit 'free general elections by secret ballot'. But, since Ho Chi-minh, the leader of the North, was denied this anticipated method of uniting the whole of Vietnam it is not surprising that he would be forced to use military means, even though he waited at least until 1958 before doing so.

States. For over two years now, the U.S. Government has, with its air and naval forces, carried the war to the Democratic Republic of Vietnam, an independent and sovereign country.

The U.S. Government has committed war crimes, crimes against peace and against mankind. In South Vietnam, half a million U.S. and satellite troops have resorted to the most inhuman weapons and the most barbarous methods of warfare, such as napalm, toxic chemicals and gases, to massacre our compatriots, destroy crops, and raze villages to the ground. In North Vietnam, thousands of U.S. aircraft have dropped hundreds of thousands of tons of bombs, destroying towns, villages, factories, roads, bridges, dykes, dams, and even churches, pagodas, hospitals, schools. In your message, you apparently deplored the sufferings and destructions in Vietnam. May I ask you: Who has perpetrated these monstrous crimes? It is the U.S. and satellite troops. The U.S. Government is entirely responsible for the extremely serious situation in Vietnam.

The U.S. war of aggression against the Vietnamese people constitutes a challenge to the countries of the socialist camp, a threat to the national-independence movement, and a serious danger to peace in Asia and the world.

The Vietnamese people deeply love independence, freedom and peace. But in the face of the U.S. aggression, they have risen up, united as one man, fearless of sacrifices and hardships: they are determined to carry on their Resistance until they have won genuine independence and freedom and true peace. Our just cause enjoys strong sympathy and support from the peoples of the whole world including broad sections of the American people.

The U.S. Government has unleashed the war of aggression in Vietnam. It must cease this aggression. That is the only way to the restoration of peace. The U.S. Government must stop definitively and unconditionally its bombing raids and all other acts of war against the Democratic Republic of Vietnam; withdraw from South Vietnam all U.S. and satellite troops: recognize the South Vietnam National Front Liberation; and let the Vietnamese people settle themselves their own affairs. Such is the basic content of the four-point stand of the Government of the Democratic Republic of Vietnam, which embodies the essential principles and provisions of the 1954 Geneva

Agreements on Vietnam. It is the basis of a correct political solution to the Vietnam problem.

In your message, you suggested direct talks between the Democratic Republic of Vietnam and the United States. If the U.S. Government really wants these talks, it must first of all stop unconditionally its bombing raids and all other acts of war against the Democratic Republic of Vietnam. It is only after the unconditional cessation of the U.S. bombing raids and all other acts of war against the Democratic Republic of Vietnam that the Democratic Republic of Vietnam and the United States could enter into talks and discuss questions concerning the two sides.

The Vietnamese people will never submit to force; they will never accept talks under the threat of bombs.

Our cause is absolutely just. It is to be hoped that the U.S. Government will act in accordance with reason.

Sincerely,

DOCUMENT 23. EXTRACTS RELATING TO THE 1962 CUBAN MISSILE CRISIS, FROM MISS MARJORIE M. WHITMAN'S *Digest of International Law*, VOL. 5, PP. 444–8 (US DEPARTMENT OF STATE, WASHINGTON, 1965)

Soviet Offensive Missiles in Cuba

On October 22, 1962, President Kennedy reported to his 'fellow citizens' that 'This Government, as promised, has maintained the closest surveillance of the Soviet military buildup on the island of Cuba', that 'Within the past week unmistakable evidence has established the fact that a series of offensive missile sites is now in preparation on that imprisoned island', and that 'The purpose of these bases can be none other than to provide a nuclear strike capability against the Western Hemisphere'. The characteristics of these new missile sites indicated, he explained, two distinct types of installations: several included medium-range ballistic missiles capable of carrying nuclear warheads for a distance of more than 1,000 nautical miles; additional sites 'not yet completed' appeared to be designed for intermediate-range ballistic missiles capable of traveling more than twice as far and capable of striking most of the major cities in the Western Hemisphere, ranging as far north as Hudson Bay, Canada, and as far south as Lima, Peru. In addition, he said, jet bombers, capable of carrying nuclear weapons were being uncrated and assembled in Cuba, while the necessary airbases were being prepared.

President Kennedy stated that 'only last month, after I had made clear the distinction between any introduction of ground-to-ground missiles and the existence of defensive anti-aircraft missiles, the Soviet Government publicly stated on September 11 that, and I quote, "The armaments and military equipment sent to Cuba are designed exclusively for defensive purposes",[1] and that 'That statement was false.' He continued:

> Only last Thursday, as evidence of this rapid offensive buildup was already in my hand, Soviet Foreign Minister Gromyko told me in my office that he was instructed to make it clear once again, as he said his Government had already done, that Soviet assistance to Cuba, and I quote, 'pursued solely the purpose of contributing to the defence capabilities of Cuba,' that, and I quote him, 'training by Soviet specialists of Cuban nationals in handling defensive armaments was by no means offensive,' and that 'if it were otherwise,' Mr Gromyko went on, 'the Soviet Government would never become involved in rendering such assistance.' That statement also was false.

Quarantine of Cuba

'Acting, therefore, in the defence of our own security and of the entire Western Hemisphere', the President stated that he had directed that the following initial steps be taken immediately:

[1] It must be recalled that in April 1961 Cuba did suffer an invasion from the United States—the 'Bay of Pigs' invasion—when 1,400 Cuban exiles, trained and equipped by the CIA (American Central Intelligence Agency), embarked from Florida and invaded Cuba in an abortive attempt to overthrow Castro. Thus, since this might be repeated, the Cuban Government had some ground for acquiring defensive missiles. But President Kennedy clearly regarded the particular missiles acquired as 'offensive' rather than 'defensive', i.e. designed to threaten the US rather than defend Cuba. Upon this distinction hangs the whole of the US justification to establish the naval blockade in self-defence. But it is obviously a very difficult distinction to make.

First: To halt this offensive buildup, a strict quarantine on all offensive military equipment under shipment to Cuba is being initiated. All ships of any kind bound for Cuba from whatever nation or port will, if found to contain cargoes of offensive weapons, be turned back. This quarantine will be extended, if needed, to other types of cargo and carriers. We are not at this time, however, denying the necessities of life as the Soviets attempted to do in their Berlin blockade of 1948.[1]

Second: I have directed the continued and increased close surveillance of Cuba and its military buildup. The Foreign Ministers of the OAS [Organization of American States] in their communique of 3 October rejected secrecy on such matters in this hemisphere. Should these offensive military preparations continue, thus increasing the threat to the hemisphere, further action will be justified. I have directed the Armed Forces to prepare for any eventualities; and I trust that, in the interest of both the Cuban people and the Soviet technicians at the sites, the hazards to all concerned of continuing this threat will be recognized.

Third: It shall be the policy of this nation to regard any nuclear missile launched from Cuba against any nation in the Western Hemisphere as an attack by the Soviet Union on the United States, requiring a full retaliatory response upon the Soviet Union.

Fourth: As a necessary military precaution I have reinforced our base at Guantanamo, evacuated today the dependents of our personnel there, and ordered additional military units to be on a standby alert basis.

Fifth: We are calling tonight for an immediate meeting of the Organ of Consultation, under the Organization of American States, to consider this threat to hemispheric security and to invoke articles 6 and 8 of the Rio Treaty in support of all necessary action. The United Nations Charter allows for

[1] This naval blockade of course carried the risk of a naval confrontation between US warships and the Soviet cargo ships carrying the missiles and warheads, which were accompanied by Soviet submarines. However, it was a very restrained response to the threat and was decided upon only after several days of debate by President Kennedy: it is clear that some of his advisers preferred either an invasion of Cuba or an air-strike to destroy the missile bases. See Theodore C. Sorensen, *Kennedy*, Harper & Row, New York, 1965, p. 682.

regional security arrangements—and the nations of this hemisphere decided long ago against the military presence of outside powers. Our other allies around the world have also been alerted.

Sixth: Under the Charter of the United Nations, we are asking tonight that an emergency meeting of the Security Council be convoked without delay to take action against this latest Soviet threat to world peace. Our resolution will call for the prompt dismantling and withdrawal of all offensive weapons in Cuba, under the supervision of UN observers, before the quarantine can be lifted.

Seventh and finally: I call upon Chairman Khrushchev to halt and eliminate this clandestine, reckless, and provocative threat to world peace and to stable relations between our two nations. I call upon him further to abandon this course of world domination and to join in an historic effort to end the perilous arms race and transform the history of man. He has an opportunity now to move the world back from the abyss of destruction—by returning to his Government's own words that it had no need to station missiles outside its own territory, and withdrawing these weapons from Cuba—by refraining from any action which will widen or deepen the present crisis—and then by participating in a search for peaceful and permanent solutions.'

On October 22, 1962, the United States requested an urgent meeting of the Council of the Organization of American States.[1] . . .

Also, on October 22, 1962, the United States, through Adlai E. Stevenson, US Representative to the United Nations, addressed a letter to the President of the Security Council (Valerian A. Zorin), requesting an urgent meeting of the Security Council to deal with the dangerous threat to the peace and security of the world caused by the secret establishment in Cuba by the Soviet Union of launching bases and the installation of long-range ballistic missiles capable of carrying thermonuclear warheads to most of North and South America[2]. . . .

[1] This meeting characterized the situation as an aggression—but not an armed attack and resolved to inform the Security Council.
[2] The Security Council held four meetings but adopted no formal resolution. The

An exchange of messages between Nikita S. Khrushchev, Chairman of the Council of Ministers of the U.S.S.R., and President John F. Kennedy, on October 26, 27, and 28, 1962, evolved a formula with respect to the Cuban crisis. In his communication on October 27, in reply Chairman Khrushchev's letter of October 26 (not yet published), President Kennedy stated:

> As I read your letter, the key elements of your proposals—which seem generally acceptable as I understand them—are as follows:
>
> 1. You would agree to remove these weapons systems from Cuba under appropriate United Nations observation and supervision; and undertake, with suitable safeguards, to halt the further introduction of such weapons systems into Cuba.
>
> 2. We, on our part, would agree—upon the establishment of adequate arrangements through the United Nations to ensure the carrying out and continuation of these commitments—(a) to remove promptly the quarantine measures now in effect and (b) to give assurances against an invasion of Cuba. I am confident that other nations of the Western Hemisphere would be prepared to do likewise.

In his reply on October 28, Chairman Khrushchev assured President Kennedy that instructions had been issued 'to take appropriate measures to discontinue construction of the aforementioned facilities, to dismantle them, and to return them to the Soviet Union' and that 'we are prepared to reach agreement to enable U.N. representatives to verify the dismantling of these means'. Immediately following this statement, he added: 'Thus in view of the assurances you have given and our instructions on dismantling, there is every condition for eliminating the present conflict'.

President Kennedy replied to Chairman Khrushchev's message of October 28 (which had been broadcast prior to delivery) on the same day. In his reply, President Kennedy stated: 'I consider my letter to you of October twenty-seventh and your reply of today as firm undertakings on the part of both our

---

Council did, however, afford to the two parties a forum in which they could test world reactions to their respective positions and, outside the meetings, a great deal of activity was begun with the UN Secretary-General playing the role of intermediary. It was thus that, within four days, the basis of an understanding was able to be worked out.

governments which should be promptly carried out. I hope that the necessary measures can at once be taken through the United Nations, as your message says, so that the United States in turn will be able to remove the quarantine measures now in effect.'

On November 2, 1962, President Kennedy reported to the American people 'the conclusions which this Government has reached on the basis of yesterday's aerial photographs', as well as other indications, namely, that the Soviet 'missiles and related equipment are being crated, and the fixed installations at these sites are being destroyed'. The United States, he said, 'intends to follow closely the completion of this work through a variety of means, including aerial surveillance, until such time as an equally satisfactory international means of verification is effected'. 'The continuation of these measures in air and sea, until the threat to peace posed by these offensive weapons is gone, is', he stated, 'in keeping with the resolution of the OAS [Organization of American States], and it is in keeping with the exchange of letters with Chairman Khrushchev of October 27th and 28th'.

On November 20, 1962, President Kennedy stated that he had been informed by Chairman Khrushchev that all of the IL-28 bombers 'now in Cuba' will be withdrawn in 30 days; and that Khrushchev had also agreed that these planes 'can be observed and counted as they leave'. Mr Kennedy stated that he had 'this afternoon instructed the Secretary of Defense to lift our naval quarantine'.

DOCUMENT 24. STATEMENT ON MILITARY INTERVENTION IN CZECHOSLOVAKIA, PUBLISHED BY THE SOVIET NEWS AGENCY *Tass*, MOSCOW, 21 AUGUST 1968

Tass is authorized to state that Party and Government leaders of the Czechoslovak Socialist Republic have asked the Soviet Union and other allied States to render the fraternal Czechoslovak people urgent assistance, including assistance with armed forces. This request was brought about by the threat which has arisen to the socialist system in Czechoslovakia, and to the statehood established by the Constitution. The threat emanates from the counter-revolutionary forces which have entered into collusion with foreign forces hostile to socialism.

The events in and around Czechoslovakia were repeatedly the subject of exchanges of views between leaders of fraternal socialist countries, including the leaders of Czechoslovakia. These countries are unanimous in that the support, consolidation and defence of the peoples' socialist gains is a common internationalist duty of all the socialist states. This common stand was solemnly proclaimed in the Bratislava Statement.

The further aggravation of the situation in Czechoslovakia affects the vital interests of the Soviet Union and other socialist states, the interests of the security of the States of the socialist community. The threat to the socialist system in Czechoslovakia constitutes at the same time a threat to the mainstays of European peace.

The Soviet government and the governments of the allied countries—the People's Republic of Bulgaria, the Hungarian People's Republic, the German Democratic Republic, the Polish People's Republic—proceeding from the principles of unseverable friendship and co-operation, and in accordance with the existing contractual commitments, have decided to meet the above-mentioned request for rendering necessary help to the fraternal Czechoslovak people.

This decision is fully in accord with the right of states to individual and collective self-defence envisaged in treaties of alliance concluded between the fraternal socialist countries.[1] This decision is also in line with vital interests of our countries in safeguarding European peace against forces of militarism, aggression and revanche which have more than once plunged the peoples of Europe into wars.

DOCUMENT 25. ARTICLE ON 'SOVEREIGNTY AND INTERNATIONAL DUTIES OF SOCIALIST COUNTRIES' IN *Pravda*, 25 SEPTEMBER 1968 (TRANSLATED BY NOVOSTI, SOVIET PRESS AGENCY)

In connection with the events in Czechoslovakia, the question

---

[1] This is quite contrary to the usual Soviet position that self-defence exists only against an actual armed attack, for there had certainly been no armed attack on Czechoslovakia by any western power. The Warsaw Pact of 1955—the Soviet bloc equivalent of NATO—speaks quite specifically in Article 4 of 'an armed attack in Europe'.

of the correlation and interdependence of the national interests of the socialist countries and their international duties acquire particular topical and acute importance.

The measures taken by the Soviet Union, jointly with other socialist countries, in defending the socialist gains of the Czechoslovak people are of great significance for strengthening the socialist community, which is the main achievement of the international working class.

We cannot ignore the assertions, held in some places, that the actions of the five socialist countries run counter to the Marxist-Leninist principle of sovereignty and the rights of nations to self-determination.

Abstract Approach Seen

The groundlessness of such reasoning consists primarily in that it is based on an abstract, nonclass approach to the question of sovereignty and the rights of nations to self-determination.

The peoples of the socialist countries and Communist parties certainly do have and should have freedom for determining the ways of advance of their respective countries.

However, none of their decisions should damage either socialism in their country or the fundamental interests of other socialist countries, and the whole working class movement, which is working for socialism.

This means that each Communist party is responsible not only to its own people, but also to all the socialist countries, to the entire Communist movement. Whoever forgets this, in stressing only the independence of the Communist party, becomes one-sided. He deviates from his international duty.

One-Sidedness Opposed

Marxist dialectics are opposed to one-sidedness. They demand that each phenomenon be examined concretely, in general connection with other phenomena, with other processes.

Just as, in Lenin's words, a man living in a society cannot be free from the society, one or another socialist state, staying in a system of other states composing the socialist community, cannot be free from the common interests of that community.

The sovereignty of each socialist country cannot be opposed

to the interests of the world of socialism, of the world revolutionary movement. Lenin demanded that all Communists fight against small-nation narrow-mindedness, seclusion and isolation, consider the whole and the general, subordinate the particular to the general interest.

The socialist states respect the democratic norms of international law. They have proved this more than once in practice, by coming out resolutely against the attempts of imperialism to violate the sovereignty and independence of nations.

It is from these same positions that they reject the leftist, adventurist conception of 'exporting revolution', of 'bringing happiness' to other peoples.

However, from a Marxist point of view, the norms of law, including the norms of mutual relations of the socialist countries, cannot be interpreted narrowly, formally, and in isolation from the general context of class struggle in the modern world. The socialist countries resolutely come out against the exporting and importing of counterrevolution.

Opposing Systems Stressed

Each Communist party is free to apply the basic principles of Marxism-Leninism and of socialism in its country, but it cannot depart from these principles assuming, naturally, that it remains a Communist party.

Concretely, this means, first of all, that, in its activity, each Communist party cannot but take into account such a decisive fact of our time as the struggle between two opposing social systems—capitalism and socialism.

This is an objective struggle, a fact not depending on the will of the people, and stipulated by the world's being split into two opposite social systems. Lenin said: 'Each man must choose between joining our side or the other side. Any attempt to avoid taking sides in this issue must end in fiasco.'

It has got to be emphasized that when a socialist country seems to adopt a 'non-affiliated' stand, it retains its national independence, in effect, precisely because of the might of the socialist community, and above all the Soviet Union as a central force, which also includes the might of its armed forces. The weakening of any of the links in the world system of socialism directly affects all the socialist countries, which cannot look indifferently upon this.[1]

NATO Threat Seen

The antisocialist elements in Czechoslovakia actually covered up the demand for so-called neutrality and Czechoslovakia's withdrawal from the socialist community with talking about the right of nations to self-determination.

However, the implementation of such 'self-determination', in other words, Czechoslovakia's detachment from the socialist community, would have come into conflict with its own vital interests and would have been detrimental to the other socialist states.

Such 'self-determination', as a result of which NATO troops would have been able to come up to the Soviet border, while the community of European socialist countries would have been split, in effect encroaches upon the vital interests of the peoples of these countries and conflicts, as the very root of it, with the right of these people to socialist self-determination.

Discharging their international duty towards the fraternal peoples of Czechoslovakia and defending their own socialist gains, the U.S.S.R. and the other socialist states had to act decisively and they did act against the antisocialist forces in Czechoslovakia.

Gomulka is Quoted

Comrade W. Gomulka, First Secretary of the Central Committee of the Polish United Workers party, commented figuratively on this score when he said:

'We tell those friends and comrades of ours in the other countries who think they are upholding the righteous cause of socialism and the sovereignty of the peoples by condemning and protesting against the entry of our troops into Czechoslovakia: When the enemy mines our house, the community of socialist states, with dynamite, it is our patriotic, national

[1] This appears to be the crux of it. Presumably the USSR feared that the liberalization being introduced in Czechoslovakia would spread to other Socialist countries and thus, ultimately, undermine the Soviet hegemony and Soviet interpretation of the proper way in which, politically and economically, Communism may develop.

and international duty to obstruct this by using the means that are necessary.

People who 'disapprove' of the actions of the allied socialist states are ignoring the decisive fact that these countries are defending the interests of all of world socialism, of the entire world revolutionary movement.

The system of socialism exists in concrete form in some countries, which have their own definite state boundaries; this system is developing according to the specific conditions of each country. Furthermore, nobody interferes in the concrete measures taken to improve the socialist system in the different socialist countries.

However, the picture changes fundamentally when a danger arises to socialism itself in a particular country. As a socialist system, world socialism is the common gain of the working people of all lands; it is indivisible and its defence is the common cause of all Communists and all progressives in the world, in the first place, the working folk of the socialist countries.

'Rightist' Aim Described

The Bratislava statement of the Communist and Workers' parties says of socialist gains that 'support, consolidation and defence of these gains, won at the price of heroic effort and the self-sacrifice of each people, represents a common international duty and obligation for all the socialist countries.'

What the right-wing antisocialist forces set out to achieve in recent months in Czechoslovakia did not refer to the specific features of socialist development or the application of the principle of Marxism-Leninism to the concrete conditions obtaining in that country, but constituted encroachment on the foundations of socialism, on the basic principles of Marxism-Leninism.

This is the nuance that people who have fallen for the hypocritical nonsense of the antisocialist and revisionist elements still cannot understand. Under the guise of 'democratization' these elements were little by little shaking the socialist state, seeking to demoralize the Communist party and befog the minds of the masses, stealthily hatching a counterrevolutionary coup, and they were not duly rebuffed inside the country.

Could Not Stand Aside

Naturally the Communists of the fraternal countries could not allow the socialist states to be inactive in the name of an abstractly understood sovereignty, when they saw that the country stood in peril of antisocialist degeneration.

The actions in Czechoslovakia of the five allied socialist countries accords also with the vital interests of the people of the country themselves.[1]

Socialism, by delivering a nation from the shackles of an exploiting regime, insures the solution of the fundamental problems of the national development of any country that has embarked upon the socialist road. On the other hand, by encroaching upon the main stays of socialism, the counterrevolutionary elements in Czechoslovakia undermined the very foundations of the country's independence and sovereignty.

Formal observance of the freedom of self-determination of a nation in the concrete situation that arose in Czechoslovakia would mean freedom of 'self-determination' not of the popular masses, the working people, but of their enemies.

The antisocialist path, 'neutrality', to which the Czechoslovak people were pushed would bring it to the loss of its national independence.

World imperialism, on its part, supported the antisocialist forces in Czechoslovakia, tried to export counterrevolution to that country in this way.[2]

The help to the working people of Czechoslovakia by other socialist countries, which prevented the export of counterrevolution from abroad, constitutes the actual sovereignty of the Czechoslovak socialist republic against those who would like to deprive it from its sovereignty and give up the country to imperialism.

Political Means Exhausted

The fraternal Communist parties of the socialist countries were for a long time taking measures, with maximum self-restraint

[1] This was not the view of the Czechoslovak Parliament, see Document 26.
[2] This is a question of fact, of which no proof is given. Did the liberalization developments in Czechoslovakia stem from the genuine wishes of the Czechoslovak people or, as here alleged, from imperialist subversion?

and patience, to help the Czechoslovak people with political means to stop the onslaught of antisocialist forces in Czechoslovakia. And only when all such measures were exhausted did they bring armed forces into the country.

The soldiers of the allied socialist countries now in Czechoslovakia proved by their actions indeed that they have no other tasks than the tasks of defending socialist gains in that country.

They do not interfere in the internal affairs of the country, are fighting for the principle of self-determination of the peoples of Czechoslovakia not in words but in deeds, are fighting for their inalienable right to think out profoundly and decide their fate themselves, without intimidation on the part of counterrevolutionaries, without revisionists and nationalist demagogy.

Class Approach to Law

Those who speak about the 'illegal actions' of the allied socialist countries in Czechoslovakia forget that in a class society there is not and there cannot be non-class laws.

Laws and legal norms are subjected to the laws of the class struggle, the laws of social development. These laws are clearly formulated in Marxist-Leninist teaching, in the documents jointly adopted by the Communist and Workers' parties.

Formally juridical reasoning must not overshadow a class approach to the matter. One who does it, thus losing the only correct class criterion in assessing legal norms, begins to measure events with a yardstick of bourgeois law.[1]

Such an approach to the question of sovereignty means that, for example, the progressive forces of the world would not be able to come out against the revival of neo-Nazism in the Federal Republic of Germany, against the actions of butchers Franco and Salazar, against reactionary arbitrary actions of 'black colonels' in Greece, because this is 'the internal affair' of 'sovereign' states.

---

[1] Does this suggest that all the rules of international law and of the UN Charter must give way before the over-riding aims of Communism? If this is really so, then hopes for 'peaceful coexistence', based upon the common observance of basic rules of conduct, are very faint indeed.

Vietnam Example Cited

It is characteristic that both the Saigon puppets and their American protectors also regard the notion of sovereignty as prohibiting support for the struggle of progressive forces.

They proclaim at every crossroads that the socialist countries, which are rendering help to the Vietnamese people in their struggle for independence and freedom, are violating the sovereignty of Vietnam. Genuine revolutionaries, being internationalists, cannot but support progressive forces in all countries in their just struggle for national and social liberation.

The interests of the socialist community and of the whole revolutionary movement, the interests of socialism in Czechoslovakia demand complete exposure and political isolation of the reactionary forces in that country, consolidation of the working people and consistent implementation of the Moscow agreement between the Soviet and Czechoslovak leaders.

There is no doubt that the actions of the five allied socialist countries in Czechoslovakia directed to the defence of vital interests of the socialist community, and the sovereignty of socialist Czechoslovakia first and foremost, will be increasingly supported by all those who have the interest of the present revolutionary movement, of peace and security of peoples, of democracy and socialism at heart.

DOCUMENT 26. DECLARATION OF THE NATIONAL ASSEMBLY OF CZECHOSLOVAKIA PROTESTING AGAINST THE INVASION OF CZECHOSLOVAKIA, 22 AUGUST 1968

The National Assembly of the Czechoslovak Socialist Republic, duly elected by the Czechoslovak people as the supreme organ of State power of a sovereign State and duly summoned by the President of the Republic,

categorically protests to the Governments and Parliaments of the Five States of the Warsaw Treaty (the USSR, GDR, Poland, Hungary and Bulgaria) and, before the entire world public declares

1. that no constitutional organ of the Czechoslovak Socialist

Republic was authorized to act or give consent to, or invite, the armies of the five States of the Warsaw Treaty to come to Czechoslovakia,

2. that it considers the occupation of Czechoslovakia as an arbitrary act of violence on international scale which is in flagrant contradiction with the principles of the treaties of alliance between Czechoslovakia and the said States,

3. that it lodges a most emphatic protest to the Governments and Parliaments of these countries who have jointly perpetrated this occupation and demands immediate discontinuance of the acts of violence against Czechoslovakia, and its population, as well as immediate withdrawal of the troops and normalization of international relations,

4. that it considers the present situation as critical, endangering all agreements and treaties sofar concluded between Czechoslovakia and the said States,

5. that it is determined to undertake all necessary steps for the safeguarding of sovereignty of the Czechoslovak people. It warns that all responsibility for the moral consequences of the occupation, liable to affect the world communist movement, shall fully rest with the heads of Governments of the countries participating in the occupation of Czechoslovakia,

6. that it considers the Government of Premier Ing. Oldřich Černík whom it had voted confidence in May of this year, as the only legitimate Government of Czechoslovakia and demands his immediate restoration to function.

DOCUMENT 27. EXTRACTS FROM STATEMENT BY US REPRESENTATIVE REIS IN THE UN SPECIAL COMMITTEE ON FRIENDLY RELATIONS, ETC., 12 SEPTEMBER 1968 (US DEPT STATE BULL., 14 OCTOBER 1968, PP. 396–401)

Prohibitions against Use of Force

Fourth, the actions of the Soviet Union and its partners have violated a cornerstone of the charter—the prohibition of the threat or use of force in international relations about which my delegation spoke earlier today. Article 2, paragraph 4, of the charter lays down this legal obligation in the following terms:

All Members shall refrain in their international relations from the threat or use of force against the territorial integrity or political independence of any state, or in any other manner inconsistent with the Purposes of the United Nations.

The invasion of Czechoslovakia constituted a massive use of force against the territorial integrity of Czechoslovakia. It was equally a use of force against the political independence of Czechoslovakia. The continuing occupation is likewise a continuing use of force against Czechoslovak territorial integrity and political independence. Moreover, the invasion and occupation are completely inconsistent with the purposes of the United Nations, purposes which, as laid down in article 1 of the charter, include the maintenance of international peace and security, the peaceful settlement of disputes, the development of friendly relations based on respect for the principle of self-determination, international cooperation, respect for human rights and fundamental freedoms, and the development of the United Nations as a center for harmonizing national action to attain these joint goals.

The very agreements the Soviet Union has forced upon Czechoslovakia as a condition of her return to a form of 'normalization' acceptable to the Soviet Union violate the principles that the U.S.S.R. agreed to, and indeed promoted, only this spring at the Vienna Conference on the Law of Treaties. The U.S.S.R.-Czechoslovak arrangements are surely open to a claim of invalidity on the basis of coercion of the representatives of Czechoslovakia. Article 48 of the emerging convention on the law of treaties as reported by the Committee of the Whole and urgently supported by the U.S.S.R. states that:

The expression of a State's consent to be bound by a treaty which has been procured by the coercion of its representatives through acts or threat directed against him personally shall be without any legal effect.

A claim of invalidity could also be based squarely on article 49—again, urged by the U.S.S.R.—that:

A treaty is void if its conclusion has been procured by the threat or use of force in violation of the principles of the Charter of the United Nations.

Self-Determination and Nonintervention

Fifth, the Soviet-led invasion, occupation, and political control of Czechoslovakia constitute a violation of the principle of equal rights and self-determination of peoples. They constitute a violation of the right of the people of Czechoslovakia to determine their future in conditions of peace and tranquillity. The fundamental right of self-determination—and the duty of others to respect it—is a right of all peoples everywhere. That right, too, has been denied the people of Czechoslovakia by the invasion and occupation.

Sixth, the invasion and occupation constitute intervention in the internal affairs of Czechoslovakia. For years the Soviet Union has stated on every occasion that the basis of its state policy, and the basis of that 'peaceful coexistence' which is its lifeblood in international affairs, lies in the twin principles of the equal sovereignty of every state and the consequent right of every state to be free from intervention in its internal affairs. The Warsaw Pact proclaims these high goals as rights and obligations of all pact members, rights and obligations expressly flowing to and from the Eastern European parties and governing the relations between the Eastern European parties as among themselves. In the preamble to the pact, the parties recite their motivation in the following words:

> being desirous of further promoting and developing friendship, co-operation and mutual assistance in accordance with the principles of respect for the independence and sovereignty of states and of non-interference in their internal affairs.

And in article 8 they undertake explicitly noninterference obligations. That article provides that:

> The Contracting Parties declare that they will act in a spirit of friendship and co-operation with a view to further developing and fostering economic and cultural intercourse with one another, each adhering to the principle of respect for the independence and sovereignty of the others and non-interference in their internal affairs.

Indeed, it is difficult to find a single agreement to which the Soviet Union is a party that does not reiterate the sovereignty of the contracting parties and their right to determine their own futures. What do these people mean by such commitment?

Nor have the Soviet Union and its partners confined themselves to violations of international legal obligations. Their actions are contemptuous of the clearly expressed political will of the General Assembly as proclaimed in the Declaration on the Inadmissibility of Intervention in the Domestic Affairs of States and the Protection of Their Independence and Sovereignty, Resolution 2131, adopted by the General Assembly in 1965. The proud words of the Soviet Union in sometimes claiming parentage of this resolution must be put alongside the facts of invasion and occupation. We need only remind the Committee that the very first principle of the nonintervention declaration states that:

No State has the right to intervene, directly or indirectly, for any reason whatever, in the internal or external affairs of any other State. Consequently, armed intervention and all other forms of interference or attempted threats against the personality of the State or against its political, economic and cultural elements, are condemned.

The nonintervention declaration goes on to state, in paragraph 5, that:

Every State has an inalienable right to choose its political, economic, and social and cultural systems, without interference in any form by any other State.

The principles of state conduct, too, have been violated by the Soviet invasion and occupation.

Definition of Aggression

A comparison of Soviet words and deeds would be incomplete without some reference to the efforts of the U.S.S.R. to bring about an authoritative definition of the concept of 'aggression'. The facts of invasion and occupation fare poorly with Soviet words and Soviet proposals. The current Soviet definition of the concept of aggression proclaims that invasion cannot '. . . be justified by any arguments of a political, strategic, or economic nature. . . . In particular the following may not be used as justifications':

A. The internal position of any State, as for example: . . .
(b) Alleged shortcomings of its administration; . . .
(d) Any revolutionary or counter-revolutionary movement, civil war, disorders or strikes;
(e) The establishment or maintenance in any State of any political, economic or social system.

Yet such defense as the Soviet Union has sought to raise in answer to the charge of intervention in the internal affairs of Czechoslovakia has been based on just such assertions and alleged 'justifications'.

No Legal Basis for Soviet Action

Mr. Chairman, the Soviet Union has not tried to provide a serious and coherent legal defense of its actions. What possible legal rights have been suggested in defense of the invasion and occupation of Czechoslovakia?

SUGGESTED STUDY QUESTIONS

1. Do the great powers demonstrate a genuine adherence to the principle of the abolition of war or do they merely pay lip-service to the principle?
2. Is there any evidence to suggest that the USA and the USSR have reached an informal understanding about their respective spheres of influence within which they will have a free hand without fear of intervention from the other?
3. Describe any occasion on which there arose a real risk of war between great powers since 1945 and the factors which led to the avoidance of war.
4. Does the present system of inter-State relations seem 'safe' in the sense that it contains adequate checks to ensure that war does not break out between great powers without either side really intending this to happen? If not, how could it be made more 'safe'?
5. Do you think that the present bipolar balance (between the USA and the USSR) will be seriously upset by the growing power of China and, if so, with what likely results?

FURTHER READING

ACHESON, DEAN G., *Power and Diplomacy*, London: Hutchinson, 1967.

FULBRIGHT, J. W., *The Arrogance of Power*, London: Cape, 1967.

HAYTER, SIR WILLIAM, *The Diplomacy of the Great Powers*, New York: Harper Bros, 1961.

KISSINGER, H. A., *The Necessity for Choice*, New York: Harper Bros, 1961.

MORGENTHAU, HANS J., *Politics among Nations*, 3rd ed., New York: Alfred A. Knopf, 1960.

WEINTAL, E. and BARTLETT, C., *Facing the Brink: A Study of Crisis Diplomacy*, London: Hutchinson, 1967.

PART V

The Era of Technology, Aid, Development and Equity

The last two decades have seen an obsession with the East-West rift as a threat to peace. However, within recent years there has been an increasing awareness that world peace can never be assured if there exists between nations and people a glaring imbalance of economic welfare. The discrepancy between the richer, developed northern hemisphere and the poor, under-developed southern hemisphere has therefore led to concern about the 'North-South' rift, or the 'rich and poor' gap. Just as, in State societies, an unfair and inequitable distribution of wealth tends to breed unrest, violence and civil war, so in international society will economic injustice lead to violence.

The contemporary concern with the problem of the under-developed nations owes much, therefore, to self-interest in the sense of a wish to avoid a potentially dangerous threat to world peace. Thus, Professor Gardner, in the extract quoted below, is at pains to demonstrate to the American people that foreign aid is not simply an act of charity but very much in America's own interest and an integral part of America's foreign policy. Obviously, this is not the only motive: there are those who are shocked—as a matter of conscience and humanity—by the state of affairs in which the *per capita* income for the developed world is $1,200–3,000 per annum whilst, for two-thirds of humanity in the underdeveloped world, it is $100 or less. There are also those who see in the underdeveloped world vast resources and vast potential consumer markets which will only become available (to the benefit of the developed States as well as the indigenous people of the underdeveloped areas) if investment, technology and aid are applied. The channels of aid are now many. They range from bilateral aid (one country assisting another) to degrees of multilateral aid. The Common Market, OECD (the Organization of Economic Co-operation and Development), Comecon (the Soviet-bloc economic organization), the Organization of American States, the Colombo Plan, are 'regional' groupings of States concerned with aid and development: on a global level we have the UN and the family of specialized agencies.

The UN family embarked upon a first development decade in the 1960–70 era but, having fallen miserably short of its target, is already planning a second decade in the seventies. Some of the problems of massive programmes of aid and development are highlighted in the extracts from Secretary-General U Thant's statement and from the UNCTAD report by Dr Prebisch and the later UNCTAD report in 1968. Lack of national planning by recipient states, lack of expert personnel to execute plans, the adverse pattern of trade which brings higher returns to the producer of manufactured goods (the developed countries) and relatively lower returns to the exporters of primary products (the developing countries) and, above all, the sheer inadequacy in the amount of aid: these are partly the reasons for failure, and failure is measured by the higher growth rate of the developed countries. The 'gap' is widening rather than narrowing.

There are contributing factors. Many States, including underdeveloped States, waste enormous resources in men and materials in providing armaments and maintaining large armed forces. The population growth is more rapid in the underdeveloped countries, so that advances are dissipated amongst an ever-increasing population, and birth control is notoriously difficult to introduce for reasons which may be religious, political, social and educational. Forecasting population growth is a most inaccurate science, for there are so many variables affecting both mortality and fertility. However, from a world population of just over 3,000 million in 1960 it is estimated that, by A.D. 2000, the world population will be between 5,000 and 7,000 million.[1] Disturbingly, the growth

[1] The UN study in 1958, *The Future Growth of World Population*, forecast an increase to a figure between 4,900 million to 6,900 million. During the 1965 World Population Conference, Professor Boyarsky gave a more conservative estimate of 4,626 million plus or minus 410 million (UN Doc. E/CONF. 41/3, vol. III).

rate is faster in the underdeveloped countries, those who can least afford it, so that development has to grow at an even faster rate if the general standard of living is to improve.[1]

The 'population explosion' represents a threat not only to the increased standards of living which are the aim of the development programmes but also to food resources. The question 'Can we feed the world's population?' does not admit of any glib answer. The FAO has shown that in 1962 in areas containing 60 per cent of the world's population the food supplies were not sufficient to provide even 2,200 calories per person per day: 10 to 15 per cent of the people of the world were said to be undernourished 'and up to half suffer from hunger or malnutrition or both'.[2] With an increase in world population aid will therefore be needed simply to keep people from hunger, let alone diminish the gap between the rich and poor nations in terms of standard of living.

Thus, whilst those who ask 'Are we sitting on a time-bomb?' are perhaps unnecessarily alarmist and underrate the contribution which technology can make to a solution of these problems, it is nevertheless true that these problems have extreme relevance to the central aim of keeping world peace.

DOCUMENT 28. EXTRACTS FROM *In Pursuit of World Order* BY RICHARD N. GARDNER, CH. 5, 'THE DECADE OF DEVELOPMENT' (PRAEGER, NEW YORK, 1964)

Foreign policy is not only concerned with survival, or with the maintenance of peace and security. It is also concerned with the promotion of welfare—both with material well-being and with nonmaterial goals essential to the fullest development of the human personality. The promotion of these economic and social objectives is not merely desirable for its own sake; it is vitally related to the pursuit of peace. The founders of the United Nations recognized in the Charter that to 'save succeeding generations from the scourge of war' it is necessary to

[1] Professor Boyarsky's estimates were that the following increases would occur from 1960 to A.D. 2000: USSR, 214 to 333 million; W. Europe, 309 to 415 million; China, 714 to 1,072 million; India, 432 to 689 million.
[2] FAO, *Third World Food Survey*, 1963: introduction by the Secretary-General. However his estimate of population in 2000 was probably high, i.e. double the 1963 figure.

'promote social progress and better standards of life in larger freedom'.

The promotion of the general welfare through economic and social co-operation now occupies more than four-fifths of the men and money in the United Nations system. It is the concern not only of the General Assembly, the Economic and Social Council, and the U.N. Secretariat, but of fourteen specialized and affiliated agencies, four regional economic commissions, and four special programs. This vast network of activity is supplemented by vital regional economic institutions in the North Atlantic Community, in the inter-American system, and elsewhere, and even by some world-wide arrangements outside the U.N. system. . . .

Let us begin with some facts about the present distribution of world income. The facts are well known, but they bear repeating. In the United States, the average annual income is about $3,000. In the other developed countries of the free world, it is about $1,200. In the less developed countries as a whole, it is about $150. In the vast majority of the less developed countries—a majority that includes two-thirds of humanity— it is less than $100.

There are many ways of dramatizing the meaning of these cold statistics. For example, U.S. Gross National Product in the three years 1961–63 increased by $100 billion—from $500 billion to $600 billion—an increase that is more than the combined national products of 84 members of the United Nations. Or perhaps this is best put in everyday terms: The average person in most less developed nations has to spend per day on all his needs—food, clothing, shelter, health, education—about what the average American spends when he goes to his corner drugstore to buy a pack of cigarettes.

Let us admit that such monetary comparisons of living standards around the world are subject to a margin of error. Economists have no way of taking precisely into account the differences in internal purchasing power of national currencies, or the fact that persons in rural and agricultural societies tend to consume a large part of their own production, which never receives a market valuation. Even allowing for a substantial margin of error, however, it remains clear that the conditions of life facing the mass of humanity are not compatible with minimum standards of human dignity.

Much is written these days about the importance of 'closing the gap' between the rich and the poor countries of the world. If this is intended to mean a closing of the gap in absolute terms, it is almost certainly not a feasible objective. Growth rates are superimposed on huge existing absolute disparities. In the less developed countries as a whole, national income has been growing at about 3 per cent a year, population at about 2 per cent a year, per capita income at about 1 per cent a year. For most of the less developed countries, therefore, the average annual increase in per capita income has been about $1. In the United States, per capita income has been increasing annually by close to $100. If present trends continue, average annual per capita income between now and the year 2000 will grow from $3,000 to about $6,000 in the United States, from $1,200 to about $2,400 in other developed countries of the free world, and from less than $100 to less than $150 in the majority of the less developed countries. Thus the absolute gap will more than double. Even if we could achieve a doubling of the present annual growth rate of per capita income in the less developed countries—a formidable assignment—the gap would still double in absolute terms. . . .

The poverty of the less developed countries is an old story. What is new is their determination to do something about it. This determination—aptly termed 'the revolution of rising expectations'—has brought to a large part of the world a turbulence and upheaval unique in history. Urgent demands for economic and social improvement are the dominant facts of life today in the poor countries of Asia, the Middle East, Africa, and Latin America. There is no longer any question of whether these countries will develop themselves—the only question is how. . . .

For some, the principal purpose of foreign aid is humanitarian—it is an indispensable expression of the brotherhood of man. For others, the purpose of foreign aid is economic—it is to assure access to the raw materials and growing markets that are important to the growth and prosperity of the developed countries. For still others, the purpose of foreign aid is political —it is to influence the less developed countries in a favorable direction and prevent the spread of Communism. All of these viewpoints are wrong if they are designed to provide the sole explanation for a foreign-aid program. All of them are right if they are designed to express one of its purposes. For foreign aid has many purposes, just as has foreign policy.

Perhaps the best way to see the many purposes involved in foreign aid is to contemplate the central choice now facing the developed and less developed countries. For the less developed countries, there are three possible sources of the capital needed for their economic development: domestic, Communist, and free world. The relative emphasis they place on these three sources will profoundly affect their economic and political evolution, and hence the economic and political evolution of the whole world.

A good part of the capital needs of the underdeveloped countries can and must be supplied from domestic sources. But for most of these countries existing production is barely sufficient to cover current consumption needs. Only a small margin of production can be channeled into the formation of capital. If these countries despair of obtaining sufficient capital from abroad, they will be more likely to adopt totalitarian measures at home. They may seek development by ruthlessly suppressing consumption and by forcibly mobilizing capital and labor. They may succumb to a militant and embittered nationalism. For them, development will be likely to occur in a climate in which freedom cannot survive. For us, this could mean the loss of important raw materials and markets, a vast erosion of world power, and the end of an opportunity to further the cause of human freedom.

A second source of capital for the underdeveloped countries is the Communist world. We need not fear Communist aid to these countries as long as it is relatively small in comparison with the investment of the West. But when the Communist world—Soviet or Chinese—becomes the main source of trade or foreign capital for an underdeveloped country, it will use this leverage to try to bring it into the Communist orbit. Should this strategy prove successful in the case of some of the larger underdeveloped countries, the Communists would alter in their favor the balance of political and economic power. The free world cannot afford to let this happen.

The third and last source of capital is the industrialized North Atlantic Community and Japan. Aid from this source represents the only chance for many less developed countries to achieve a tolerable rate of economic development without sacrificing human values or becoming dependent on the Communist bloc. Moreover, this aid is one of the most effective ways to build a bridge between the developed and the less developed countries and achieve a reciprocal influencing of values and institutions.

Thus foreign aid has a direct bearing on security and prosperity. But we should not restrict our calculations to material considerations alone. There is a very special respect in which foreign aid can promote nonmaterial ends. For the people of the United States, currently enjoying a power and prosperity unique in history, a foreign-aid programme represents an opportunity to express their natural idealism, their concern for the brotherhood of man and the dignity of the individual. . . .

To say this does not mean that we must be crusaders for an ideology, that we should seek to impose our political, economic, and social institutions on other people. To the other people of the world we must never say 'be like us', but 'be what you want to be'. Our purpose is to help men everywhere towards security, prosperity, and freedom, through institutions suited to their own traditions and environments.

In short, foreign aid is a matter of both politics and economics, of self-interest and ideals.

DOCUMENT 29. EXTRACT FROM U THANT, SECRETARY-GENERAL OF THE UNITED NATIONS, IN *The UN Development Decade: Proposals for Action* (UNITED NATIONS PUBLICATION, NEW YORK, 1962)

The main economic objective for the decade is to create conditions in which the national incomes of the developing countries not only will be increasing by 5 per cent yearly by 1970, but will also continue to expand at this annual rate thereafter. If this can be done, and if the population of the developing countries continues to rise at its present rate of 2 to $2\frac{1}{2}$ per cent yearly, personal living standards can be doubled within twenty-five to thirty years. If, however, the growth of population should be even more rapid by the end of the decade than it is now—and there are indications that in a number of countries the annual rate of increase is already 3 per cent or higher—it will take correspondingly longer to double living standards. . . .

A better understanding of the nature of development has resulted in the clarification of a number of issues as being irrelevant to the fundamental problems of development; for example, the demarcation of the public and private sectors in economic life, agricultural development *versus* industrial development, and education *versus* vocational training. There has perhaps been less progress in recognizing the nature of the relationship between aid policies and trade policies, but even here there are signs that a more enlightened view may be making headway.

Meanwhile, there has been increasing appreciation of the need for a number of new approaches. These include:

1. The concept of national planning—for social as well as for economic development. This is central to all the proposals for intensified action by the United Nations system during the development decade outlined in this report. Former objections to planning, based largely on a misunderstanding of the role envisaged for the private sector in most development plans, have died away. It is now generally appreciated that the purpose of a development plan is to provide a programme of action for the achievement of targets based on realistic studies of the resources available. Planning is proving to be a potent tool for the mobilization of existing and latent resources—human and material, public and private, domestic and external—available to countries for the achievement of their development aims. It has been shown that vigorous efforts are more likely to result if national and sectoral objectives are defined and translated into action programmes.

2. There is now greater insight into the importance of the human factor in development, and the urgent need to mobilize human resources. Economic growth in the advanced countries appears to be attributable, in larger part than was previously supposed to human skills rather than to capital. Moreover, the widening of man's horizons through education and training, and the lifting of his vitality through better health, are not only essential pre-conditions for development, they are also among

its major objectives. It is estimated that the total number of trained people in the developing countries must be increased by at least 10 per cent a year if the other objectives of the decade are to be achieved.

3. One of the most serious problems facing the developing countries is increasing under-employment and unemployment. This increase is not confined to countries already experiencing population pressures, although rapidly rising population is undoubtedly a major aggravating factor. Far-reaching action will be required if the fruits of economic progress are to benefit all the inhabitants of the world.

4. The disappointing foreign trade record of the developing countries is due in part to obstacles hindering the entry of their products into industrial markets, and in part to the fact that production of many primary commodities has grown more rapidly than demand for them. It is appreciated that 'disruptive competition' from low-income countries may be felt by established industries in high-income countries. Yet, precisely because they are so advanced, the high-income countries should be able to alleviate any hardships without shifting the burden of adjustment to the developing countries by restricting the latter's export markets. A related problem to be solved is that of stabilizing the international commodity markets on which developing countries depend so heavily. Progress could certainly be made if the main industrial countries were to devote as much attention to promoting trade as to dispensing aid.

5. The acceptance of the principle of capital assistance to developing countries is one of the most striking expressions of international solidarity as well as enlightened self-interest. If such assistance increases to, and maintains, a level of 1 per cent of the national incomes of the advanced countries during the development decade, as suggested by the General Assembly, this will represent yet another essential contribution to the success of the decade. At the same time, there is a need for pragmatism and flexibility in determining the forms of capital flows and aid, in relation both to the needs of the developing countries and to the shifting balance of payments position of assisting countries.

6. . . . . It is estimated that total expenditure on pre-investment work must rise to a level of about $1 billion a year by 1970, if

the objectives of the decade are to be reached. This is about double the present rate of expenditure.

7. A crucial area for intensified pre-investment activity is the surveying and development of natural resources, including water, minerals and power. In the development of water resources, in particular, the United Nations system may have a significant part to play. Nearly all the world's great rivers flow through several countries, and their development is a problem requiring regional and international co-operation.

8. The potentialities of modern technology and new methods of research and development for attacking the problems of the developing countries are as yet only dimly perceived. Since the Second World War it has become clear that new techniques permit the solution of most scientific and technical problems once they are correctly posed. . . . It also seems desirable to stimulate research on the social problems of developing countries entering upon a period of rapid social change.

9. If the skills of the advanced countries are to be successfully adapted to the problems and conditions of the developing countries, the former must be willing and able to make available the necessary resources of skilled personnel. Indeed, it may be that the shortage of such highly skilled personnel, rather than shortage of material resources or finance, will be the greatest obstacle to action in the development decade unless new steps are taken. Technical co-operation field workers or field-teams should no longer be isolated but work in close contact with those institutions in the advanced countries which have most knowledge of the problems they will encounter. Ways must also be found for the foreign experts to participate in setting up institutions which will take over and carry forward their work when they leave.

The successes of the United Nations development decade in achieving its objectives will depend in large part on the application of such new approaches. Precisely because they are new, all their implications cannot yet be fully seen. They may be expected to change many existing attitudes and approaches.

DOCUMENT 30. EXTRACT FROM A REPORT BY DR PREBISCH, SECRETARY-GENERAL OF THE UN CONFERENCE ON TRADE AND DEVELOPMENT (UNCTAD), 'TOWARDS A GLOBAL STRATEGY OF DEVELOPMENT', TD/3/REV. I, 1968

34. This frustration is very understandable. The growth rate of these countries during the Development Decade has not reached the annual figure of 5 per cent which was set as the minimum target. Actually the average rate for fifty-four countries, representing 87 per cent of the population of the developing world as a whole was only 4·5 per cent per annum from 1960 to 1965.

35. Giving a simple average rate, however, always entails the risk of misinterpretation. Although the picture of international co-operation has been a discouraging one, this co-operation has not been completely ineffective, and there are countries which have encountered external conditions that promoted their development.

36. Where this has happened, the results are usually favourable, as is apparent from an analysis of the composition of this average. Among the fifty-four countries mentioned, there is a group of eighteen with an average growth rate of 7·3 per cent per annum, while the rate for fifteen countries was scarcely 2·7 per cent per annum. In the former—those of relatively speedy growth—exports increased at an annual rate of 8·7 per cent,* whereas in the latter—where growth was relatively slow—they expanded by only 3·3 per cent. Between these two extremes there were twenty-one countries whose average growth rate was 4·9 per cent and whose exports increased by 4·8 per cent per annum.

37. The dynamic effect of exports in the peripheral countries is thus very obvious. When they expand slowly, they hold back development, and they stimulate it if they gather speed. But exports are only one of the dynamic external factors, although a very important one. Another, as is common knowledge, is the inflow of finance from the industrial centres. The amount of this contribution also helps to explain the disparate growth rates: the countries of faster growth received an annual average financial contribution of $8·54 per capita,† and those of

* Between 1959–60 and 1964–5.
† In the period 1961–5. [Original footnotes.]

slower growth $2·37. The countries in the middle group received $5·96 per capita.

38. The importance of trade and international financial co-operation in the dynamic of development is thus obvious. Undoubtedly there are other fundamental factors which determine the rate of growth, but it is no mere coincidence that the countries whose exports expand very slowly and which receive a very small volume of international finance per capita are also those which show a lower growth rate, whereas those which receive a large volume of finance and whose exports rise at a relatively satisfactory pace develop with most speed.

39. These comparisons may serve to dispel the not infrequent belief that the flow of international finance is being wasted. No specific cases of this happening have been mentioned when financial co-operation has been provided for strictly economic reasons and without political or military implications.

40. There have been, on the other hand, notorious cases of wastage of domestic resources that could have been put to productive use. This risk always exists, but it would be reduced to a minimum if international financial co-operation were closely linked to rational development planning.

41. This last remark also applies to the actual sources of financial co-operation. A stage has been reached where a flow of resources commensurate with the dimensions of the development problem is inconceivable, if the country requiring the resources does not have a programme which clearly shows its determination to apply the resources effectively, i.e., to observe strict discipline in development.

42. As the Under-Secretary-General for Economic and Social Affairs of the United Nations recently stated, 'We can no longer cherish the illusion that the affluent societies will in the future provide, either *automatically*, or in response to our exhortations, the surplus needed to finance adequately the development of the Third World. It is true that it has become a habit to cite certain particularly eloquent orders of magnitude, to mention, for example, that $4 billion more would be enough to enable us to reach the 1 per cent target, solemnly proclaimed by this Assembly, and to compare this figure of $4 billion to that of $1,300 billion produced by the industrial countries as a whole. But these calculations do not take us very far. In fact these countries are

already feeling a heavy pressure of demand on their resources and will feel it even more in the years ahead. The general rise in the standard of living is showing up more startlingly than heretofore the social blemishes which they contain. Urban concentration has given rise to quasi-monstrous phenomena. The need for education is far from satisfied. All this gives rise to urgent claims on their resources. It is probably only through deliberate and, so far as possible, concerted policies that assistance to the under-developed countries will find its rightful place, that it will rise a few notches in the hierarchy of preoccupations and priorities for action, that it will imbue the process of decision-making on trade, on the balance of payments and on budgetary and monetary policy.'

DOCUMENT 31. EXTRACT FROM THE REPORT OF THE SECOND SESSION OF THE UN CONFERENCE ON TRADE AND DEVELOPMENT, NEW DELHI, FEBRUARY–MARCH 1968: VOL. I, *Report and Annexes*, PART ONE—INTRODUCTION (UNITED NATIONS, NEW YORK)

Recent Trends in World Trade and Development

22. The second session of the Conference took place in a setting of changing trends in world trade and development. The Final Act, after affirming that an expansion of the trade of developing countries was a prerequisite for their accelerated economic development had briefly described a number of the salient world economic trends hampering their rate of economic progress and reflecting inadequacies in the structure of international economic relationships. The further evolution of trends in economic growth, international trade and development finance, as well as developments in international trading, economic and monetary policies since the first session of the Conference, and in relation to the experience of earlier years, are outlined below.

23. During the first six years of the present decade the following changes occurred in the rhythm of growth of the world's main economic regions as compared with the experience of the preceding quinquennium. The developed market economies succeeded in raising their average annual rate of growth of gross national product (GNP) from 3·2 per cent in

the latter half of the 1950s to about 5 per cent in the period 1960–1966. The real material product of the socialist countries of Eastern Europe rose at an annual rate of 8·1 per cent between 1955 and 1960 and by nearly 7 per cent in the 1960s. The average annual rate of economic growth of developing countries, in terms of total real product, in the period 1955–1960 was 4.6 per cent and in the period 1960–1965 it was 4.5 per cent. During the first quinquennium of the United Nations Development decade the developing countries succeeded in passing the 5 per cent target growth rate only once, in 1964. Since then their expansion has been slower; in 1965 the combined GDP of the developing countries rose by less than 4 per cent, and by some 4·5 per cent in 1966. Thus, the economic growth of the developing countries, far from accelerating, has tended to fall back from the disappointing long-term average rate of 4·6 per cent which obtained during the ten years preceding 1964; indeed, their economic growth has been inadequate in recent years so that there is now little prospect of attaining the minimum growth target of 5 per cent for the developing countries at the end of the Development Decade. The fact that developing countries have been unable as yet to reach this modest goal gives rise to concern, inasmuch as the 1960s have been a relatively dynamic decade elsewhere.

24. The inadequacy of this pace of growth in the developing countries becomes still clearer when the increase in output is related to the increase in population. Between 1958 and 1965 the annual rates of increase of population were 2·5 per cent in the developing countries, 1·2 per cent in the developed market-economy countries and 1·6 per cent in the socialist countries. The faster rate of increase in the population of the developing world is one of the factors explaining why the gap between *per capita* income in the developing and developed countries has continued to widen. In the first two years following the first session of the Conference, income *per capita* rose at the annual average of 3·5 per cent in the developed market-economies and by nearly 6 per cent in the socialist economies of Eastern Europe. In the developing countries, however, the corresponding rate was below 2 per cent, a disturbingly low figure. In the period 1960–1965, the corresponding rates of growth for those groups of countries were 3·6 per cent, 5·5 per cent and 2·0 per

cent respectively. Behind these broad tendencies in aggregate magnitudes of GDP and *per capita* income there has been a marked diversity in the growth record of the developing countries, and regions. A number of these countries achieved a conspicuously better rate of growth than average, while others, including some of the most populous countries, experienced low rates of growth. A comparison of five-year averages shows that the majority of the population of the developing world lives in those regions where economic growth has been slowest in the latter periods; in the years 1955–1960, 33 per cent of the entire population of the developing world lived in countries whose national output *per capita* grew at a yearly average of less than 1.5 per cent; in the 1960–1965 period the proportion of population living in countries with such low growth rates has risen to 66 per cent.

25. The pace of world trade expansion has quickened in the 1960s—rising to an annual rate of 8 per cent from 1960 to 1966 from 6·4 per cent in the latter half of the 1950s, although a certain slackening has set in since 1964. About 52 per cent of world trade in 1966 consisted of trade among the developed market-economies, and the tendency has been for the proportion of their intra-group trade to rise still higher: in 1966 it constituted as much as three-fourths of their total trade. Trade between developed market-economies and socialist countries has been growing much faster than world trade as a whole: from 1960 to 1966 exports from developed market-economies to the socialist countries grew at an average annual rate of 11·6 per cent, and the expansion of the opposite flow has been equally fast. But the share of such exchanges in total world trade is still small—2·8 per cent in 1966, indicating that the potential for further expansion is considerable. The developed market-economy countries raised their share of world trade from 61 per cent in 1950 to about 70 per cent in 1966, and the socialist countries of Eastern Europe from 8 per cent in 1950 to 10·2 per cent in 1966, with virtually no change thereafter.

26. The share of developing countries in total world trade has steadily declined: from just under 31·2 per cent in 1950 it had fallen to 19·1 per cent in 1966; if oil exports are excluded, the decline over the same period was from 24·4 per cent to just over 14 per cent. Exchanges within the group of developing

countries have steadily diminished as a share of total world trade to about 3 per cent in 1966, such exchanges representing only 16 per cent of the total trade of the group, but this declining tendency seems to have been arrested in recent years, mainly owing to the successes in trade expansion of the two integration systems in Latin America.

27. The variety of growth rates by commodity classes goes far towards explaining the diversity in the trading performance of different areas; and, in this respect, trading experience in the first half of the 1960s has provided further evidence of long-term trends in world trade which operate to the relative disadvantage of the majority of developing countries. In particular, the share of primary commodities in total world trade has continued to contract, while that of manufactured products has maintained a rising trend. Moreover, those primary commodities which experienced higher growth rates of exports than average—for example, some temperate-zone food-stuffs and certain synthetic substitutes such as plastic materials—are mainly exported by developed countries; thus, between 1960 and 1965 the value of exports of primary products from developed countries increased at an annual average rate of 6·3 per cent, as compared with 3·5 per cent in respect of such exports from developing countries. World exports of raw materials have been most severely affected by structural changes in international trade, rising in value by only 3 per cent a year between 1960 and 1965; food exports have fared better, with an annual increase of 4·6 per cent in volume terms and, thanks to higher average prices, by 6·3 per cent in value; and exports of fuel, though rising at a rate below the average for world trade, have been the most dynamic segment of trade in primary commodities. Exports of manufactures have been the spearhead of progress in world exports, with the highest rates of growth, in value terms occurring in such products as chemicals, machinery and transport equipment.

28. In consequence, the countries whose exports consist mainly of manufactured products have stood to benefit most from the buoyant expansion of demand for them. Both the developed market economy countries and the socialist countries of Eastern Europe have participated in this dynamic growth, the most sought-after manufactures mentioned above

accounting for more than one-third of the total exports of each of these groups of countries. The commodity structure of exports from developing countries offers a stark contrast, inasmuch as the share of the slowest growing group of exports—raw materials—accounted for 28 per cent of their total exports in 1960 (23 per cent in 1965), food for no less than 30 per cent (29 per cent in 1965). The remainder consisted of fuel (28 per cent in 1960 and 31 per cent in 1965), with all manufactures accounting for only 14 per cent in 1960 and 17 per cent in 1965.

29. The growth of exports from developing countries has therefore been relatively slow—6 per cent per annum on average between 1960 and 1966, as against rates of 8·8 per cent for exports from developed market-economies and 8·3 per cent in respect of those from the socialist countries of Eastern Europe. Thus, notwithstanding the substantial improvement that has occurred in the 1960s in the export performance of developing countries, their export growth has lagged appreciably behind the average for world trade, with the resultant contraction of their share in world trade to 19·1 per cent in 1966 that has already been noted. The flow of exports from developing countries to developed market-economy countries has risen during the 1960s at an annual average rate of 5·8 per cent, but this growth has not sufficed to prevent a decline in the share of imports from developing countries from 24 per cent of total imports into these countries in 1960 to 20 per cent in 1966. An opposite change occurred in the share of imports from developing countries in the total imports of socialist countries of Eastern Europe, the faster growth of the former imports, at a rate of 12·8 per cent a year, resulting in an increase in the developing countries' share from 7·4 per cent in 1960 to 10 per cent in 1966. This enlargement of market outlets in the socialist countries of Eastern Europe was, however, more than offset by the relative decline, noted above, experienced in the large markets of the developed market-economy countries, which absorb over 70 per cent of all exports from the developing world.

30. The problems posed by the sluggish export growth of the developing countries have been aggravated by the adverse movement of their terms of trade. Apart from a short-lived improvement in 1963–1964, the trend in the terms of trade of

developing countries has been downward. Although the magnitude of the deterioration by 1966 varies according to the reference year chosen, the direction of change is beyond dispute; for example, taking 1954 as a base, the deterioration amounted to 13 per cent; taking 1955 as a base, it was 10 per cent; taking 1960 as a base it was 4 per cent. The loss borne by the developing countries on account of the worsening in their terms of trade was equivalent to a considerable part of the aid received by them, although the extent of the loss varies according to the reference period chosen for estimation. Thus, taking as a base for estimation the average export and import prices ruling in the years 1953–1957, the average annual magnitude of this loss has been put at nearly $2.2 billion, or an appreciable proportion—roughly one-fifth—of the annual net capital flow into developing countries from all sources in the years 1961–1965. Another manifestation of these unfavourable price developments in the trade of developing countries is provided by comparing rates of change in the volume, value and purchasing power of their exports. Despite an annual increase in the volume of exports of some 5 per cent in the 1955–1965 decade as a whole, the declining unit values of exports brought the growth in the value of exports below that of their volume. There was, furthermore, a simultaneous rise in import prices, the net outcome of these movements being a consistently lower rise in the purchasing power of exports than the increase in the value of exports: over the decade 1955–1965 the purchasing power of exports went up by as little as 3·4 per cent a year, or 1·8 per cent if exports of petroleum are excluded.

31. The import capacity of developing countries depends not only on the revenue earned by their exports and the prices that have to be paid for imports, but also on their net capital inflow. In this sphere neither the volume nor the conditions of capital flows have matched the expectations or requirements of the developing countries. A mounting burden of external indebtedness, much of it a short-term liability, has resulted. The annual gross flow of official capital towards the developing countries through bilateral channels grew from approximately $5·1 billion in 1961 to $6·7 billion in 1966, an increase of 5 per cent a year over the five-year period. However, the flow net of rising amortization and interest charges, failed to rise

by more than 2·5 per cent a year. Further, the share of the total capital outflow from developed market-economies to developing countries had fallen from 0·87 per cent of their combined GNP in 1961 to 0·72 per cent in 1965, and appears to have fallen again to 0·63 per cent in 1966; although provisional data indicate that there may have been some recovery in 1967. As for the commitments of financial resources by the socialist countries to the developing countries and multilateral agencies, such aggregative data as exist for the group as a whole suggest that they have undergone marked fluctuations in the past ten years, total gross disbursements during the 1960s having been estimated at about $300–500 million a year.

32. Plainly, there is not an advance towards, but retrogression from, the terms of the recommendation in annex A.IV.2 of the Final Act, which states that 'Each economically advanced country should endeavour to supply in the light of the principles of annex A.IV.1 financial resources to the developing countries of a minimum net amount approaching as nearly as possible to 1 per cent of its national income . . .'.

33. Awareness of the difficulties caused by such tendencies was reflected in the following unanimously adopted Agreed Statement on the Problems of Development, issued on 19 April 1967 by representatives of all groups of countries meeting under the auspices of UNCTAD: 'It is a matter of concern that the flow of financial resources from developed countries, in support of the developing countries' efforts, has failed in recent years to keep pace with the growth in the national incomes of the developed countries, even though most developing countries could immediately put into effective use a greater volume of external assistance' (see para. 16 above and document TD/7, and Corr. 1, para. 16).

34. As regards the terms of aid, there has been an overall deterioration, notwithstanding an improvement in the practices of some aid-giving countries. Grants, as a percentage of gross official disbursements by countries members of the Development Assistance Committee (DAC) of OECD declined from 73 per cent in 1962 to 61 per cent in 1965; the weighted average interest rate on official loans accorded by these countries softened to 3 per cent in 1964, but by 1965 was again up to the 3.6 per cent rate obtaining in 1962; similarly, the

average maturity of new loan commitments had shortened to twenty-two years in 1965, following a short-lived improvement from twenty-four to twenty-eight years between 1962 and 1964; finally, the grace periods attaching to loan commitments shortened, on a weighted average, from 6.9 years in 1964 to 5.4 years in 1965. In addition, the recent increase in the practice of tying aid to purchases from certain capital-exporting countries has tended not only to add to the costs of some recipient countries but also to reduce the efficiency of the assistance and its beneficial influence on economic growth in developing countries.

35. For many developing countries, one result of these changes has been a further increase in accumulated indebtedness and, as a corollary, of the burden of debt-servicing: according to estimates made by the staff of IBRD, the total accumulated indebtedness of developing countries slightly exceeded $40 billion at the end of 1965, having increased by 17 per cent over 1964; in 1966 there was a substantial further increase, certainly exceeding $4 billion. Recent years have seen a sharp increase in one major component of this indebtedness—private export credits—to record levels; in 1966 the annual increase in such credits, with maturity of five years or less, amounted to $487 million, or nearly 30 per cent above the previous ceiling attained in 1960. A similar increase has occurred in export credits with longer maturities. While these global figures include very different situations so far as individual countries are concerned, on both the lending and borrowing sides, there is no doubt that the aggregate debt-servicing commitments of the developing countries have increased sharply in recent years, to reach an annual rate in the mid-1960s of $4·2 billion, equivalent to about 12 per cent of merchandise exports as compared with 6 per cent ten years earlier.

SUGGESTED STUDY QUESTIONS

1. If you were a politician trying to impress upon the general public of a developed country the need to allocate a greater share of the resources of that country to the aid and development of underdeveloped countries, how would you present your case?

2. What are the major problems facing a developing country in trying to improve its standard of living?
3. What are the major problems confronting potential donors wishing to give aid to developing countries?
4. What are the respective advantages and disadvantages of multilateral and bilateral aid?
5. How would you account for the disappointing results of the first UN Development Decade?
6. In what ways could the failure to solve the rich-poor gap between nations constitute a threat to world peace?

FURTHER READING

ARNOLD, H. J. P., *Aid for Development*, London: Bodley Head, 1965.
BLACK, EUGENE R., *The Diplomacy of Economic Development*, Cambridge, Mass.; Harvard University Press, 1960.
GARDNER, R. N., *In Pursuit of World Order*, New York: Praeger, 1964.
HOFFMAN, PAUL R., *World Without Want*, New York: Harper Bros, 1962.
MYRDAL, GUNNAR, *Rich Lands and Poor*, New York: Harper Bros, 1958.
WARD, BARBARA, *The Rich Nation and the Poor Nation*, New York: W. W. Norton, 1962.

PART VI

Arms Control and Disarmament

THE CASE FOR DISARMAMENT

The primary argument for disarmament is the threat of catastrophic war which is necessarily posed by antagonistic States having unfettered control of highly destructive armaments. Some idea of the destructiveness of nuclear weapons is conveyed in Document 32, the Secretary-General's Report in 1968. A secondary argument is the wasteful employment of human and material resources involved in an almost entirely non-productive activity: this is all the more lamentable in view of the enormous tasks of aid and development which lie waiting and unfulfilled. This is really the point made in the Secretary-General's earlier report in 1962 on the economic and social consequences of disarmament, from which extracts are given in Document 33. Yet a third argument is the moral one, namely that a commitment to the possibility of violence and destruction on such a scale must be immoral, whatever the ends sought to be achieved. Or, in simpler language, it cannot be morally justified to defend one's political beliefs—whether they be 'democratic', 'communist' or whatever—if the price is the slaughter of millions of people.

The counter-arguments do not accept that armaments heighten the risk of war; indeed, they would suggest that the very destructive force of nuclear weapons constitutes a deterrent to war. This, of course, assumes a degree of sanity amongst all world leaders and implies that no country would risk a nuclear war in order to defeat the opposing forces: but is it clear that, for example, China would not, at some future stage, take this risk in the belief that from the ruins it would be communism which would emerge triumphant? More practical counter-arguments turn on the unreliability of the safeguards involved in disarmament. Could we be sure that the other side was truly keeping its side of any disarmament agreement?

Whatever the pros and cons, in fact both the USA and the USSR are agreed in principle on disarmament. They issued a Joint Statement in September 1961, agreeing upon certain basic principles for future multilateral negotiations on disarmament and calling for the co-operation of other States in reaching 'early agreement on general and complete disarmament in a peaceful world'.[1]

In fact, both sides have filed quite detailed treaty proposals for general and complete disarmament:[2] this was done first in 1962 (though some amendments came later) and these two drafts have since formed the basis of the discussions in the Geneva disarmament talks in the eighteen-Nation Committee on disarmament. These two proposals are, regrettably, too lengthy to permit inclusion in the documents within this section. However, it is vital that some comparison of them be made in order to show what the differences of opinion are, for these differences are so great that for the last nine years no real progress has been made in producing agreed proposals.

THE RATE AND QUANTUM OF DISARMAMENT

The question 'How fast and by what degrees shall we disarm?' is vital if only because the answers to this question must allay the distrust inevitable in disarmament: both sides will want to maintain a 'balance' as they disarm for they will not risk the other acquiring an overwhelming superiority at any stage.

The Soviet draft has three stages:

---

[1] Text in UN Doc. A/4879 of 20 September 1961: or in *Documents relating to disarmament etc.* (1962), Cmnd. 1694, p. 9.

[2] For the Soviet Draft Treaty see *Further docs. relating to the Conference of the 18 Nation Committee on disarmament*, Miscellaneous No. 5, Cmnd. 1958 (1963), Doc. No. 1. For the USA 'Outlines of Basic Provisions of a Treaty, etc.', see *ibid.*, Miscellaneous No. 22, Cmnd. 1792 (1962), p. 53; Cmnd. 1957, pp. 15–16; Cmnd. 2353, p. 14; Cmnd. 2353, pp. 14–15. The full texts are given in Marion H. McVitty, *Current Disarmament Proposals as of March 1, 1964* and see also her booklet *A Comparison and Evaluation of Current Disarmament Proposals*: both are published by the World Law Fund, 11 West 42nd St., New York 36, in 1964.

Stage I (18 months)

Elimination of most[1] delivery vehicles for nuclear weapons, elimination of foreign bases, reduction of armed forces and conventional arms and military expenditures to a level of 1·9 million men for each of the two powers, the USA and the USSR (other States *pro rata*). 30 per cent reduction of arms— by destruction or conversion to peaceful uses and proportionate reduction of arms production and military expenditures. Adoption measures to safeguard security of States, i.e., inspection by IDO (International Disarmament Organization), control over rocket launching, agreement on non-proliferation of nuclear weapons, ban on nuclear testing, ban on large-scale manoeuvres, creation of a UN Force, etc.

Stage II (24 months)

Elimination of *all* nuclear weapons and stockpiles, *all* chemical, biological and radiological weapons. Reduction of armed forces to one million each for the USA and the USSR (and *pro rata* for rest). Further reductions in military expenditures, conventional arms and manufactures by 35 per cent.

Stage III (12 months)

Completion in the sense of eliminating all military production and establishments and, eliminating *all* military forces save for agreed levels of 'national security forces' equipped only with light firearms.

The USA's basic outlines reflect a more cautious, gradual approach, thus:

Stage I (3 years)

A 30 per cent reduction 'across the board', of all aircraft, missile systems, tanks, artillery, ships, etc. Armed forces reduced to 2·1 million each. Halt production of fissionable materials for nuclear weapons and transfer agreed quantities of U-235 to peaceful uses. Halt *all* nuclear tests. Establish IDO and UN Peace Force.

Stage II (3 years)

A 50 per cent reduction of remaining armaments and armed

---

[1] Originally the Soviets proposed destruction of *all* delivery vehicles so as to offset the danger of concealed, stockpiled warheads (which could not then be delivered). But the USA opposed this because this would upset the 'balance' by leaving the USSR with a superiority in conventional arms. The USSR therefore agreed to the retention of some delivery rockets by the USA and USSR.

forces. Reduction of nuclear weapons to agreed percentages[1] and 50 per cent reduction of delivery vehicles. Dismantling of agreed military bases. UN Police Force to be established.

Stage III (to be completed as soon as possible)

Elimination of *all* nuclear weapons, delivery vehicles and all remaining armaments and manufacture and the build up of a UN Peace Force to a strength 'so that no state could challenge it'.

It must also be noted that in the US draft the transition from one stage to the next would not be automatic but would depend on a decision of the Control Council of the IDO which either the USA or the USSR could veto if they doubted that the other had fulfilled its obligations. In contrast, the USSR visualizes a well-nigh automatic transition from stage to stage.

VERIFICATION

Obviously, it is essential for the parties to be satisfied that the agreed disarmament steps are actually being taken and, in principle, both the USA and the USSR are agreed on an international inspectorate: in their Joint Statement of 1961 they agreed:

> This International Disarmament Organisation and its inspectors should be assured unrestricted access without veto to all places as necessary for the purpose of effective verification.

However, beyond this general principle there is considerable disagreement about the techniques of implementation.

Machinery of Control

Both agree on the creation of an IDO within the framework of the UN with three organs, namely a Conference of all Parties (one State equals one vote), a Control Council and a Secretariat.

The principal difficulty is the Control Council, for although

---

[1] In the Soviet plan all nuclear weapons would be destroyed by this time, since the stages are much shorter.

the Soviets do not demand a veto there they do demand 'proper representation of the three principal groups of States existing in the world' and a two-thirds voting rule. The USA does not propose any detailed voting procedure but it is apprehensive that the Soviets could muster an effective blocking vote, sufficient to stop a two-thirds majority. Hence, the USA is worried about the Council becoming paralysed in the same manner as the Security Council has been.

In the Secretariat, the USA wants a strong Administrator whereas the USSR wants a 'troika', a directorate of three persons (one East, one West, one 'non-aligned') and this the USA fears would also lead to a stalemate. Thus the basic question which worries the USA is 'Could the IDO organs, especially the Control Council, be guaranteed to take the necessary decisions?'

The other important point is that the Soviets see all enforcement measures, i.e. punitive military action against a delinquent State, being taken not by the Control Council but by the Security Council, so that a veto would certainly apply to these.

The Inspection Process

Inspection is the key to control for, without foolproof inspection, no party will be sure that the other is keeping its side of the bargain.

Although the Soviet draft is full of references to inspection there is no indication of precisely how it would work. One major difference is that the USA wants not only inspection of the measures of disarmament but *also* inspection of what armaments have been retained (and note that in the US Stage I both sides could retain 70 per cent of their armaments). The USSR is adamantly opposed to this and regards this as a device by which the USA, using the IDO inspectorate, would engage in widespread espionage within the Soviet Union. Thus, the basic issue here is whether one inspects disarmament *or* disarmament plus the arms retained by each party and this is very much reflected in the article by Grinyov quoted in Document 34.

It must be conceded that an inspection of both disarmament

and arms retained would be a gigantic task: indeed, there is considerable doubt whether it could ever be done with real accuracy.[1]

Of course, physical 'on-site' inspection within a State's territory would not be the only form of inspection. There are techniques for inspection by satellites using photographic or other recording devices, there is the suggestion for 'black boxes',[2] there are statistical techniques based upon analysis of figures for budgets, production quotas, imports and exports, etc., and, doubtless, the scientists will devise many more. But it is likely that some physical, on-site inspection will be essential within a State's territory and, clearly, the sheer size of the task is prodigious. Hence, there is the proposal for 'zonal inspection'[3] by which each party's territory would be divided into zones and, prior to inspection, would declare precisely what armaments each zone contained. The actual inspection would be of a zone selected at random at the last minute by the inspectorate so that they would sample the State's honesty rather than attempt an inspection of its entire territory.

However, even if the task could be made physically manageable, several difficult questions remain. Would the inspectorate be of neutral, international civil servants or would it be comprised of national groups with each State inspecting its prime adversary? Would the inspectorate have a right to enter a State's territory, or a particular military base, factory or installation at any time or only upon notice? Would the reports from

[1] The UK submitted to the eighteen-Nation Conference a paper entitled 'The Technical Possibility of International Control of Fissile Material Production', ENDC/60, 31 August 1962, in which it was suggested that even with a staff of 10,000, including 1,500 scientists, the *current* production of plutonium could be checked to an accuracy of 1–2 per cent and of U 235 to 1 per cent but that declaration of stockpiles could only be checked to an accuracy of 10–15 per cent for plutonium or 80 per cent for U 235. This is presumably the 'British document' referred to by Grinyov in Document 34 below.
[2] Seismographic recording devices to detect underground nuclear testing: these would be positioned in a State's territory and later removed for examination.
[3] US 'Basic Outlines, etc', Sec. G.3; and see Louis Sohn, 'Progressive Zonal Inspection: Basic Issues' in Seymour Melman, *Disarmament: its Politics and Economics*, American Academy of Arts and Sciences, 1962. The Clark-Sohn draft Treaty establishing a World Disarmament and World Development Organization (1962) envisages a step-by-step reduction, with one tenth of the State's territory being inspected in each of ten years and with a one-tenth reduction in arms each successive year, but with the proviso that each stage has to be completed by *all* States before proceeding to the next stage.

the inspectorate be screened or vetted by the Secretariat before being submitted to the Control Council?

One needs to know a good deal about the practical operation of the inspection process before passing any judgment on its reliability and, unhappily, the USSR has been reluctant to discuss this in detail as yet. The Soviet argument, not entirely convincing, is that first we must agree on what precisely is to be inspected.

Sanctions and Responses

The USSR is quite clear in that it will be for the Security Council, acting under its powers under Chapter VII of the Charter, to take the necessary sanctions for any breach of the Disarmament Treaty. Under Chapter VII the forces would remain national contingents, under national control although earmarked and pledged for UN use. Understandably, the USA, though very vague in its own draft on this issue, has misgivings given the past record of the Security Council and the veto. This also presupposes a formidable UN Force which, so far, the UN has never been able to create under Chapter VII.[1]

Perhaps this problem is less than it seems. Ideally, one would hope to see institutionalized sanctions, taken by a UN organ on behalf of the entire community. However, the more effective sanctions might be unilateral, that is to say any of the following measures taken by individual States:

(i)   a refusal to proceed further with disarmament;
(ii) reciprocal non-compliance—i.e. the adversary ignores the precise rule ignored by the other State;
(iii) a decision to begin re-arming;
(iv) the use of force.

If, in fact, the threat of these unilateral responses were

[1] The Clark-Sohn emphasis on a strong World Police Force is indicative of the importance they attach to guarantees of security which they believe are a sounder basis than mutual trust. In addition the executive organ, with power to commit the Force, would be the Executive Council of the new Organization, not the Security Council, and would be without the veto although subject to the final control of the General Conference of all States. Moreover, the Clark-Sohn draft contemplates enforcement by the Police Force directly against individuals, whilst the Soviet and the US drafts appear to regard this as entirely a matter for the national authorities acting under national legislation.

adequate to make States keep to the agreement, it would follow that the main problem would remain that of verification, for it would still be absolutely essential to know whether a breach had been committed or not.

This somewhat inadequate summary may suffice to show the kind of difficulties which have so far precluded any real progress with disarmament. And there are yet other problems such as the reluctance of China to participate (see Document 35), the need to control space research and the need to take concerted action to forestall the adverse economic consequences of disarmament.

COLLATERAL MEASURES

Having thus reached something of an impasse over general and complete disarmament, the major powers, particularly the USA and USSR, have nevertheless devoted themselves to certain collateral problems and intermediate measures of restraint and arms control. Here they had some success. They have achieved the following:

(i) 1959 Antarctica Treaty bans nuclear tests and military bases in Antarctica;

(ii) 1963 Partial Test Ban Treaty signed (Document 36): this forbids testing in the atmosphere, outer space and underwater but *not* underground testing and, in any event, neither China[1] nor France has signed it;

(iii) 1967 Treaty concerning the Exploration of Outer Space: this bans the placing of nuclear weapons in space;

(iv) February 1967 Treaty banning nuclear weapons in Latin America;

(v) July 1968 Nuclear non-Proliferation Treaty signed (Document 37).

These are no mean achievements and still further progress is possible. In November 1969 the US and USSR began talks in Helsinki to try to achieve a halt in the construction of their enormously expensive missiles and anti-missiles systems. But,

[1] See Document 35 below for the Chinese justification of their refusal to sign this treaty.

in the final analysis, these are very minor achievements when compared to the main task of general and complete disarmament. Obviously progress takes time, but have we the time to wait or will we see catastrophe before we see sense?

DOCUMENT 32. EXTRACTS FROM 'THE EFFECTS OF THE POSSIBLE USE OF NUCLEAR WEAPONS AND THE SECURITY AND ECONOMIC IMPLICATIONS FOR STATES OF THE ACQUISITION AND FURTHER DEVELOPMENT OF THESE WEAPONS', REPORT BY THE SECRETARY-GENERAL OF THE UN, 1968 (UNITED NATIONS, NEW YORK)

Interdiction targets

37. Were such weapons ever to be used in a war, it is also quite certain that they would not be restricted to the battle zone itself—even if it were assumed that there would not be what is usually referred to as a strategic exchange. It is part of the concept of tactical nuclear warfare that in a purely military campaign they would also be used outside the area of contact in order to impede the movement of enemy forces, the operation of air forces and so on. The objectives which would be attacked in order to achieve these effects are generally called interdiction targets. Theoretical studies of operations of this kind provide a picture of 'deep' nuclear strikes whose effects would be hardly distinguishable from a strategic nuclear exchange in which both sides set out from the start to destroy each other's major centres of population. To illustrate what is implied, reference can be made to a single strike in one such study in which it was assumed that the railway installations in a major transport centre were attacked by a single twenty-kiloton bomb, or a single 100-kiloton bomb, in order to make the centre impassable to troops and supplies, and thereby to assist the land battle elsewhere. The railway centre chosen for this study was a city with 70,000 inhabitants living in 23,000 houses in an area of some fifty sq. km. . . .

38. The estimated inescapable collateral effects of bombing a single railway centre in such a programme of attacks indicate that most of the industrial and commercial property in the middle of the town would have been destroyed. Fire would have consumed not only houses but also the large buildings and

factories not immediately destroyed by the explosion. A twenty-kiloton bomb in an 'interdiction' attack on a town which was a communications centre—and few, if any communication centres are not towns—would kill about a quarter of the 70,000 inhabitants, while a 100-kiloton attack would kill about half. . . . A programme of 'interdiction' attacks on targets behind the zone of contact of opposing armies, if such a programme included communication centres as well as airfields, supply depots, armament factories and so on, would be no different in its effects from those of a widespread so-called strategic nuclear exchange between two opposing Powers.

Deterrence of War

39. Nuclear weapons constitute one of the dominant facts of modern world politics. They are at present deployed in thousands by the nuclear weapon Powers, with warheads ranging from kilotons to megatons. We have already witnessed the experimental explosion of a fifty to sixty-megaton bomb, i.e., of a weapon with about 3,000 times the power of the bomb used in 1945 against Japan. Hundred-megaton devices, weapons about 5,000 times the size of those used in 1945, are no more difficult to devise. They could be exploded just outside the atmosphere of any country, in order utterly to destroy hundreds, even thousands, of square kilometres by means of blast and spreading fire. It has been suggested on good authority that in certain geographical circumstances multi-megaton weapons could also be exploded in ships near coastlines in order to create enormous tidal waves which would engulf the coastal belt.

40. The effects of all-out nuclear war, regardless of where it started, could not be confined to the Powers engaged in that war. . . . The extent and nature of the hazard would depend upon the numbers and type of bombs exploded. Given a sufficient number, no part of the world would escape exposure to biologically significant levels of radiation. To a greater or lesser degree, a legacy of genetic damage could be incurred by the world's population.

41. It is to be expected that no major nuclear Power could attack another without provoking a nuclear counter-attack. It

is even possible that an aggressor could suffer more in retaliation than the nuclear Power it first attacked. In this lies the concept of deterrence by the threat of nuclear destruction. Far from an all-out nuclear exchange being a rational action which could ever be justified by any set of conceivable political gains, it may be that no country would, in the pursuit of its political objectives, deliberately risk the total destruction of its own capital city, leave alone the destruction of all its major centres of population; or risk the resultant chaos which would leave in doubt a government's ability to remain in control of its people. But the fact that a state of mutual nuclear deterrence prevails between the Super Powers does not, as we know all too well, prevent the outbreak of wars with conventional weapons involving both nuclear and non-nuclear weapon nations; the risk of nuclear war remains as long as there are nuclear weapons.[1]

42. The basic facts about the nuclear bomb and its use are harsh and terrifying for civilization; they have become lost in a mass of theoretical verbiage. It has been claimed that the world has learnt to live with the bomb; it is also said there is no need for it to drift unnecessarily into the position that it is prepared to die for it. The ultimate question for the world to decide in our nuclear age—and this applies both to nuclear and non-nuclear Powers—is what short-term interests it is prepared to sacrifice in exchange for an assurance of survival and security.

DOCUMENT 33. EXTRACT FROM *The Economic and Social Consequences of Disarmament*, VOL. I, REPORT OF THE SECRETARY-GENERAL OF THE UNITED NATIONS, UN DOC. E/3593/REV. I, 1962

Chapter 8
Summary and Conclusions

166. The present level of military expenditure not only represents a grave political danger but also imposes a heavy economic and social burden on most countries. It absorbs a

[1] The point made here appears to be that a State fighting a war with conventional weapons, and losing, might be tempted to win by a sudden strike with nuclear weapons.

large volume of human and material resources of all kinds, which could be used to increase economic and social welfare throughout the world—both in the highly industrialized countries, which at the present time incur the bulk of the world's military expenditures, and in the less developed areas.

Resources devoted to military purposes

167. There appears to be general agreement that the world is spending roughly $120 billion annually on military account at the present time. This corresponds to about one-half of the total gross capital formation throughout the world. It is at least two-thirds of—and according to some estimates, of the same order of magnitude as—the entire national income of all the under-developed countries.

168. It is important that countries, in preparing to disarm, should take stock of the various resources that disarmament would release for peaceful uses. In the major military powers, military production is highly concentrated in a few industry groups. In those countries that rely upon imports for their supplies of military goods or in which the major part of military expenditure is for the pay and subsistence of the armed forces, rather than for their equipment, the resources devoted to military purposes consist essentially of manpower and foreign exchange.

The peaceful use of released resources

169. There are so many competing claims for usefully employing the resources released by disarmament that the real problem is to establish a scale of priorities. The most urgent of these claims would undoubtedly already have been largely satisfied were it not for the armaments race.

170. Increased personal consumption might well absorb a large share of the released resources. A substantial portion of them, however, would be used for expansion of productive capacities because only such expansion can provide a firm basis for further increases in consumption. In the less developed countries, the utilization of released resources for capital formation must be considered vitally important. . . .

172. The release of scientific and technical manpower would

make it possible to encourage programmes of basic scientific research in fields which have hitherto been neglected. Disarmament would also open up possibilities for joint international ventures of an ambitious kind, such as the utilization of atomic energy for peaceful purposes, space research the exploration of the Arctic and Antarctic for the benefit of mankind and projects to change the climates of large areas of the world.

173. Thus, though it would take active decisions by Governments in the light of national and international needs to set in motion the necessary programmes for employing the released resources, it seems abundantly clear that no country need fear a lack of useful employment opportunities for the resources that would become available to it through disarmament.

Impact on national production and employment

174. Disarmament would raise both general problems of maintaining the over-all level of economic activity and employment and specific problems in so far as manpower or productive capacity might require adaptation to non-military needs. In the economic life of all countries, shifts in the pattern of demand and in the allocation of productive resources are continually occurring. The reallocation of productive resources which would accompany disarmament is in many respects merely a special case of the phenomenon of economic growth.

175. The post-war conversion was a much larger one and involved a more rapid transfer of resources than total disarmament would require at present. Nevertheless, huge armies were quickly demobilized without a significant rise in unemployment in most countries. . . .

Structural problems of conversion

179. Even with the successful maintenance of total effective demand during a period of disarmament, significant problems of adjustment would remain in specific sectors and areas of the economy. The resources now supplying military requirements could be adapted to peace-time needs partly by shifts within industries and plants. . . .

180. Hypothetical studies on the assumption that military

expenditure is replaced wholly by increases in expenditure on other kinds of goods and services suggest that in the event of very rapid disarmament some 6 or 7 per cent (including the armed forces) of the total labour force in the United States and $3\frac{1}{2}$ to 4 per cent in the United Kingdom would have to find civilian instead of military employment or change their employment from one industry group to another. These shifts would be small if spread out over a number of years and would be greatly facilitated by the normal process of turnover. The higher the rate of growth of the economy, the easier the process of adaptation.

181. Under-developed countries generally have been meeting their requirements for military goods and services by imports, so that their disarmament would release foreign exchange rather than industrial workers. It would also free members of the forces, many with useful skills and training. . . .

182. In the centrally planned economies, where productive capacity is usually fully utilized, it would be necessary to convert plants producing military equipment to production of durable consumer goods and of such investment goods as can be produced in them with only minor retooling. This could be done rapidly.

183. Some special problems would arise with regard to re-employment and training of manpower and reorientation of scientific research. . . .

184. In industries depending heavily on military orders, many of the employees possess a level of skill that should find gainful employment in other branches of production, so long as over-all effective demand is rising. . . .

185. The task of shifting scientific and technical personnel to non-military fields of research in some countries would be considerable. No reduction in the actual employment of scientific and technical personnel need be feared, however, because the demand for civilian research would increase rapidly.

Impact on international economic relations

186. Disarmament would be bound to have favourable effects on the development of international relations. The political *détente* that would accompany an international dis-

armament programme would in itself imply that nations were willing to reconsider their economic relations with one another. . . . An important consequence of this would be a substantial increase in trade between the centrally planned economies and the rest of the world.

187. Since disarmament may be expected to result in an acceleration of economic growth, it should stimulate the growth of demand for primary production in general. Accelerated economic growth would be still more powerful in increasing total demand for manufactures. . . .

Effects on the volume and framework of aid for economic development

190. National efforts and international co-operation in the development of the under-developed countries have so far not brought about the desired acceleration of economic growth. A much larger volume of resources could be allocated to investment for productive development in these countries even if only a fraction of the resources currently devoted to military purposes were used in this way. Disarmament could thus bring about a marked increase in the rate of growth of real income in the poorer parts of the world. . . .

Some social consequences

194. In a disarmed world, a general improvement could be expected in the level of living, including an increase in leisure. With the end of the armaments race, Governments would accord social objectives a higher priority. . . .

DOCUMENT 34. EXTRACT FROM 'SOVIET EFFORTS FOR DIS- ARMAMENT' BY O. GRINYOV, IN *International Affairs* (MOSCOW), DECEMBER 1967

In what way do the Soviet and U.S. approaches to this problem differ?

First, as to the concept of universal and complete disarmament. The Soviet programme envisages complete abolition of all armed forces and all types of armaments. Thus, when universal and complete disarmament is achieved all states will be without soldiers or armaments, which means that the menace of war will be removed once and for all. . . .

The Western powers, on the contrary, have always endeavoured to preserve freedom of action to continue the arms race and are doing so today. For this purpose they want to institute control over existing armaments instead of concluding an agreement on universal and complete disarmament.[1] Their proposals for a percentage reduction of armaments are formulated so as to allow the Western powers to have more than enough modern means for an armed attack[2] at any stage of disarmament. At times, it is not clear whether the speeches of the U.S. delegates on the Committee are about disarmament or about creating a more favourable balance of forces for the NATO countries.

Second, as regards nuclear disarmament. Is it possible to imagine universal and complete disarmament without eliminating nuclear weapons? A ridiculous question, indeed. Yet for five years the negotiating sides have before them a folder with a U.S. disarmament project according to which the fate of nuclear weapons, the cardinal problem of disarmament, is placed entirely at the discretion of experts who would have to decide at the very peak of the disarmament process whether or not it was possible to control the destruction of atomic bombs. But if they say no? Will nuclear weapons then remain in the arsenals of countries even after 'universal and complete disarmament'? That seems quite possible.[3] In the Committee's archives there is a British document[4] which attempts to prove that such control is impossible. This stand is officially supported by the U.S. and other Western delegations.

Third, as regards control. The Soviet Union proposes that from the outset all disarmament measures should be subjected to strict and effective international control, the extent of which would correspond to the extent and nature of the disarmament

[1] This is the basic disagreement referred to above at p. 175.
[2] Or defence against a State which has cheated? The more gradual, cautious approach is merely an indication of the American distrust of the Soviets.
[3] It is difficult to see how this remark is justified on the US proposals which, in the third stage, do contemplate the elimination of nuclear weapons. Possibly the author is thinking of the US reservation on whether the UN Force should retain some such weapons?
[4] Presumably ENDC/60, dated 31 August 1962.

measures at each stage. The Soviet recommendations envisage genuine control over all steps in disarmament at each of the three stages of the programme for universal and complete disarmament.[1]

The Western powers counterpose to this a control which in effect is aimed at collecting intelligence information. They suggest establishing at the very outset control over rockets, artificial satellites of the Earth, armed forces and so forth, with the states retaining all their armed forces and armaments, including rockets and nuclear weapons. It is clear that control without disarmament would not be conducive to strengthening peace. On the contrary, it would make it easier for the aggressor to carry out his plans threatening the security of the peoples.

Fourth, as regards the destruction of nuclear delivery means. During the very first stage, the Soviet Union suggested withdrawing from armaments all means of delivery, stopping their production and destroying them, thus making it impossible from the beginning of disarmament for any country to attack another country with atomic or hydrogen weapons.

The U.S.A. and its allies rejected the Soviet proposal, alleging that they required some sort of additional guarantees for their security and had to retain a certain amount of delivery means even after the first stage of disarmament. But when the Soviet Government suggested that the U.S.S.R. and the U.S.A. retain an agreed limited number of rockets until disarmament is completed, the U.S.A. rejected this compromise proposal too.

Fifth, as regards dismantling military bases on foreign territory. The Soviet Union suggested dismantling all military bases on foreign territory and withdrawing all foreign troops stationed in other countries simultaneously with the destruction of delivery means. This measure would place the Soviet Union and other socialist countries, on the one hand, and the Western powers, on the other, on an equal footing from the point of view of security.[2]

The Western proposals say nothing about dismantling mili-

---

[1] Actually, the Soviet Draft Treaty is extremely vague on how the inspection process would work.

[2] This the western powers would deny: they would contend that, geographically, the western alliance is far more scattered than the Soviet bloc and thus, to afford adequate defence, requires the use of bases by NATO powers in various parts of the world.

tary bases on foreign territory although it is common knowledge that these bases serve aggressive purposes and as such are one of the principal causes of international tension. It is perfectly obvious that an agreement on universal and complete disarmament is out of the question if it does not provide for the dismantling of military bases on foreign territory.

The entire course of negotiations in the 18 Nation Committee shows that the Western powers do not want to solve the problem of universal and complete disarmament.

DOCUMENT 35. CHINESE STATEMENT ON ARMS CONTROL, 22 NOVEMBER 1964[1]

New Starting Point for Efforts to Ban Nuclear Weapons Completely

More than a month ago, the Chinese Government, simultaneous with its announcement of the explosion of China's first atom bomb, solemnly declared to the whole world that China will never at any time and under any circumstances be the first to use nuclear weapons. The Chinese Government also formally proposed to the world's governments that a summit conference of all countries be convened to discuss the question of the complete prohibition and thorough destruction of nuclear weapons, and that, as the first step, the conference should reach an agreement to the effect that the nuclear powers and those countries which may soon become nuclear powers undertake not to use nuclear weapons, neither to use them against nonnuclear powers and nuclear-free zones, nor against each other. . . .

Tripartite Treaty: a Cover for U.S. Nuclear War Preparations[2]
Some people say that the tripartite treaty for the partial suspension of nuclear testing is the first step towards the complete prohibition of nuclear weapons.

This claim has been utterly refuted by what has happened in

[1] This translation of the 22 November 1964 *People's Daily* editorial is reproduced in its entirety as it appeared in the *Peking Review*, Vol. VII, No. 48 (27 November 1964), pp. 12–14. It is reproduced from *Communist China and Arms Control* by M. H. Halperin and D. H. Perkins (Harvard University Press, Cambridge, Mass., 1965).
[2] This is the Chinese argument for not adhering to the Test Ban Treaty.

the last year and more. As everybody knows, the tripartite treaty was signed when the United States had already acquired enough technical data on atmospheric nuclear testing. This treaty in no way hampers the United States from continuing to use, manufacture and stockpile nuclear weapons, nor from conducting underground nuclear testing to develop tactical nuclear weapons, still less proliferating nuclear weapons under the smokescreen of the so-called multilateral nuclear force. On the contrary, the United States is using the tripartite treaty to pinion other countries, including those possessing nuclear weapons, so as to obtain nuclear superiority for continuing its policy of nuclear blackmail and threats. . . .

A Complete Test Ban now only Strengthens U.S. Nuclear Monopoly

Some people say that the complete prohibition of nuclear weapons can begin with the complete banning of nuclear testing.

On the face of it, such a ban sounds slightly better than a partial ban. In actual fact, there is little difference. The United States has carried out hundreds of nuclear tests of various kinds and possesses a huge nuclear arsenal. Under such circumstances, even a complete ban on nuclear testing will still leave this U.S. nuclear overlord intact. . . . Far from enjoying peace and security as a result of a complete ban on nuclear testing, the world, on the contrary, will be subjected to even more serious nuclear threats by the U.S. nuclear overlord. . . . Isn't it clear as daylight whom a complete ban on nuclear testing will benefit?

Proposal to Destroy Delivery Means Complicates Issue

Some people[1] say that destruction of the delivery vehicles of nuclear weapons can be taken as a primary measure for realizing the complete prohibition of nuclear weapons.

At first glance, such opinion seems to be not entirely senseless. But after a careful study, it is not difficult to see that this suggestion has a serious weakness. Devils are devils, whether they have long or short legs. Conventional weapons can launch nuclear bombs as well as the intercontinental ballistic missile.

[1] This is the Soviet view.

And ordinary aircraft can carry nuclear weapons as well as strategic bombers.[1] . . . The proposal to first of all destroy the means of delivery in effect confuses the question of complete prohibition of nuclear weapons with the question of reduction of conventional arms and thus greatly complicates the issue. Moreover, this proposal will inevitably involve the question of control which is the great obstacle to arms reduction deliberately put up by the United States during the disarmament talks. . . . If the complete prohibition of nuclear weapons should begin with the destruction of the means of delivery only heaven knows when this goal will ever be attained.

Not to Use Nuclear Weapons: the Effective Step towards Complete Prohibition

As the first step towards the complete prohibition of nuclear weapons, it is necessary to get at the real key question and not be bogged down by some minor and side issues. . . .

It is precisely in the light of these principles that the Chinese Government has proposed that the various countries should agree to undertake not to use nuclear weapons, as the first step towards the complete prohibition of nuclear weapons. The Chinese government proposal is reasonable and practicable.[2]

It is very easy for the countries possessing nuclear weapons to do this provided they harbour no aggressive intentions. After they have undertaken not to use nuclear weapons, it will no longer be necessary for them to continue nuclear testing and the production of nuclear weapons. The United States will then be unable always to intimidate others with nuclear weapons nor set up nuclear bases and spread nuclear weapons in other countries under this or that pretext. Then, the stockpiling of nuclear weapons will become unnecessary.

As for those countries which do not possess nuclear weapons, they will have no need to develop their own or import them from other countries, since the countries possessing nuclear weapons and those which may soon possess them will undertake

[1] This rather ignores the fact that it is easier to construct defensive systems against aircraft than against intercontinental ballistic missiles.
[2] This proposal has adherents within the USA: see R. W. Tucker, 'No First Use of Nuclear Weapons: a Proposal' in R. Falk and S. Mendlovitz, *The Strategy of World Order*, The World Law Fund, New York, 1966, vol. 3, p. 233.

not to use nuclear weapons, not to use them against non-nuclear countries. . . .

No question of control is involved in undertaking first of all not to use nuclear weapons. So long as the countries concerned have peaceful intentions, agreement can be reached quickly. Therefore this is simple and can be easily carried out. . . .

To undertake first of all not to use nuclear weapons is the only realistic and effective step towards complete prohibition.[1] The Chinese Government has taken the lead in declaring that at no time and under no circumstances will it be the first to use nuclear weapons, and it is willing to reach an international agreement guaranteeing against their use. The question now is whether the U.S. Government is willing to make the same commitment. . . .

China will Not Take Part in Geneva Disarmament Talks

It seems that the U.S. authorities have no desire either to hold a world summit conference or to reach a bilateral agreement with China against the use of nuclear weapons. They have been declaring, evidently with an ulterior motive, that they have no objection to China's participation in the Geneva disarmament talks, thus trying to substitute the 18-nation disarmament talks for a summit conference of all countries.[2]

We would like to point out that the Geneva disarmament talks are conducted within the framework of the United Nations. Over the past 15 years, the United States has deprived China of its legitimate rights in the United Nations by various sinister and despicable means. Now that China has nuclear weapons, the United States wants to drag her into the affairs of the United Nations. What is behind all this? Frankly speaking, China will have nothing to do with the United Nations as long as the latter fails to restore to the representative of the People's Republic of China the legitimate rights as the representative of the sole legal government of the Chinese people and as long

---

[1] But all this presupposes that States will keep their word not to use nuclear weapons first. This seems an extremely naïve faith in the value of such declarations and is unlikely to satisfy States who require somewhat more effective guarantees against nuclear war.
[2] But would a world conference, at this stage, really help to iron out the differences between the USA and USSR? This is doubtful.

as the illegal status of the representative of the Chiang Kai-shek clique is not nullified. This stand of ours is absolutely unalterable.[1] . . .

The Geneva 18-nation disarmament conference is in fact still under the manipulation and control of the United States and can in no way reflect the aspirations of the peoples. . . . We thank the U.S. Government for its generosity in not opposing China's participation in the Geneva disarmament conference, but we must tell it frankly that it will not have the pleasure of our company.

All Countries Must Have Their Say

There is also the suggestion that the five countries possessing nuclear weapons should hold negotiations to discuss questions concerning nuclear weapons. We do not approve of this proposal either.

The reason is that the question at present is primarily one of a certain nuclear power posing a threat to all non-nuclear countries. . . .

DOCUMENT 36. TREATY BANNING NUCLEAR-WEAPON TESTS IN THE ATMOSPHERE, IN OUTER SPACE AND UNDER WATER, SIGNED IN MOSCOW, 5 AUGUST 1963

The Governments of the United Kingdom of Great Britain and Northern Ireland, the Union of Soviet Socialist Republics, and the United States of America, hereinafter referred to as the 'Original Parties',

Proclaiming as their principal aim the speediest possible achievement of an agreement on general and complete disarmament under strict international control in accordance with the objectives of the United Nations which would put an end to the armaments race and eliminate the incentive to the production and testing of all kinds of weapons, including nuclear weapons,

Seeking to achieve the discontinuance of all test explosions

[1] The Chinese pique about exclusion from the UN is understandable, but it will require a majority vote in the Security Council and a two-thirds vote in the General Assembly to seat Communist China in those two organs.

of nuclear weapons for all time, determined to continue negotiations to this end, and desiring to put an end to the con-
tamination of man's environment by radioactive substances,

Have agreed as follows:

Article 1. 1. Each of the Parties to this Treaty undertakes to
prohibit, to prevent, and not to carry out any nuclear weapon
test explosions, or any other nuclear explosion, at any place
under its jurisdiction or control:

(*a*) in the atmosphere; beyond its limits, including outer
space; or under water, including territorial waters or high
seas; or

(*b*) in any other environment if such explosion causes
radioactive debris to be present outside the territorial limits
of the State under whose jurisdiction or control such explosion is conducted. It is understood in this connection that the
provisions of this subparagraph are without prejudice to the
conclusion of a treaty resulting in the permanent banning
of all nuclear test explosions, including all such explosions
underground, the conclusion of which, as the Parties have
stated in the Preamble to this Treaty, they seek to achieve.

2. Each of the Parties to this Treaty undertakes furthermore
to refrain from causing, encouraging, or in any way participating in, the carrying out of any nuclear weapon test explosion,
or any other nuclear explosion, anywhere which would take
place in any of the environments described, or have the effect
referred to, in paragraph 1 of this Article. . . .

Article 4. This Treaty shall be of unlimited duration.

Each Party shall in exercising its national sovereignty have
the right to withdraw from the Treaty if it decides that extraordinary events, related to the subject matter of this Treaty,
have jeopardised the supreme interests of its country. It shall
give notice of such withdrawal to all other Parties to the Treaty
three months in advance.

DOCUMENT 37. TREATY ON THE NON-PROLIFERATION OF NUCLEAR
WEAPONS, ANNEXED TO GENERAL ASSEMBLY RESOLUTION

A/RES/2373 (XXII) ADOPTED 12 JUNE 1968 BY 95 VOTES TO 4 WITH 21 ABSTENTIONS[1]

The States concluding this Treaty, hereinafter referred to as the 'Parties to the Treaty', . . . *have agreed* as follows:

Article 1. Each nuclear-weapon State Party to the Treaty undertakes not to transfer to any recipient whatsoever nuclear weapons or other nuclear explosive devices or control over such weapons or explosive devices directly, or indirectly; and not in any way to assist, encourage, or induce any non-nuclear-weapon State to manufacture or otherwise acquire nuclear weapons or other nuclear explosive devices, or control over such weapons or explosive devices.

Article 2. Each non-nuclear-weapon State Party to the Treaty undertakes not to receive the transfer from any transferor whatsoever of nuclear weapons or other nuclear explosive devices or of control over such weapons or explosive devices directly, or indirectly; not to manufacture or otherwise acquire nuclear weapons or other nuclear explosive devices; and not to seek or receive any assistance in the manufacture of nuclear weapons or other nuclear explosive devices.

Article 3. 1. Each non-nuclear-weapon State Party to the Treaty undertakes to accept safeguards, as set forth in an agreement to be negotiated and concluded with the International Atomic Energy Agency in accordance with the Statute of the International Atomic Energy Agency and the Agency's safeguards system, for the exclusive purpose of verification of the fulfilment of its obligations assumed under this Treaty with a view to preventing diversion of nuclear energy from peaceful uses to nuclear weapons or other nuclear explosive devices. Procedures for the safeguards required by this article shall be followed with respect to source or special fissionable material whether it is being produced, processed or used in any principal nuclear facility or is outside any such facility. The safeguards required by this article shall be applied on all source or special fissionable material in all peaceful nuclear activities within

[1] The wide abstentions are largely due to the feeling of middle powers that they are being deprived of the right to acquire nuclear weapons whilst the major powers do have them and show little sign of proceeding to general nuclear disarmament.

the territory of such State, under its jurisdiction, or carried out under its control anywhere.

2. Each State Party to the Treaty undertakes not to provide: (a) source or special fissionable material, or (b) equipment or material especially designed or prepared for the processing, use or production of special fissionable material, to any non-nuclear-weapon State for peaceful purposes, unless the source or special fissionable material shall be subject to the safeguards required by this article.

3. The safeguards required by this article shall be implemented in a manner designed to comply with Article 4 of this Treaty, and to avoid hampering the economic or technological development of the parties or international co-operation in the field of peaceful nuclear activities, including the international exchange of nuclear material and equipment for the processing, use or production of nuclear material for peaceful purposes in accordance with the provisions of this article and the principle of safeguarding set forth in the preamble.

4. Non-nuclear-weapon States Party to the Treaty shall conclude agreements with the International Atomic Energy Agency to meet the requirements of this article either individually or together with other States in accordance with the Statute of the International Atomic Energy Agency. Negotiation of such agreements shall commence within 180 days from the original entry into force of this Treaty. For States depositing their instruments of ratification or accession after the 180-day period, negotiation of such agreements shall commence not later than the date of such deposit. Such agreements shall enter into force not later than eighteen months after the date of initiation of negotiations.

Article 4. 1. Nothing in this Treaty shall be interpreted as affecting the inalienable right of all the Parties to the Treaty to develop research, production and use of nuclear energy for peaceful purposes without discrimination and in conformity with Articles 1 and 2 of this Treaty.

2. All the Parties to the Treaty undertake to facilitate, and have the right to participate in, the fullest possible exchange of equipment, materials and scientific and technological information for the peaceful uses of nuclear energy. Parties to the Treaty in a position to do so shall also co-operate in contribut-

ing alone or together with other States or international organizations to the further development of the applications of nuclear energy for peaceful purposes, especially in the territories of non-nuclear-weapon States Party to the Treaty, with due consideration for the needs of the developing areas of the world.

Article 5. Each Party to the Treaty undertakes to take appropriate measures to ensure that, in accordance with this Treaty, under appropriate international observation and through appropriate international procedures, potential benefits from any peaceful applications of nuclear explosions will be made available to non-nuclear-weapon States Party to the Treaty on a non-discriminatory basis and that the charge to such Parties for the explosive devices used will be as low as possible and exclude any charge for research and development. Non-nuclear-weapon States Party to the Treaty shall be able to obtain such benefits, pursuant to a special international agreement or agreements, through an appropriate international body with adequate representation of non-nuclear-weapon States. Negotiations on this subject shall commence as soon as possible after the Treaty enters into force. Non-nuclear-weapon States Party to the Treaty so desiring may also obtain such benefits pursuant to bilateral agreements.

Article 6. Each of the Parties to the Treaty undertakes to pursue negotiations in good faith on effective measures relating to cessation of the nuclear arms race at an early date and to nuclear disarmament, and on a Treaty on general and complete disarmament under strict and effective international control.

Article 7. Nothing in this Treaty affects the right of any group of States to conclude regional treaties in order to assure the total absence of nuclear weapons in their respective territories. . . .

Article 10. 1. Each Party shall in exercising its national sovereignty have the right to withdraw from the Treaty if it decides that extraordinary events, related to the subject matter of this Treaty, have jeopardized the supreme interests of its country. It shall give notice of such withdrawal to all other Parties to the Treaty and to the United Nations Security Council three months in advance. Such notice shall include a statement of the extraordinary events it regards as having jeopardized its supreme interests.

2. Twenty-five years after the entry into force of the Treaty, a Conference shall be convened to decide whether the Treaty shall continue in force indefinitely or shall be extended for an additional fixed period or periods. This decision shall be taken by a majority of the Parties to the Treaty.

SUGGESTED STUDY QUESTIONS

1. What benefits would flow from general and complete disarmament? What risks would a great power run in agreeing to, and carrying out, such disarmament?
2. What kinds of short-term measures of arms control or partial disarmament might be considered feasible pending agreement on general and complete disarmament?
3. Explain and comment critically on the Chinese position on disarmament.
4. 'Inspection is the key to disarmament.' Comment.
5. Are there special features of nuclear weapons which make them different from conventional weapons of mass destruction?
6. If mankind has possessed, but not used, nuclear weapons for the past twenty-five years does this not suggest that a nuclear stalemate will continue and that nuclear weapons in fact are a deterrent to war?

FURTHER READING

BLACKETT, P. M. S., *Studies of War: Nuclear and Conventional*, New York: Hill and Wang, 1962.

BULL, HEDLEY, *The Control of the Arms Race: Disarmament and Arms Control in the Missile Age*, New York: Praeger, 1961.

Current Disarmament Proposals, published by World Law Fund, 11 West 42nd St., New York 36, N.Y.

KAHN, HERMAN, *On Thermonuclear War*, Princeton: Princeton University Press, 1961.

KAHN, HERMAN, *Thinking about the Unthinkable*, New York: Horizon Press, 1962.

LARSON, A. (ed.), *A Warless World*, New York: McGraw-Hill, 1962.

RUSSELL, BERTRAND, *Common Sense and Nuclear Warfare*, New York: Simon and Schuster, 1959.

VAN SLYCK, PHILIP, *The Control of National Power*, Boston: Beacon Press, 1964.

PART VII

The Future Structure of International Society

Very considerable thought has to be given to the possibilities of creating a structure for international society which will afford surer guarantees of peace and a decent life to mankind than does the present structure of nation-States, loosely co-ordinated through international organizations like the UN.

Doubtless, in the Middle Ages, the English barons and their lieges saw little prospect of a central, law-enforcing agency and disliked whatever prospect they did contemplate. But 'the King's Peace' came and, by degrees, a central authority became the rule. Yet the nation-State is, historically, a fairly recent creation and, to judge by its record in maintaining world peace, not a very successful one. Must we assume that centralization of authority stops at the nation-State? Why not centralize still further in a World Authority?

It would be foolish to underestimate the problems involved, but equally foolish to assume that the present structure, based on the sovereign, nation-State, embodies the ultimate in human wisdom. If, then, mankind will contemplate possible alternatives there are perhaps three basic alternatives:

1. The present UN system—gradually improved but still resting on the basis of the sovereign member States retaining unfettered military power.

2. The present UN system—but radically improved and embodying first arms control and later general disarmament, thus conferring the overriding military power to the UN.

3. A totally changed system—embodying a new Federal Constitution for the world and relegating the present nation-States to component units within the federal system.

In the documents which follow, we see an attempt to explore alternatives (2) and (3). Rejecting the efficacy of (1), they give serious thought to the many problems involved. Document 38 gives extracts from this Clark-Sohn plan, taken from an outline of this plan first published in 1958 and revised in 1962,[1] and from the 'Borgese' plan, published by the Center for the Study of Democratic Institutions in 1965.[2] These extracts are designed to show contrasts between alternative (2)—which is the Clark-Sohn plan—and alternative (3)—the Borgese plan. They illustrate only the barest essentials of the two plans in their thinking about the essentials of the scheme, i.e. allocation of powers, the legislature, the executive, the judiciary, the armed forces and finance. The extracts are minimal, for reasons of space, and scarcely do credit to the detailed work of the full plans. Readers are especially recommended to study in detail the full Clark-Sohn plan. However, these extracts may suffice to set in train intelligent thought about the possibilities and the problems and it is with this purpose that a comparison is made. A comparison of the two drafts prepared by Clark and Sohn on the one hand and Elisabeth Mann Borgese on the other serves to illustrate some of the basic problems.

The Clark and Sohn concept of the powers to be entrusted to the revised UN is narrower than Borgese's concept for the new World Government: her 'powers' stretch into domains such as the regulation of commerce, transportation and communication, control of emigration and immigration, etc. Not all will be directly related to the maintenance of peace—which is the Clark and Sohn criterion—but a case can be made out to show that all the matters envisaged by Borgese would be more efficiently and harmoniously regulated at the international level rather than by nation-States, often competing in their interests and conceding co-operation only as a last resort.

The 'legislature' under the Clark and Sohn plan becomes the Assembly with a new voting formula based on population as

[1] Grenville Clark and Louis B. Sohn, *World Peace through World Law*, Harvard University Press, Cambridge, Mass., 1962, second ed. (revised), a book of 370 pages. This plan is a comprehensive study of the way in which the United Nations Charter might be revised so as to provide a more effectively functioning organization for maintaining world peace.

[2] Although, basically, first drafted by Elisabeth Mann Borgese in 1948.

opposed to the present 'one State—one Vote' principle: and the representatives become, ultimately, directly elected by the people. The Borgese plan is much more complex, with a system of nine regional Electoral Colleges which nominate candidates for the legislature, the World Council, of ninety-nine members.[1] Again, the representation is based on population rather than any other criterion. Obviously this poses problems for States like the UK, for on this criterion they become dwarfed by India, China, etc. The counter-argument is that representation ought to reflect the realities of world power, although this is notoriously difficult to measure and possibly not a very sound criterion. The other feature of the Clark-Sohn plan which must be stressed is that the Assembly would assume primary responsibility for the maintenance of world peace: it is virtually a reversal of roles with the Security Council. It must be recalled that the Soviet Union presently opposes any transfer of power to the Assembly,[2] so that the difficulties of acceptance are considerable.

So far as the Executive is concerned, under the Clark and Sohn plan this becomes the servant of the Assembly (although in practice the relationship might prove very different) and the members are still State representatives. The Borgese plan is totally different, with an Executive rather like the US President, although the President would be assisted by a Chancellor and Cabinet. Although appointed by the legislature, the President would not be removable on a vote of no confidence: that would only apply to the Chancellor and Cabinet. Clearly, the Borgese plan moves much further into the realm of true world federalism, diminishing far more the power of the individual States.

The judicial system under the Clark and Sohn plan provides not only for a strengthened International Court, with com-

[1] Under the Borgese plan this World Council would have three special advisory bodies, namely:
(a) a House of Nationalities and States, with representatives from each, for the safeguarding of local institutions and autonomies and the protection of minorities;
(b) a syndicate or functional Senate, for the representation of syndicates and unions or occupational associations and any other corporate interests of transnational significance, as well as for mediation or arbitration in non-justiciable issues among such syndicates or unions or other corporate interests;
(c) an Institute of Science, Education and Culture.
[2] Above, pp. 88–9.

pulsory jurisdiction over disputes which the Assembly directs shall be referred to it as likely to endanger international peace, but also for a World Equity Tribunal and a World Conciliation Board. The former would deal, equitably, with *non-legal* situations dangerous to peace and the latter with similar situations but by the different process of conciliation. In addition regional UN courts would try individuals for offences against international peace. All of this, of course, demands a degree of subordination by States to impartial adjudication which is far beyond their present contemplation.

The Borgese plan goes even further, with a typically federal structure of Supreme Court, five 'Benches' or divisions dealing with different types of cases, lower Federal Courts and a World Attorney—an individual called 'The Tribune of the People' who safeguards before these courts the rights of the people and the principles embodied in the World Constitution.[1] The assertion of criminal jurisdiction over *individuals* is common to both plans in so far as this is necessary to prosecute offences which threaten international peace: these might range from breaches of the disarmament treaty (e.g. raising a private army) to inciting war or racial violence. So far, this kind of international criminal jurisdiction is only in a very elementary stage so that, by reference to present practice, both plans are highly ambitious. But the principle was accepted at Nuremburg, as we have seen,[2] and a draft Code of Offences against the Peace and Security of Mankind and draft Statute for an International Criminal Court have already been drafted (but *not* adopted) under UN auspices. Surely, in principle, this is the right solution, for 'crimes against international law are committed by men, not by abstract entities' (Nuremburg). One cannot expect States to punish men who may well be the very leaders of those States!

The armed forces under the Clark and Sohn plan become a UN Peace Force of between 200,000 to 600,000 and a Reserve of between 600,000 and 1,200,000. It of course presupposes

---

[1] Though not nearly so extensive, a somewhat analogous role is played by the European Commission of Human Rights in cases before this European Court of Human Rights; also by the two Advocates-General before the Court of the European Communities.

[2] Above, p. 12.

general and complete disarmament[1] so that it would be the sole *military* force in the world. The Borgese plan is less specific about size but equally presupposes that the Federal Forces would constitute the only true military force, with the component units of the federation entitled to no more than limited militias. Control over the Federal Forces is assigned to a Chamber of Guardians, whereas the Clark and Sohn plan uses the Assembly. Certainly the problem of political control will be acute if ever this one World Force obtains what is virtually a monopoly of military power: the fear of a world military dictatorship will ensure that very considerable thought will have to be given to appropriate political safeguards.

In the financing of their plans, Clark and Sohn present comprehensive proposals of which the essential feature is that States collect taxes to be assigned to the UN. Costly as the figures may appear, they would represent an enormous saving over what is currently spent on armaments by the nation-States. The Borgese plan is not much different except that, being based upon a federal concept, the World Government would legislate directly and raise taxes on its own authority without needing to rely on States to do so on its behalf.

A final question is whether either plan can be implemented, if at all, only by gradual evolution or whether a 'big step'—a radical change to one or other plan (or a similar plan)—can be made in a short space of time. Many believe that the 'big step' would only be possible in the wake of a catastrophic Third World War: this would be needed to shock mankind into acceptance of radical change. This is an appalling prospect and one is perhaps justified in hoping that, provided sufficient people think about the problem and possibilities, transition will occur peaceably and in time to avoid such a catastrophe.

DOCUMENT 38. EXTRACTS FROM GRENVILLE CLARK AND LOUIS B. SOHN'S INTRODUCTION TO *World Peace through World Law* (HARVARD UNIVERSITY PRESS, CAMBRIDGE, MASS., 1962) AND FROM E. M. BORGESE's *Constitution for the World*, 1947–8 (CENTER FOR THE STUDY OF DEMOCRATIC INSTITUTIONS, SANTA BARBARA, CALIFORNIA, 1965)

[1] A matter to which the plan devotes the whole of Annex I.

1. Powers

The powers of the world organization should be restricted to matters directly related to the maintenance of peace. All other powers should be reserved to the nations and their peoples. This definition and reservation of powers is advisable not only to avoid opposition based on fear of possible interference in the domestic affairs of the nations, but also because it is wise for this generation to limit itself to the single task of preventing international violence or the threat of it. If we can accomplish that we should feel satisfied and could well leave to later generations any enlargement of the powers of the world organization that they might find desirable.

(Clark and Sohn)

The jurisdiction of the World Government as embodied in its organs of power shall extend to:

(a) The control of the observance of the Constitution in all the component communities and territories of the Federal World Republic, which shall be indivisible and one;

(b) The furtherance and progressive fulfillment of the Duties and Rights of Man in the spirit of the foregoing Declaration, with their specific enactment in such fields of federal and local relations as are described hereinafter (Art. 27 through 33);

(c) The maintenance of peace; and to that end the enactment and promulgation of laws which shall be binding upon communities and upon individuals as well,

(d) the judgment and settlement of any conflicts among component units, with prohibition of recourse to interstate violence,

(e) the supervision of and final decision on any alterations of boundaries between states or unions thereof,

(f) the supervision of and final decision on the forming of new states or unions thereof,

(g) the administration of such territories as may still be immature for self-government, and the declaration in due time of their eligibility therefor,

(h) the intervention in intrastate violence and violations of law which affect world peace and justice,

THE FUTURE STRUCTURE OF INTERNATIONAL SOCIETY

(i) the organization and disposal of federal armed forces,

(j) the limitation and control of weapons and of the domestic militias in the several component units of the World Republic;

(k) The establishment, in addition to the Special Bodies listed hereinafter (Art. 8 and 9), of such other agencies as may be conducive to the development of the earth's resources and to the advancement of physical and intellectual standards, with such advisory or initiating or arbitrating powers as shall be determined by law;

(l) The laying and collecting of federal taxes, and the establishment of a plan and a budget for federal expenditures,

(m) the administration of the World Bank and the establishment of suitable world fiscal agencies for the issue of money and the creation and control of credit,

(n) the regulation of commerce affected with federal interest,

(o) the establishment, regulation, and, where necessary or desirable, the operation of means of transportation and communication which are of federal interest;

(p) The supervision and approval of laws concerning emigration and immigration and the movements of peoples,

(q) the granting of federal passports;

(r) The appropriation, under the right of eminent domain, of such private or public property as may be necessary for federal use, reasonable compensation being made therefor;

(s) The legislation over and administration of the territory which shall be chosen as Federal District and of such other territories as may be entrusted directly to the Federal Government.

2

The powers not delegated to the World Government by this Constitution, and not prohibited by it to the several members of the Federal World Republic, shall be reserved to the several states or nations or unions thereof.

(Borgese)

2. Legislature

The purpose is, by abolishing the present system of one vote for each member Nation, to substitute a more equitable system, and thus to make the nations more willing to confer upon the General Assembly the limited yet considerably increased powers that it would need.

The proposed plan of representation takes account of relative populations but is qualified by the important provisions that no nation, however large, shall have more than thirty Representatives and that even the smallest nation shall have one Representative. The upper limit of thirty would be imposed partly because weighted representation is not likely to be accepted by the smaller nations unless the differences in representation between the majority of the nations and the largest nations are kept within moderate limits, and also because without some such limitation, the General Assembly would be of so unwieldy a size as to be unable to transact business. At the other extreme the purpose is to ensure that even the very small nations shall have some voice.

The proposed formula divides the ninety-nine nations, generally recognized in early 1960 as independent states or likely to be so recognized by 1965, into six categories according to relative populations, with representation as follows:

The   4 largest nations . . . . . . 30 Representatives each . . 120
The   8 next largest nations . . 15 Representatives each . . 120
The 20 next largest nations . .   6 Representatives each . . 120
The 30 next largest nations . .   4 Representatives each . . 120
The 34 next largest nations . .   2 Representatives each . .   68
The   3 smallest nations . . . .   1 Representative each . .   3
——   ———
   99 nations   551 Representatives

It is proposed that the populations of colonial and semi-colonial areas (i.e., the non-self-governing territories and dependencies, including territories under trusteeship administration) shall not be counted in determining the representation of the independent states but that, in order to afford equal treatment to the estimated approximately 95 million people (in 1965) of these areas, they shall be entitled to representation in proportion to population on the same average basis as the people of the member Nations. It is assumed that as of July 1965 this method would entitle these areas as a whole to seventeen Representatives. The General Assembly would allocate these Representatives among the various territories or groups of territories, taking into account their relative populations.

Of the assumed 568 Representatives, 551 would therefore represent the assumed ninety-nine independent states, while the non-self-governing and trust territories would have 17 Representatives.

The four most populous nations of the world—the People's Republic of China, India, the Soviet Union and the United States—would each have the maximum of thirty Representatives; and even the smallest nation (Iceland) would have one Representative. The 568 Representatives would represent a total estimated world population (as of July 1965) of 3,172,156,000, or an average of about 5,600,000 for each Representative.

The effect would be that, with relation to population, the smaller nations would still have a disproportionately large voice, but not nearly as much so as under the present system of one vote for each member Nation irrespective of population.

Over a period of years, the authors have studied many plans for determining representation by various formulas that would take account of such factors as relative literacy, relative wealth as measured by per capita income, etc. We have concluded, however, that the introduction of any such other factors would raise so many complications and involve such uncertain and invidious distinctions that it is wiser to hold to the less elaborate formula herein proposed.

We have also studied numerous suggestions for a bicameral world legislature in which the nations would have voting power in one house in proportion to their populations, but equal voting power in the other house irrespective of their size. Modifications of this plan in the shape of a system of double voting in a single house have also been studied. After weighing these alternatives, we conclude that the one-chamber solution herein proposed (together with representation which takes account of relative populations, but is modified by the proposed system of categories and the proposed maximum and minimum number of Representatives) is not only simpler, but also is probably as fair an arrangement as any other. However, we hold no dogmatic views on this difficult subject, the essential point being that there must be some radical, yet equitable, change in the present system of representation in the General Assembly as a basis for conferring upon the Assembly certain essential, although carefully limited, powers of legislation which it does not now possess.

As to the method of selection of the Representatives, it is proposed that a system of full popular election shall be gradually introduced. This would be done under a three-stage plan providing: (a) that in the first stage all the Representatives would be chosen by the respective national legislatures of the member Nations; (b) that in the second stage at least half the Representatives would be chosen by popular vote of those persons qualified to vote for the most numerous branch of the national legislature; and (c) that in the third stage all the Representatives would be chosen by the same sort of popular vote. The first two stages would normally be of twelve years each (three four-year terms of the General Assembly) but could each be extended by eight years by a special vote of the Assembly. The popular election of all the Representatives would, therefore, normally become mandatory twenty-four years after the ratification of the revised Charter and in any case not later than forty years after the revised Charter comes into force.

With regard to the terms of service of the Representatives, it is proposed that they shall serve for four years.

Concerning the procedure for voting in the General Assembly, it is proposed in place of the present method: (a) that a majority of all the Representatives then in office must be present in order to constitute a quorum; (b) that, except as to certain 'important' and 'special' questions, decisions shall be made by a majority of the Representatives present and voting; (c) that on these 'important' questions which would be specifically defined, decisions shall be by a 'special majority' consisting of a majority of all the Representatives then in office, whether or not present and voting; and (d) that in respect of several 'special' questions, also specifically defined, there shall be even larger special majorities which in one instance would require the affirmative vote of three fourths of all the Representatives in office including two thirds of the Representatives from those nations entitled to fifteen or more Representatives, i.e., the twelve largest nations.

(Clark and Sohn)

The Federal Convention shall consist of delegates elected directly by the people of all states and nations, one delegate for each million of population or fraction thereof above one-half million, with the proviso that the people of any extant state, . . . ranging between 100,000 and 1,000,000, shall be entitled to elect one delegate, but any such state with a population below 100,000 shall be aggregated for federal electoral purposes to the electoral unit closest to its borders.

The delegates to the Federal Convention shall vote as individuals, not as members of national or otherwise collective representations [except as specified hereinafter, Art. 46, paragraph 2, and Art. 47].

The Convention shall meet in May of every third year, for a session of thirty days.

5

The Federal Convention shall subdivide into nine Electoral Colleges according to the nine Societies of kindred nations and cultures, or Regions, wherefrom its members derive their powers, such Regions being:

1. The continent of Europe and its islands outside the Russian area, together with the United Kingdom if the latter so decides, and with such overseas English- or French- or Cape Dutch-speaking communities of the British Commonwealth of Nations or the French Union as decide to associate (this whole area here tentatively denominated *Europa*);

2. The United States of America, with the United Kingdom if the latter so decides, and such kindred communities of British, or Franco-British, or Dutch-British, or Irish civilization and lineage as decide to associate (*Atlantis*);

3. Russia, European and Asiatic, with such East-Baltic or Slavic or South-Danubian nations as associate with Russia (*Eurasia*);

4. The Near and Middle East, with the States of North Africa, and Pakistan if the latter so decides (*Afrasia*);

5. *Africa*, south of the Sahara, with or without the South African Union as the latter may decide;

6. *India*, with Pakistan if the latter so decides;

7. China, Korea, Japan, with the associate archipelagoes of the North- and Mid-Pacific (*Asia Minor*);

8. Indochina and Indonesia, with Pakistan if the latter so decides, and with such other Mid- and South-Pacific lands and islands as decide to associate (*Austrasia*);

9. The Western Hemisphere south of the United States (*Columbia*).

Each Electoral College shall nominate by secret ballot not more than three candidates, regardless of origin, for the office of President of the World Republic. The Federal Convention in plenary meeting, having selected by secret ballot a panel of three candidates from the lists submitted, shall elect by secret ballot one of the three as President, on a majority of two-thirds.

If three consecutive ballots have been indecisive, the candidate with the smallest vote shall be eliminated and between the two remaining candidates a simple majority vote shall be decisive.

Each Electoral College shall then nominate by secret and proportional ballot twenty-seven candidates, originating from the respective Electoral Area or Region, for the World Council; with the proviso that one-third and not more than one-third of the nominees shall not be members of the Federal Convention; and the nine lists having been presented to the Federal Convention, the Federal Convention in plenary meeting shall select by secret and proportional ballot nine Councilmen from each list, with the same proviso as above.

The Federal Convention shall also elect by secret and proportional ballot, on nominations, prior to the opening of the Convention, by such organizations of world-wide importance and lawfully active in more than three Regions as shall be designated [for the first election by the United Nations Assembly and subsequently] by the Council, eighteen additional members, regardless of origin; and the total membership of the World Council shall be thus ninety-nine.

7

The primary power to initiate and enact legislation for the Federal Republic of the World shall be vested in the Council.

The tenure of the Council shall be three years.

The Council shall elect its Chairman, for its whole tenure of three years.

Councilors shall be re-eligible.

(Borgese)

3. The Executive

(3) *The Executive Council.* It is proposed to abolish the present Security Council and to substitute for it an Executive Council, composed of seventeen Representatives elected by the General Assembly itself. This new and highly important organ would not only be chosen by the Assembly, but would also be responsible to and removable by the Assembly; and the Council would serve for the same four-year terms as the Representatives in the Assembly.

Special provision would be made for representation of the larger nations, whereby the four largest nations (China, India, the U.S.A. and the U.S.S.R.) would each be entitled at all times to have one of its Representatives on the Council; and four of the eight next largest nations (Brazil, France, West Germany, Indonesia, Italy, Japan, Pakistan and the United Kingdom) would in rotation also be entitled to representation, with the proviso that two of these four shall always be from nations in Europe and the other two from nations outside Europe. The remaining nine members would be chosen by the Assembly from the Representatives of all the other member Nations and the non-self-governing and trust territories under a formula designed to provide fair representation for all the main regions of the world and to ensure that every member Nation, without exception, shall in due course have a Representative on this all-important Council.

In contrast to the voting procedure of the present Security Council, whereby any one of the five nations entitled to 'permanent' membership has a veto power in all nonprocedural matters, the decisions of the new Executive Council on 'important' matters (as defined in paragraph 2 of revised Article 27) would be by a vote of twelve of the seventeen Representatives composing it, with the proviso that this majority shall include a majority of the eight members of the Council from the twelve member Nations entitled to fifteen or more Representatives in the Assembly and a majority of the nine other members of the Council. All other decisions would be by a vote of any twelve members of the Council.

This Executive Council would constitute the *executive arm* of the strengthened United Nations, holding much the same relation to the General Assembly as that of the British Cabinet to the House of Commons. Subject to its responsibility to the Assembly, the new Council would have broad powers to supervise and direct the disarmament process and other aspects of the whole system for the maintenance of peace provided for in the revised Charter.

(Clark and Sohn)

10

The executive power, together with initiating power in federal legislation, shall be vested in the President. His tenure shall be six years.

The President shall not have membership in the Council.

The President shall not be re-eligible. He shall not be eligible to the Tribunate of the People until nine years have elapsed since the expiration of his term.

No two successive Presidents shall originate from the same Region.

11

The President shall appoint a Chancellor. The Chancellor, with the approval of the President, shall appoint the Cabinet.

The Chancellor shall act as the President's representative before the Council in the exercise of legislative initiative. The Chancellor and the Cabinet members shall have at any time the privilege of the floor before the Council.

But no Chancellor or Cabinet member shall have a vote or shall hold membership in the Council, nor, if he was a member of the Council at the moment of his executive appointment, shall he be entitled to resume his seat therein when leaving the executive post unless he be re-elected at a subsequent Convention.

No one shall serve as Chancellor for more than six years, nor as Cabinet member for more than twelve, consecutive or not.

No three Cabinet members at any one time and no two successive Chancellors shall originate from the same Region.

The Council shall have power to interrogate the Chancellor and the Cabinet and to adopt resolutions on their policies.

The Chancellor and the Cabinet shall resign when the President so decides or when a vote of no confidence by the absolute majority of fifty or more of the Council is confirmed by a second such vote; but no second vote shall be taken and held valid if less than three months have elapsed from the first. . . .

14

Any legislation of the Council can be vetoed by the President within thirty days of its passage. But the Council can overrule the veto if its new vote, by a majority of two-thirds, finds support, within sixty days of the President's action, in the majority of the Grand Tribunal [and no such support shall be required during the tenure of the first President].

15

The President can be impeached on grounds of treason to the Constitution, or usurpation of power, or felony, or insanity, or other disease impairing permanently his mind.

The vote of impeachment shall be final when three-quarters of the Council and three-quarters of the Grand Tribunal concur and the majority of the Supreme Court validates the legality of the proceedings.

(Borgese)

4. The Judiciary

(7) *The Judicial and Conciliation System.* In accordance with the conception that the *abolition* of national armaments is indispensable to genuine peace, and that if such armaments are abolished other means must be simultaneously provided for the adjudication or settlement of international disputes and for 'peaceful change', provision is made for a world system of conciliation and adjudication.

In proposing such a system, recognition is given to the existence of two main categories of international disputes, namely: (1) those disputes which are capable of adjudication through the application of legal principles, and (2) the equally or more important category of disputes which cannot be satisfactorily settled on the basis of applicable legal principles.

With respect to those international disputes which are susceptible of settlement upon legal principles, it is proposed to empower the General Assembly to *direct* the submission of any such dispute to the International Court of Justice whenever the Assembly finds that its continuance is likely to endanger international peace. In case of such submission, the Court would have compulsory jurisdiction to decide the case, even if one of the parties should refuse to come before the Court.

The International Court of Justice would also be given authority to decide questions relating to the interpretation of the revised Charter; and to decide disputes involving the constitutionality of laws enacted thereunder. Compulsory jurisdiction would also be conferred upon the Court in certain other respects as, for example, any dispute relating to the interpretation of treaties or other international agreements, or as to the validity of any such treaty or agreement alleged to conflict with the revised Charter.

In respect of the enforcement of the judgments of the International Court of Justice, it is proposed that the General Assembly (or in certain special circumstances the Executive Council) could direct economic sanctions or, in the last resort, action by the United Nations Peace Force to ensure compliance. Any such action would, however, be limited, if at all possible, to air or naval demonstrations and would involve actual military operations against a noncomplying nation only if absolutely necessary.

With regard to the other main category of international disputes, i.e., those inevitable disputes which are not of an exclusively legal nature, it is proposed to establish a new tribunal of the highest possible prestige, to be known as the World Equity Tribunal. To this end it is proposed that the Tribunal shall be composed of fifteen persons elected by the General Assembly pursuant to safeguards and an elaborate procedure designed to ensure the choice of individuals whose reputation, experience and character would furnish the best assurance of impartiality and breadth of view. . . .

In ordinary circumstances this World Equity Tribunal could not make binding decisions, as distinguished from recommendations, except with the consent of the parties. But provision is made that if the General Assembly votes by a large special majority, i.e., by a three-fourths majority of all the Representatives then in office (including two thirds of all the Representatives from the twelve largest nations), that the carrying out of the Tribunal's recommendations is essential for the preservation of peace, the recommendations of the Tribunal shall become enforceable by the same means as a judgment of the International Court of Justice.

The purpose of this important departure is to supplement other methods for settling *nonlegal* international disputes (such as negotiation, conciliation and agreed arbitration) by providing an impartial world agency of so high a stature that, under exceptional conditions involving world peace, its recommendations may be given the force of law.

Through the adoption of these proposals in respect of both legal and nonlegal international disputes, world institutions would at last exist whereby *any* nation could be compelled to submit *any* dispute dangerous to peace for a final and peaceful settlement; and the world would no longer be helpless, for lack of adequate machinery, to deal by peaceful means with any and all dangerous disputes between nations.

In order to provide means for the trial of individuals accused of violating the disarmament provisions of the revised Charter or of other offences against the Charter or laws enacted by the General Assembly, and to provide safeguards against possible abuse of power by any organ or official of the United Nations, provision is also made for regional United Nations courts, inferior to the International Court of Justice, and for the review by the International Court of decisions of these regional courts.

The proposal is for not less than twenty or more than forty such regional courts to have jurisdiction in regions to be delineated by the General Assembly, each regional court to be composed of not less than three or more than nine judges. . . .

The regional United Nations courts, together with the International Court of Justice, would introduce a regime of genuine and enforceable world law in respect of all *legal* questions likely to endanger world peace, while the World Equity Tribunal would, as above mentioned, provide means for the authoritative and compulsory settlement of nonlegal situations seriously dangerous to peace.

In addition to these judicial agencies, it is proposed to establish a World Conciliation Board which could be voluntarily availed of by the nations, or to which the General Assembly could refer any international dispute or situation likely to threaten peace. The functions of this new Board would be strictly confined to mediation and conciliation; and, if it failed to bring the disputing nations to a voluntary settlement, resort could be had to the International Court of Justice or the World Equity Tribunal, as might be most suitable in view of the nature of the issues involved. . . .

(8) *Enforcement and Penalties*. The plan envisages a variety of enforcement measures, including the prosecution in United Nations regional courts of individuals responsible for a violation of the disarmament provisions.

In order to aid the Inspection Service in the detection and prosecution of any such violators, it is proposed to have a civil police force of the United Nations with a strength not exceeding 10,000. This force would be under the general direction of an Attorney-General of the United Nations. . . .

(Clark and Sohn)

The Grand Tribunal and the Supreme Court

16

The supreme judiciary power of the World Republic shall be vested in a Grand Tribunal of sixty Justices, with the President of the World Republic as Chief Justice and Chairman, and the Chairman of the Council as Vice-Chairman ex-officio.

The President as Chief Justice shall appoint the Justices of the Grand Tribunal and fill the vacancies, subject to vetoes by the Council on majorities of two-thirds. He shall have power to overrule any such veto if he finds support in a two-thirds majority of the Justices in office [except that no such power shall be vested in the first President]. . . .

18

The sixty Justices shall be assigned twelve to each of five Benches:

the First Bench to deal with constitutional issues between the primary organs and powers of the World Government as well as with all issues and cases in which the Tribune of the People shall decide to appear in his capacity of World Attorney and defender of the Rights of Man;

the Second Bench to deal with issues and conflicts between the World Government and any of its component units, whether single States or unions thereof or Regions, as well as with issues and conflicts of component units of the World Republic among themselves;

the Third Bench to deal with issues and conflicts between the World Government and individual citizens or corporations or unions or any other associations of citizens;

the Fourth Bench to deal with issues and conflicts among component units, whether single States or unions of States or Regions, and individual citizens or corporations or unions or any other associations of citizens when such issues and conflicts affect the interpretation or enactment of federal law;

the Fifth Bench to deal with issues and conflicts, when they affect the interpretation and enactment of federal law, either among individual citizens or among corporations, unions, syndicates, or any other collective organizations of citizens and interests.

Each Region shall be represented in each Bench by at least one member and not more than two.

19

The Supreme Court shall be of seven members: five representing one each Bench, with the Chief Justice as their Chairman and the Chairman of the Council as their Vice-Chairman ex-officio; and the active membership of the Benches shall thus remain of eleven each.

No two members of the Supreme Court shall originate from the same Region.

20

The Supreme Court shall distribute the cases among the five Benches of the Grand Tribunal according to competences as specified hereinbefore [Art. 18].

Cases where competences overlap or are otherwise doubtful shall be referred to such Bench or Benches jointly as the Supreme Court shall decide.

The Supreme Court shall have power to modify the rules of assignment for the five Benches as specified in Art. 18, subject to approval by the majority of the Council and by a two-thirds majority of the Grand Tribunal concurrently.

21

It shall be the office and function of the Supreme Court to review the decisions of the Benches, within three months of their issuance, said decisions to become effective upon registration by the Court, or, when annulled, to be returned for revision each to the Bench which judged the case, or to another, or to others jointly as the Court may decide; annulment to be pronounced in cases of unfair trial or faulty procedure, and also for reasons of substance when final appeal was filed by the losing party, if the Court at its own discretion choose to take cognizance thereof, or by the Tribune of the People, whose demand shall be mandatory.

22

The Grand Tribunal, with the approval of the Supreme Court, shall establish Lower Federal Courts in such number and places as conditions in the component units of the World Republic shall require, and a Federal Appellate Court in each Region. It shall also determine the rules and competences of such courts, and appoint their officials on the basis of competitive examinations. . . .

The Tribune of the People and the World Law

26

The Federal Convention, after electing the Council, shall elect by secret ballot the Tribune of the People as a spokesman for the minorities. . . .

27

It shall be the office and function of the Tribune of the People to defend the natural and civil rights of individuals and groups against violation or neglect by the World Government or any of its component units; to further and demand, as a World Attorney before the World Republic, the observance of the letter and spirit of this Constitution;[1] and to promote thereby, in the spirit of its Preamble and Declaration of Duties and Rights, the attainment of the goals set to the progress of mankind by the efforts of the ages. . . .

33

Every individual or group or community shall have the right of appeal against unjust application of a law, or against the law itself, gaining access through the inferior courts, local or federal, to the superior and the Grand Tribunal, and securing the counsel and support of the Tribune of the People when the Tribune so decides; and, if a law or statute is found evidently in conflict with the guarantees pledged in the foregoing articles or irreparably in contradiction with the basic principles and intents of the World Republic as stated in the Preamble to this Constitution and in its Declaration of Duties and Rights, the Grand Tribunal shall have power to recommend to the Supreme Court that such law or statute be declared, and the Supreme Court shall have power to declare it, null and void.

(Borgese)

5. The Armed Forces

(6) *A World Police Force.* The plan is framed upon the assumption that not even the most solemn agreement and not even the most thorough inspection system, or both together, can be *fully* relied upon to ensure that every nation will always carry out and maintain complete disarmament and refrain from violence under all circumstances. Moreover, it must be recognized that even with the complete elimination of all *military* forces there would necessarily remain substantial, although strictly limited and lightly armed, internal police forces and that these police forces, supplemented by civilians armed with sporting rifles and fowling pieces, might conceivably constitute a serious threat to a neighboring country in the absence of a well-disciplined and heavily armed world police. . . .

[1] Articles 28 to 32 proceed to set out certain basic, constitutional guarantees by reference to which an appeal to annul any law can be made. Note also that Annex VII to the Clark and Sohn plan is a Bill of Rights.

Annex II provides in detail for the organization and maintenance of the proposed United Nations Peace Force—for its recruitment and pay, its terms of service, its maximum and minimum strength, and for its training, equipment, disposition and functions. This Peace Force would consist of two components—a standing component and a Peace Force Reserve—both of which would, save in the most extreme emergency, be composed solely of volunteers.

The standing component would be a full-time force of professionals with a strength of between 200,000 and 600,000, as determined from year to year by the General Assembly. The proposed term of service for its enlisted personnel would be not less than four or more than eight years, as determined by the General Assembly, with provision for the re-enlistment of a limited number of especially well-qualified personnel.

In respect of the composition of the standing component, assurance would be provided through various specific limitations in Annex II that it would be recruited mainly, although not exclusively, from the smaller nations. . . .

The units of the standing component would be stationed throughout the world in such a way that there would be no undue concentration in any particular nation or region, and, on the other hand, so as to facilitate prompt action for the maintenance of peace if and when required. . . .

As distinguished from the active or standing component, the Peace Force Reserve would have no organized units whatever, but would consist only of individuals partially trained and subject to call for service with the standing component in case of need. It would have a strength of between 600,000 and 1,200,000, as determined by the General Assembly. . . .

It is contemplated that the United Nations Peace Force shall be regularly provided with the most modern weapons and equipment, except that its possession or use of biological, chemical or any other weapons adaptable to mass destruction, other than nuclear weapons, would be forbidden, special provision being made, as hereafter mentioned, for the use of nuclear weapons in extreme circumstances. . . . The plan includes the utmost precautions for the subordination of the military direction of the Peace Force under all circumstances to civilian authority as represented by the Executive Council and the General Assembly.

(Clark and Sohn)

35

The control and use of the armed forces of the Federal Republic of the World shall be assigned exclusively to a Chamber of Guardians under the chairmanship of the President, in his capacity of Protector of the Peace. The other Guardians shall be six Councilmen elected by the Council. . . .

Officers holding professional or active rank in the armed forces of the Federal Republic, or in the domestic militia of any component unit thereof, shall not be eligible as Guardians. . . .

41

The Chamber of Guardians, assisted by a General Staff and an Institute of Technology whose members it shall appoint, shall determine the technological and the numerical levels that shall be set as limits to the domestic militias of the single communities and states or unions thereof.

Armed forces and the manufacture of armaments beyond the levels thus determined shall be reserved to the World Government.

(Borgese)

6. Finance

(10) *A United Nations Revenue System.* It would obviously be futile to establish the proposed new world institutions called for by the plan (including the United Nations Peace Force, the Inspection Service, the World Development Authority, the Nuclear Energy Authority, the Outer Space Agency, the World Equity Tribunal and the World Conciliation Board) unless a well-planned system is provided for their sufficient and reliable financial support. Such a system should also, of course, provide for the adequate support of the already existing organs and agencies of the United Nations which would be continued and, in some cases, would have enlarged functions and responsi-

bilities. These include the revised General Assembly itself, the strengthened International Court of Justice, the Economic and Social Council, the Trusteeship Council, the Secretariat and the various specialized agencies already affiliated with the United Nations.

The United Nations Peace Force, with an assumed strength for its standing component of, say, 400,000 (midway between the proposed constitutional maximum of 600,000 and minimum of 200,000) and with an assumed strength for the Peace Force Reserve of, say, 900,000 (midway between the proposed constitutional maximum of 1,200,000 and minimum of 600,000) would alone require some $9 billion annually. The minimum annual amount required for the General Assembly and Executive Council, the judicial system, the Secretariat, the Inspection Service, the Nuclear Energy Authority, the Outer Space Agency and the other organs and agencies other than the World Development Authority[1] may be estimated at $2 billion. To this should be added a large amount on the order of $25 billion which should be annually appropriated by the General Assembly for the proposed World Development Authority in order to make a real impression on the vast problem of mitigating the worst economic disparities between nations and regions.

Upon first impression, this assumed $25 billion figure for world development may appear high, but is in fact moderate if the purpose is to accomplish a substantial change in the living conditions of the more underdeveloped areas of the world. This is so because before the machinery for supplying any such amount can become operative, there will doubtless be an increase in world population to nearly 4 billion, by which time the number of people living in poverty relative to the standards of the industrialized nations will certainly be not less than 2 billion. Accordingly, the annual expenditure of

[1] The Clark and Sohn Plan envisages this authority as a major organ whose function would be to assist in the economic and social development of the underdeveloped areas of the world, primarily through grants-in-aid and interest-free loans. This authority would be under the direction of a World Development Commission of five members to be chosen with due regard to geographical distribution by the Economic and Social Council, subject to confirmation by the General Assembly. This would accord with the emphasis given in Part V of this book to the necessity for expanded aid as a contribution to world peace.

$25 billion to improve the condition of these people would represent only about $12 per capita which is little enough to accomplish any substantial improvement in their living standards.

It is apparent, therefore, that the reasonable expenses of a world authority adequately equipped to deter or suppress any international violence, to administer a comprehensive system for the peaceful settlement of all disputes and also to do something substantial for the economic betterment of the underdeveloped parts of the world, could easily run to $36 billion per annum. And while this amount would be only about one half the 1960–62 budget of a single nation—the United States—it would, nevertheless, be so large a sum that reliance for supplying it should not be placed on a system of yearly contributions by the separate governments of nearly one hundred nations. Apart from a World Development Authority, the maintenance of a high level of efficiency and morale by the proposed Inspection Service, the Peace Force and the Nuclear Energy Authority and the Outer Space Agency would be of crucial importance; and it would indeed be folly to set up these and other vital organs without reliable machinery for supplying the necessary funds. To this end, a carefully devised *collaborative* revenue system is proposed.

A chief feature of this system would be that each member Nation would assign in advance to the United Nations all or part of certain designated taxes assessed under its national laws. Each nation would undertake the entire administrative function of collecting the taxes thus assigned to the United Nations, these taxes to be paid directly to a fiscal office of the United Nations in each member Nation. In this way it would be unnecessary to create any considerable United Nations bureaucracy for this purpose.

Another important feature would be an *over-all limit* on the maximum amount of revenue to be raised in any year, namely two per cent of the gross world product (total value of all goods produced and services rendered) as estimated from year to year. . . .

The General Assembly would adopt the annual United Nations budget covering all its activities, and would determine the amounts to be supplied by the taxpayers of each member

Nation for that budget. These amounts would be allotted on the basis of each Nation's estimated proportion of the estimated gross world product in that year subject to a uniform 'per capita deduction' of not less than fifty or more than ninety per cent of the estimated average per capita product of the ten member Nations having the lowest per capita national product, as determined by the Assembly. A further provision would limit the amount to be supplied by the people of any nation in any one year to a sum not exceeding two and one half per cent of that nation's estimated national product.

Taking 1980 as an example, and assuming that the gross world product for that year was estimated at $2,600 billion, the maximum United Nations revenue which could be raised would be $52 billion. And if for the 1980 fiscal year a budget of $16 billion less than the maximum, or $36 billion, was voted, it being then estimated that the United States had 30 per cent of the gross world product, the amount which the taxpayers of the United States could be called upon to supply, allowing for the 'per capita deduction' would be about $12·2 billion. This charge upon the taxpayers of the United States, while substantial, would still be less than one third of the $40 billion to be supplied by them in 1960–61 for military purposes alone. It follows that upon the completion of national disarmament, whereby this $46 billion item would be entirely eliminated, even the maximum possible charge for the budget of the strengthened United Nations would seem relatively small. The same would be true of any other nation with large military expenses.

In addition to the provisions for the raising of annual revenue, a United Nations borrowing power would also be provided for, with the limitation that the total United Nations debt outstanding in any year shall not exceed 5 per cent of the estimated gross world product in that year.

A more detailed explanation of this revenue plan is set forth in Annex V. It is believed that the plan would be effective to provide reliable and adequate revenues for the strengthened United Nations without involving the creation of a United Nations revenue-raising bureaucracy.

(Clark and Sohn)

38

Appropriations[1] for the budget of Peace and Defence, under control of the Chamber of Guardians, as proposed by the Chamber at the beginning of each term for the whole duration thereof, shall be submitted by the President to the Council, in conformity with Art. 13. But if a state of emergency is declared, in the manner and limits as specified hereinbefore (Art. 28, last paragraph), the Chamber shall have power to demand and appropriate such additional funds as the emergency demands, subject to auditing and sanction by the Council when the emergency is closed; whereafter, if sanction is denied, the Guardians responsible shall be liable to impeachment and prosecution for usurpation of power with the same procedure as specified for the President and the Tribune of the People hereinbefore (Art. 15 and 34).

(Borgese)

SUGGESTED STUDY QUESTIONS

1. How can people be taught to think of themselves as 'world citizens' rather than citizens of particular States, and would this be beneficial in terms of promoting world peace?
2. If large, regional groupings of States are to be an intermediate step to a truly supranational world community how could these groupings be prevented from developing rivalries likely to lead to large-scale war?
3. What major problems confronting international society could best be solved by the creation of a truly supranational world authority?
4. If a world legislature were to be created on what basis could representatives be chosen and how could its powers be defined so as to preserve a reasonable degree of autonomy for national States?
5. 'Given general and complete disarmament, a world police force would be a potential world dictatorship.' Do you agree? Suggest possible checks and balances to minimize this risk.
6. How far do you see an international judicial system operating effectively in a supranational world authority? Would it (and

[1] The levying of federal taxes is a specific power conferred on the World Government in Article 1.

224

the system of laws it applied) operate only against States or against individuals?

7. Could a system of taxation be developed in a supranational authority which would not deprive the developed countries of the incentives towards even greater economic development?

8. Setting aside the more ambitious plans for a world supranational authority, in what areas of activity could supranational bodies be created so as to afford greater guarantees of world peace without eliminating the national state as we now know it?

9. 'A world authority is unthinkable so long as political ideologies differ.' Do you agree?

FURTHER READING

BURTON, J. W., *International Relations: A General Theory*, Chs. 4 and 5, Cambridge: Cambridge University Press, 1965.

CHISHOLM, B., *Prescription for Survival*, New York: Columbia University Press, 1957.

MILLARD, E. L., *Freedom in a Federal World*, 5th revised ed., New York: Oceana Publications, 1969.

MITRANY, D., *A Working Peace System*, New York: Quadrangle Books, 1966.

NEWCOMBE, H., 'Alternative Approaches to World Government', *Peace Research Review*, I (1967), p. 88.

Pacem in Terris, Encyclical of Pope John XXIII, Catholic Truth Society, 38/40 Eccleston Sq., London, S.W.1, 1963.

ROSSITER, CLINTON (ed.), *The Federalist Papers*, New York: Mentor Books, New American Library, 1964.

The United Nations: the next Twenty-Five Years, 20th Report of the Commission to Study the Organization of Peace, Chairman Louis B. Sohn, 1969.

Index

Gardner, Richard N., 150; extracts from *In Pursuit of World Order*, 152–6 (Doc.28)
General Agreement on Tariffs and Trade (GATT), 71
General Treaty for the Renunciation of War; see Kellogg-Briand Pact
Geneva Conference on . . . Peace in Indo-China, 21 July 1954: extracts from the final declaration, 120–1 (Doc. 20); 125–8, 128–30
Geneva Disarmament Talks, 172; Chinese refusal to take part, 191–2
Gentili, Alberico, natural law and 'just wars', 3
Georgia, 35
Gerassi, John, 42
German attack on the Soviet Union, 11
German invasion of Austria and Czechoslovakia, 11
German invasion of Poland, 11
Germany, 13, 119; Control Council, 120
Germany, Eastern, 81, 136, 143
Germany, Western, 142; in world government, 210
Giap, General, 128
Goa, 79
Goldstein, Walter, 68; extract from 'The Peaceful Limitation of Disputes . . .' 79–86 (Doc.14)
Gomulka, Wladyslav, 139
Great Britain and Northern Ireland, 11, 13, 18, 20, 28, 38, 94, 105, 112, 119, 120; economic and social effects of disarmament, 184; in world government, 200, 208, 210; involvement in Suez crisis (1956). 30, 55, 57, 80, 81, 116, 117; proposals for disarmament inspection, 176, 186; signatory to test-ban treaties, 196
Great powers and 'brinkmanship', 116–49 (Part IV)
Greece, 56, 92, 105, 142
Grinyov, O., 175, 176; extract from

'Soviet Efforts for Disarmament' 185–8 (Doc.34)
Gromyko, Andrei A., 131
Grotius, Hugo, natural law and 'just wars', 3
Growth rate in developing areas, 153–4, 156, 162–9 (Doc.31)
Guantanamo, US base, 132
Guatemala, 46, 79
Guerilla warfare, 43–5
Guevara, Che, extracts from writings, 42–9 (Doc.9)
Guinea, 46

Hague Convention (1907), 15–16
Hammarskjöld, Dag, 89, 111; extracts from Summary Study of the experience derived from the establishment and operation of UNEF, 94–102 (Doc.15)
Hatred, 45
Helsinki Missile Talks, 178
Hitler, Adolf, 11, 55, 63
Ho Chi-Minh, reply to President Johnson, February 1967 128–30 (Doc. 22)
House of Nationalities and States (Borgese plan), 200
Human resources in developing areas, 157–8
Hundred Years' War, 59
Hungary, 30, 39, 48, 54, 58, 79, 80, 106, 117, 118, 136, 143
Hungry bloc, 84

Iceland in world government, 206
Ideological struggles, 34, 48, 53–4, 73, 80
Imperialism, 41, 50, 52, 53, 44, 47, 55, 80, 84
India, 56, 57, 58, 80, 82, 118; assimilation of Goa, 79; estimated growth of population, 152; Chairman of International Control Commission in Indo-China, 123, 126; in world government, 200, 206, 208, 210